Praise for *Deeper into the Word: New Testament*

"We don't use words well because we coax them into meaning what we'd like them to mean rather than what they did mean. The only way to become a Bible Christian is to learn how the Bible uses words, and Keri Wyatt Kent will guide you into how to do just that. God bless this book for what it can do for Christians."

—Scot McKnight, Karl A. Olsson Professor in Religious Studies, North Park University

"The Bible says that in the beginning was the Word. Keri will help you go slower and deeper into the richness of the *logos* of God."

—John Ortberg, popular author and pastor of Menlo Park Presbyterian Church in Menlo Park, CA

"I regularly refer to favorite commentaries and reference books as I prepare talks for retreats and conferences. Keri Wyatt Kent's *Deeper into the Word* will definitely be added to my shelf of 'go to' references. She takes New Testament words, some we know well, and opens us up to deeper meanings. This is a resource every Christ follower would benefit from."

—Anita Lustrea, Host & Executive Producer of *Midday Connection*

# DEEPER *into the* WORD

OLD TESTAMENT

Keri Wyatt Kent

# Deeper *into the* Word

## Old Testament

Published by Bethany House Publishers
11400 Hampshire Avenue South
Bloomington, Minnesota 55438
www.bethanyhouse.com

Bethany House Publishers is a division of
Baker Publishing Group, Grand Rapids, Michigan

Printed in the United States of America



Library of Congress Cataloging-in-Publication Data

Kent, Keri Wyatt.
Deeper into the Word : Old Testament : reflections on 100 words from the Old Testament / Keri Wyatt Kent.
p. cm.
Summary: "Devotional that explores the context, background, and application of 100 important Old Testament words"—Provided by publisher.
Includes bibliographical references (p. ) and index.
ISBN 978-0-7642-0843-0 (pbk. : alk. paper) 1. Bible. O.T.—Terminology. 2. Bible. O.T.—Meditations. I. Title.
BS1185.K46 2011
221.7—dc23 2011026985



Cover design by Lookout Design, Inc.

Author is represented by MacGregor Literary.

11 12 13 14 15 16 17 7 6 5 4 3 2 1

# CONTENTS

# INTRODUCTION

As a writer and avid reader, I find a peculiar intimacy in friendships with people who have read the same books I have. Shared experiences, whether of a book or a real-life adventure, weave us together.

Just as I connect with friends when we read the same books, we can connect with Jesus when we read the Scriptures he read: the Old Testament. While the New Testament is the story Jesus lived, the Old Testament contains Scriptures Jesus loved. He studied them not under compulsion or duress, but with passion and joy.

Can you imagine Jesus as a little boy in Hebrew school? As the rabbi read the scroll of the first chapters of Genesis, was he filled with memories of creating giraffes? Or overcome again with the sadness of the fall—how it broke his heart? When he and his peers memorized psalms, did Jesus already know them because he'd listened to them from heaven as they were sung by his people for generations?

Many Christians I speak to long for a deeper connection to Jesus, a stronger faith. But they ignore the treasure that sits on their bookshelf or computer or electronic reader. Ironically, although the Bible is more available to American Christians at this time than any other in history, biblical literacy in the Western world is at an all-time low. If Christians read the Bible at all, they often skip the first two-thirds of it, missing out on that bond that comes from reading the same book Jesus read, loved, and memorized when he walked this earth. Ignoring the Old Testament compromises our intimacy with Jesus.

We're separated from the stories of the Old Testament by a prodigious gap of time, language, and culture. And yet, its stories (even the strange ones) are true, and its precepts remain, as the psalm says, a light to our path. It contains truth about God and about the fallibility of human nature (Old Testament characters are refreshingly flawed). The Old Testament reveals God's relentless seeking of a people to call his own, and it is full of stories, laws, rituals, and poetry, all of which point to Jesus.

This book is not an overview of the Old Testament, but rather a close-up look at one hundred English words found in the text. Because the Old Testament was written in Hebrew, each chapter will provide information on the Hebrew word or words that English word represents, as well as the historical and cultural context of those words. Each chapter is a word study designed to give us insight into the meaning of the text. My hope is that each of these hundred key words will provide an on-ramp into the Old Testament.

This book is a tool to help you better understand both the words and their context so that you can engage in the spiritual discipline of the study of God's Word. As such, it is meant to be used with the Bible rather than on its own. Think of it as a shovel to help you dig deeper, or a light to help you see better.

---

There are several ways this book can help you connect with Scripture. First, it can be used as a reference volume to look up words you come across in your own reading. For example, as you engage in daily Scripture reading, you may want to dig deeper. Cultivate the habit of reading slowly. As you read, notice which words in the text stand out to you or give you pause. Rather than trying to get through a chapter or section, read a shorter portion through a few times. When a specific word strikes you or puzzles you, use this book as a reference tool to look up words you've encountered in your daily reading.

Second, this book can be used as a model to launch your own study of specific words. If there's a word in your daily reading that is not listed in *Deeper into the Word*, you can use it in another way: as a tutorial for how to do what has been traditionally called a "word study." By reading a few chapters, you can learn this technique and try it on your own. In a word study, you take one word—say, the word *love*—and by using a concordance, either printed or online, find other verses where *love* occurs. The other verses will provide insights into the word. You can use commentaries to see what scholars say about it. You can look up the words in various Bible dictionaries or even a lexicon—which gives you the Greek or Hebrew translation of the English words (there are several available online—see the appendix for suggestions).

Third, you could read this book one chapter at a time, devotionally. Don't rush—you may want to spend several days reflecting on a chapter. Look up the verses mentioned in the chapter and read their context. Or use a concordance to find other verses that use that word. Pray and journal about how God might be asking you to live out his words. You can also use this book with others—a prayer partner or a group.

As you engage with individual words, allow them to coax you into the Old Testament itself. Explore, investigate. You may be surprised how much of Jesus you will find in the Scriptures he loved.

## ALIEN

Questions of race and origin pervade the Old Testament, which tells the story of God's choosing and leading a people to be his own. The nation of Israel is to be holy, set apart. Consequently, they would be keenly aware of the otherness of tribes and nations around them.

While God commands his people not to intermarry or adopt the religions and cultic practices of other nations, he also gives them detailed instructions about caring for foreigners. When referred to in a compassionate way, they are called *geyr*—strangers or aliens. That shouldn't surprise us, because Abraham, with whom the race began, uses that word to describe himself, and the children of Israel began their journey toward God's promise as emancipated slaves and refugees—aliens.

In Genesis 23:4, a grieving Abraham says to the Hittites, whom he is living among, "I am an alien and a stranger among you. Sell me some property for a burial site here so I can bury my dead." He negotiates to buy a field and a cave in which he can bury his wife, Sarah. The words he uses to describe himself in the Hebrew are *geyr* (or *ger*) and *toshab*. (In the King James Version, they are translated "a stranger and a sojourner.")

*Toshab*, or sojourner, appears fourteen times in the Old Testament, meaning someone who dwells in a foreign land, and is often combined with *geyr* as it is above. (See especially Lev. 25.) It typically referred to permanent non-Hebrew residents.

*Geyr* is found throughout the Old Testament. It describes someone who has come from another country, sometimes to escape difficulty, and settled in a new land. The word describes a person outside of the Hebrew community of faith, who would not have all of the privileges afforded to members of that community, but was to be treated with respect nonetheless. It describes both the people Moses led out of Egypt, and people who later lived among them.

Scholars believe that when the Israelites fled from Egypt, quite a few other people of various races escaped with them and likely traveled along with them. Exodus 12:38 says, "Many other people went up with them, as well as large droves of livestock, both flocks and herds."[1] Those foreigners were allowed, and expected to keep the law, but did not have all the privileges of full-blooded Israelites.

Exodus 22:21 states, "Do not mistreat an alien (*geyr*) or oppress him, for you were aliens (*geyr*) in Egypt." The word is also found in the Ten Commandments, in the Sabbath command, with a similar reminder of kindness to the poor and slaves, and to "the alien within your gates." They are reminded to allow the poor and slaves to rest because they were slaves in Egypt (Deut. 5:14–15).

Aliens were to be treated fairly, but also were expected to comply with the law if they were living among the Israelites. They received the protection of the law only if they were willing to live within its precepts.

"The alien who resides with you shall be to you as the citizen among you; you shall love the alien as yourself, for you were aliens in the land of Egypt: I am the LORD your God" (Lev. 19:34 NRSV).

The Hebrew word *geyr* is often grouped with two other words that describe the poor: the fatherless (*yathowm*) and the widow (*almanah*). This triad is seen repeatedly in Deuteronomy 24, instructing God's people in specific practices of compassion (gleaning, etc.) to the poor. For example, Deuteronomy 24:17 says, "Do not deprive the alien or the fatherless of justice, or take the cloak of the widow as a pledge."

Like widows and other poor people, the aliens living among the Israelites were recipients of a special third year tithe (Deut. 14:28–29; 26:12).

"When you have finished setting aside a tenth of all your produce in the third year, the year of the tithe, you shall give it to the Levite, the alien, the fatherless and the widow, so that they may eat in your towns and be satisfied" (Deut. 26:12).

While aliens were to be treated with compassion, their privileges and rights were limited: "Do not place a foreigner over you, one who is not a brother Israelite" (Deut. 17:15). However, in this verse the word translated "foreigner" is not *geyr*, but the term *iysh nokriy*. Literally, the words mean man and stranger, or a foreign man. For example, in Judges 19:12, "His master replied, 'No. We won't go into an alien (*nokriy*) city, whose people are not Israelites. We will go on to Gibeah.' "

*Nokriy* also means adulterous or different, giving it a more negative connotation. We find it paired with another word for stranger, *zuwr*. *Zuwr* means literally to turn aside (especially for lodging), hence to be foreign or strange, a stranger. "I am a stranger (*zuwr*) to my brothers, an alien (*nokriy*) to my own mother's sons" (Ps. 69:8).

God's people did not always obey the laws regarding aliens. In fact, many of the prophets chastised the Israelites for the way they ignored God's commands, including specifically the commands about how aliens were to be treated.

God's protection (and yet, expectations) of aliens should perhaps make us consider how we ought to treat aliens in our own country.

## ALTAR

The word *altar* (or *altars*) appears more than four hundred times in the Old Testament. Its meaning evolved over time.

An altar was often a pile of stones assembled to commemorate a significant act of God, or to worship him. The first altar we read about is the one that Noah built (Gen. 8:20) to thank God for keeping him safe on the ark during the flood. Abraham, Isaac, and Jacob all built altars at various times to commemorate encounters with God. Before the time of Moses, altars were usually piles of stone or dirt.

Sometimes the person building the altar would name it (Gen. 33:19–20 and Ex. 17:15, for example). In 1 Samuel 7:12 we read that Samuel set up a stone to commemorate God's miraculous help in defeating the Philistine army and named it "Ebenezer," which means stone of help.

Altars were used not only by the Israelites, but by other religious groups as well. For example, the goddess Asherah, considered the mother of all pagan gods, was worshiped with wooden columns known as *asherah* poles. In Exodus 34, we read:

> Be careful not to make a treaty with those who live in the land where you are going, or they will be a snare among you. Break down their altars, smash their sacred stones and cut down their Asherah poles. Do not worship any other god, for the LORD, whose name is Jealous, is a jealous God. (vv. 12–14)

"Do not set up any wooden Asherah pole beside the altar you build to the LORD your God, and do not erect a sacred stone, for these the LORD your God hates" (vv. 21–22). Similarly, Judges 6:31 mentions the altar of the pagan god Baal being broken down.

God gave specific rules about building altars—they were to be built with plain stones, not carved ones:

"If you make an altar of stones for me, do not build it with dressed stones, for you will defile it if you use a tool on it" (Ex. 20:25). Some scholars believe that tools were prohibited because those same tools would also be used for war (Josh. 8:31).

The instructions for the tabernacle include two altars—each a hollow box, one made of wood overlaid with bronze for burnt offerings (Ex. 38:1), a second overlaid with gold for burning incense (Ex. 37:5). The bronze altar was visible just inside the doorway of the tabernacle, while the gold incense altar was in an inner chamber, in front of the ark of the covenant, and so only seen by the priests. (See Ex. 27, 37, 38, 39, and 40 for just some of the elaborate instructions.)

The altar of acacia wood overlaid with bronze was to be four and a half feet high, seven and a half feet wide and long—a square box. When Solomon built the great temple, he made it three or four times as large. The corners had "horns"—triangular projections that looked like animal horns.

According to Leviticus 6:12–13, the fire on this altar was never allowed to go out.

The altar and the sacrifices offered on it provided a bridge between human beings and God. Here, the most amazing thing could be found: forgiveness of sins.

The specific design of the tabernacle, its curtains and courts, created a picture of God's holiness. God was said to dwell in the innermost chamber, the Holy of Holies, which could only be entered once a year by the priest for the purpose of atoning sacrifice. God could not be approached casually—he was separate, holy. Sacrifice and confession were required to even come into his presence. The Hebrew word for altar is *mizbeah*. It comes from the word *zbh*, which means slaughter. However, animals were not actually slaughtered right on the altar, but near it, and then their blood was poured on or around the altar, which was a raised platform. *Altar* also later referred to a table on which incense was burned (Ex. 30:1). One Bible dictionary notes:

> In the ancient Near Eastern world at large, the preparation and offering of food to the gods had much to do with the concept of deities as supra-human beings with human bodily needs. Food and drink were offered to keep them content and thus positively disposed toward their worshippers. Worship at the Israelite altar,

> deriving as it did from Canaanite precedents, surely included that traditional sense of attending to the needs of the Divine. More significant, however, was the Israelite understanding that the altar was a place at which one could invoke—and encounter—God.[1]

While we do not offer sacrifices in the way the ancients did, we can still encounter God in the act of sacrifice. He asks not for bulls or lambs, but for us to lay down our will, to sacrifice perhaps our comfort or selfishness, or to be generous in a sacrificial way. While we can approach the throne of grace with confidence, God still asks us to surrender our will, and all we have, to him. The daily dying to self is the sacrifice that will bring us into his presence.

## ANGEL

The first person to meet an angel in the Old Testament is a slave woman with a rather complicated pregnancy. (It's interesting that the first mention of an angel in the New Testament also involves straightening out the details of an unexpected pregnancy.) Hagar, whom we meet in Genesis 16, is bearing the son of Abram, an eighty-six-year-old not-yet-patriarch with a barren wife. Enlisted as a surrogate, she now finds herself angry.

The angel tells her to go back to Sarai and Abram, to name her child Ishmael, a portentous name, and yet she seems somehow comforted.

Although she is the first person in the biblical record to have a conversation with an angel, she has no doubt who this person represents, or in fact, is: "She gave this name to the LORD who spoke to her: 'You are the God who sees me,' for she said, 'I have now seen the One who sees me'" (Gen. 16:13–14). She is the only person in the Bible who names God.

It is an angel who calls out to Abraham—"from heaven" the

text says—to stop him from slaying his son. Interestingly, at the beginning of the chapter, God himself speaks directly to Abraham and tells him to take Isaac up the mountain to sacrifice him. It appears that the angel speaks on behalf of God.

The Hebrew word in these texts is *mal'ak*, which means a messenger or angel, someone sent over a great distance to communicate a message. It can also mean a human messenger—a king sends a *mal'ak* in 1 Kings 20:1ff. A human prophet or priest can also be referred to as a *mal'ak*.

> It can also mean an angel or heavenly messenger, in general, or more specifically, an "angel of the Lord," *mal'ak Yahweh*; or "the angel of God," *mal'ak 'elohim*. This is a theophanic manifestation—a divine being who embodies the person and authority of God himself. . . . Every occurrence of the phrase 'angel of the Lord (or God)' carries with it an important connotation, since his appearance consistently initiates or advances a stage in God's plan of salvation, whether in blessing or judgment.[1]

Angels appear in dreams or to people awake, but they always speak on behalf of God, or as if it were God speaking. In Genesis 31, for example, an angel appears to Jacob in a dream and says, among other things, "I am the God of Bethel . . ." A few paragraphs later, God himself appears directly to Jacob's father-in-law, Laban, again in a dream.

A page later, Jacob is traveling and "the angels of God met him" (Gen. 32:1). He recognizes them immediately.

Later Jacob wrestles all night with a man. When he asks his name, the man won't tell him, but gives him a new name, Israel, which means, "He struggles with God." Apparently, this man is God in disguise.

When Moses sees the burning bush, "There the angel of the LORD appeared to him in flames of fire" (Ex. 3:2). But when he goes over to look, it says, "When the LORD saw that he had gone over to look, God called to him from within the bush, 'Moses, Moses!' " (v. 4), and then he has a conversation with God. So who's in the bush? An angel, or God? Does the angel just get things started, to see if Moses will turn aside? And when he does, then God steps in?

Some scholars believe that the angel of the Lord is actually Jesus, before his human incarnation. One dictionary notes: "The relation between the Lord and the 'angel of the Lord' is often so close that it is difficult to separate the two, Gen. 16:7ff; 21:17ff. . . . This identification has led some interpreters to conclude that the 'angel of the Lord' was the pre-incarnate Christ."[2]

Was the Old Testament "angel of the Lord" the pre-incarnate Jesus? Often within one text, the angel will not only speak on behalf of God, but as if he were God. One commentary concludes: "No clear distinction can be made between this angel and Yahweh, and where human beings encounter God in the OT, they meet him not in unmasked glory but in the person of the angel of the Lord."[3]

The pillar of cloud that led the Israelites through the desert is also referred to as the angel of God (Ex. 14:19; 23:20). (See ***Cherubim***.) While some today are suspicious of belief in angels, why would the Bible include so many stories of them if these beings did not exist? The Bible says that even strangers may be angels and we don't realize it—a reminder to show God's love to everyone we encounter. Today, be aware of the activity of God and his armies, whether in the physical or spiritual realm. Be courageous, knowing that his angels are mighty and able to help in time of need.

## ARK

The Old Testament mentions two kinds of arks: a boat and a box.

The first is "an ark of gopher wood" (aka cypress wood), which Noah was instructed to make and then turn into a floating zoo as a flood destroyed the rest of humanity and animals. The Hebrew word is *tebah*, a box. The giant boat may have weighed anywhere from 19,000 to 43,000 tons.[1] Ironically, the same word is used of the small basket of bulrushes that floated among the weeds and hid baby Moses in the Nile (Ex. 2).

The second type of ark is an ark of acacia wood, also known as shittim wood. The Hebrew word is *'aron*. This was the ark of the covenant, or the ark of the testimony, which signified the presence of God and was carried with the Israelites as they traveled through the wilderness. It is mentioned 195 times in the Old Testament. It was a hollow box fashioned according to detailed instructions (Ex. 25). The stone tablets bearing the Ten Commandments were housed inside the ark, as were an omer of manna and Aaron's rod.

It is sometimes known as the ark of the LORD *Yahweh*, or the ark of *'elohim*, God. The ark's cover was fashioned of pure gold, with a cherubim at each end (Ex. 37:1–9). This cover, sometimes called the "mercy seat" (Heb. 9:5), was sprinkled with blood once a year on the Day of Atonement. It was there that the presence of the LORD dwelt.

Exodus 25 gives instructions for building the ark of the covenant, and the following chapters talk about how to build the tabernacle and the altars—all of which are oriented around the ark and designed to house and protect it. The ark was surrounded by elaborate curtains with cherubim woven into them. It was the focus of their feasts, ceremonies, and rituals.

In Joshua 3, God tells the Israelites to follow the ark, carried by the priests, into battle. When the priests carrying it step into the water of the Jordan, the water miraculously stops flowing so that they may cross on dry land. It leads the strange procession around the walls of Jericho, causing them to crumble. It symbolizes God's presence, powerful and unmistakable, leading them into battle.

But years later, in 1 Samuel 4, in an attempt to use the ark to bring God to the battlefield, the ark is captured by the Philistine army, and Israel, who has gone astray under the leadership of Eli and his sons, is defeated. Rather than following God, they were attempting to use the ark as a good-luck charm as they attacked nations when God had not directed them to do so.

Vine's Bible dictionary says of the ark: "To be before it was to be in God's presence, Num. 10:35, although his presence was not limited to the ark. . . . The ark ceased to have this sacramental function when Israel began to regard it as a magical box with sacred power (a *palladium*)."[2]

Despite their misuse of the ark and subsequent loss of it, God makes sure his people eventually recover the ark of the covenant. It brings curses, plagues, and worse to Israel's enemies (see 1 Sam. 5), and eventually it is returned to Israel (1 Sam. 6–7). King David later takes the ark to Jerusalem, but not without complications (2 Sam. 6; 1 Chron. 13). When the temple is destroyed in 586 BC, the ark is lost—and no one knows where it is now (Hollywood's adventure films not being a reliable historic record).

Both the ark that Noah built and the ark of the covenant represent the saving power of God—both his judgment and his grace. The spiritual significance of the ark as a point of connection between God and his people was yet another Old Testament symbol of the coming Messiah.

## ASSEMBLY

The Old Testament is essentially the story of a group of people—the nation of Israel. While our culture emphasizes individuals and their experience, ancient Middle Eastern culture was much more group oriented. Even today, Eastern cultures focus much less on individual needs and much more on the groups or families comprised of those individuals. The common good of the group is more highly valued than the needs of the individual, while in our culture it is the opposite.

God assembles his people and calls them to follow him, to be holy and set apart, as a group. Several Hebrew words are translated "assembly" in various versions of the Bible. Sometimes an assembly is convened like a meeting. Other times, *assembly* refers to the entire community of Israel. We often see Israel's leaders giving God's direction through the law or prophesy, and the people agree with one accord to follow God.

The word *qahal* is sometimes translated "congregation" or "community." In Exodus 12:6, it's rendered "the whole assembly of the congregation" (KJV) or "all the people of the community of Israel." A *qahal* can refer to an assembly of people or leaders convened for a specific reason, often religious. Sometimes the word refers to a group of leaders representing all of the people. A *qahal* could be convened for various purposes, but usually for religious reasons. It is often found in the phrase "the day of the assembly" (Deut. 10:4; 18:16).

Another word, *edah,* is translated "community" in modern translations and "congregation" in the King James Version. This word is similar to *qahal* but focuses on the entire people of Israel and their unity, the covenantal community. *Qahal* sometimes describes an assembly of representatives, where *edah* does not. Instead, it refers to the entire group of people. Also, *edah* could be used to describe a herd of animals, while *qahal* is not used in this way.

Both of these words are found in Leviticus 4:13: "If the whole Israelite community (*edah*) sins unintentionally and does what is forbidden in any of the LORD's commands, even though the community (*qahal*) is unaware of the matter, they are guilty."

How would the *qahal* be unaware of sin of the *edah*? This would be possible if the *qahal* were representative leaders, and the *edah* were the larger community of Israelites. The emphasis again is on the entire group, not the individuals who comprise it.

Leviticus 8:4 says, "And Moses did as the LORD commanded

him; and the assembly (*edah*) was gathered together unto the door of the tabernacle of the congregation" (KJV). The phrase "tabernacle of the congregation" is a translation of the Hebrew *ohel moed* ("tent of meeting").

Another word translated "assembly" is *atsarah* or *atsereth*: an assembly on a festival or holiday, always used with the word *solemn* (Lev. 23:36; Num. 29:35, a "solemn assembly"). This word refers not so much to the group but to the event of the group's gathering for worship or to commemorate the activity of God in their midst.

Yet another word that is sometimes translated "assembly" is *cowd*, which can also mean counsel or a group of close confidantes. We find this word, for example, in Psalm 111:1, which says: "I will extol the LORD with all my heart in the council of the upright and in the assembly."

*Cowd* is also found in Jeremiah 15:17, where the prophet reminds God that he has not kept bad company, but followed God, saying, "I sat not in the assembly of the mockers, nor rejoiced; I sat alone because of thy hand: for thou hast filled me with indignation" (KJV). The New International Version translates the phrase, "I never sat in the company of revelers." *Cowd* can also be used in a positive way, to describe confidentiality between friends (Ps. 55:14).

Yet another word translated "assembly" is *miqra*, meaning a public worship service or convocation.

It's obvious from the variety of words and the frequency of their use that community is an important theme. Assembly in the Old Testament is a foreshadowing of the church—God's people coming together as one body, in unity and confidentiality.

## BARREN

The first mention of a barren woman, suffering from infertility, is Sarai (Gen. 11:30), who, in a bit of divine irony, eventually becomes the mother of the great nation of Israel. No wonder she named her first child "laughter."

Today, a woman having trouble conceiving can seek treatment at a fertility clinic. In the ancient world, women turned instead to elaborate fertility rites and pagan worship. Don't you wonder if Sarah, while still Sarai, may have tried such things? I wonder if she, like other barren women in her day, kept a statue of Astarte, the love/fertility goddess, in her home, and offered the prescribed sacrifices and prayers in a desperate attempt to unclench her womb? Did she pray that El, the God she and Abram worshiped but did not yet truly know, would hear her prayers for a child?

She tries to hurry along the promise of God by having her husband sleep with her slave girl. This ends badly, of course. But she cannot scheme beyond the reach of grace, and God still grants her the desire of her heart, although he takes his sweet time, waiting until she is ninety years old before she gives birth to Isaac. As John Ortberg has commented, they were probably the only couple to buy diapers and Depends at the same time.

The Hebrew word for barren, when the word refers to an infertile woman, is *aqar*. Renn's dictionary points out that other partriarch wives, Rebekah and Rachel, also suffered from infertility, but eventually God intervened and gave them children (twins Jacob and Esau, and Joseph, respectively). He notes, "Barrenness is a very significant theological concept in the Old Testament. Although the verb *aqar* itself only occurs eleven times, the majority of references relate to the entire scope of God's redemptive purposes in both the old and new covenants."[1]

Old Testament heroes Samson and Samuel were also born to women who were barren until God answered their prayers for a child.

Philip Yancey notes,

> After promising to bring about a people numerous as the stars in the sky and the sand on the seashore, God then proceeds to conduct a clinic in infertility. Abraham and Sarah wait into their

> nineties to see their first child; their daughter-in-law Rebekah proves barren for a time; her son Jacob must wait fourteen years for the wife of his dreams, only to discover her barren as well. Three straight generations of infertile women hardly seems an efficient way to populate a great nation.[2]

Renn adds, "God's action of removing barrenness for certain women among his people is a distinct pointer to the powerful theological symbol of divine renewal and transformation for his people as a whole."[3]

The Old Testament also has two words that refer to ground that does not bear fruit. The word *melechah*, meaning barren land or salt land, is found in Job 24:21. The word *shakol* is translated "barren" in 2 Kings 2:19–21, where it refers to barren ground or land, but the word itself literally means to miscarry or suffer abortion (but is often used symbolically to mean barren or childless). It is most often translated "bereave," and appears twenty-five times in the text.

A similar word, *shakkul*, means bereaved of children and appears six times, including Song of Solomon 4:42; 6:6.

In the ancient world, children, especially sons, were seen as a sign of God's favor. Women could be divorced or even put to death for failing to produce male heirs. So this prophetic utterance in Isaiah 54:1 seems odd:

> "Sing, O barren (*aqar*) woman,
> you who never bore a child;
> burst into song, shout for joy,
> you who were never in labor;
> because more are the children of the desolate woman
> than of her who has a husband,"
> says the LORD.

This word picture points to the future of God's people, using barrenness as a symbol for loss of hope. This prophecy is a reminder that the end result, even when things look bleak, is in God's hands. Nothing is too difficult for God.

Paul quotes this verse in Galatians 4:27, pointing out the theological significance of this theme. Just as God used so many barren women to fulfill his promises, we too are "children of a promise," set free in Christ.

## BIND

When God gave his people Israel the law, he told them, "These commandments that I give you today are to be upon your hearts. . . . Tie them as symbols on your hands and bind them on your foreheads" (Deut. 6:6, 8).

His people took the command seriously, creating small boxes called phylacteries, which they literally tied to their hands and foreheads to show their devotion to God and the gift of Torah. The binding was both literal and symbolic, as the boxes were a physical symbol of their devotion to God.

The Hebrew word in this verse is *qasar*, one of several that can be translated "bind." We will focus on the three most commonly used: *qasar, habas*, and *asar*.

*Qasar* is found forty-four times in the Old Testament. We see it in Proverbs 6:20–21: "My son, keep your father's commands and do not forsake your mother's teaching. Bind them upon your heart forever; fasten them around your neck." In this case, *qasar* is used metaphorically to remind children to listen to and live out their parents' instruction.

However, in most of its other metaphorical uses, *qasar* often connotes a conspiracy—an alliance focused on causing trouble. (We see it frequently in the books of 1 and 2 Kings to describe political espionage.) An exception is found in 1 Samuel 18:1, where *qasar* describes the Bible's quintessential example of deep, intimate friendship, that of David and Jonathan.

The Hebrew word *habas* (also transliterated *habash*) occurs about thirty times in the Old Testament. It means to bind or wrap with a bandage. It is used in a literal sense to describe binding turbans onto the head (Ex. 29:9). It is sometimes translated "saddle" to describe binding a load or saddle onto a beast of burden (Gen. 22:3; Num. 22:21).

When used metaphorically, *habas* describes God's miraculous spiritual healing, a restoration of hope. The idea is a binding that promotes healing, as in binding wounds. It is only occasionally used in a negative way, when God refuses to heal (Ezek. 30:21; Isa. 3:7). But most often, it is a word that reminds us of the nurture and compassion of God. It's found in Isaiah 61:1: "He has sent me to bind up the brokenhearted, to proclaim freedom for the captives. . . ." It is a word rich in the imagery of healing and redemption, put in parallel with phrases of liberation. What will ultimately heal people's broken hearts? The freedom found in Christ.

This is, of course, the prophecy Jesus reads when he preaches in the synagogue in Luke 4. The implication is that this binding and healing is his mission.

But the most frequently used word translated "bind" is *asar*. It means to tie or bind, to harness or to imprison. It is used both literally and metaphorically in the text.

"At the literal level, *asar* refers to prisoners in varying contexts being bound with ropes or chains. . . . *Asar* is also used metaphorically in the sense of a 'vow.' Here the idea is that one 'binds' one's soul to a specific promise or cause."[1] It is used this way only in Numbers 30.

One dictionary notes: "Most often, *asar* suggests imprisonment and is used of such things as binding a sacrifice (Ps. 118:27) or putting a person in prison (Judg. 15–16). The ministry of the Messiah is not only to bind up the brokenhearted (*Habas*) but also to announce release for the prisoners (for 'them that are bound,' *asar*)."[2]

As it does in English, "to bind" in Hebrew can mean both to restrict or to heal. The question to consider is this: Where am I bound (imprisoned)—by persecution, by my own bad habits, by the pain of my past? And have I asked God to bind my wounds, to heal the pain that keeps me from growing toward him?

## BLESSING

Many of us long for a blessing from God, which we think will consist of him making our lives easier, our wallets fatter, or our careers more successful. But a blessing is not necessarily going to guarantee any of that. The word does mean to bestow favor in some contexts, but also to praise and worship, as it does in the Psalms and elsewhere, when we are told to bless God. "Bless the LORD, O my soul: and all that is within me, bless his holy name. Bless the LORD, O my soul, and forget not all his benefits" (Ps. 103:1–2 KJV).

The New International Version and later versions say "Praise the Lord," which is indeed what it means in this context, but the nuance of the old language illumines the text, inviting us to consider the mysterious paradox of being able to bless the giver of all blessings. While to bless the Lord means to worship him, I can't help but think that like any loving Father, God takes delight in our attention and respect for him, in our verbalizing of that by uttering blessings toward him. And the text is clear—we bless God as a heartfelt response to his blessing us.

And it is the same word, whether I am blesser or blessed—in Hebrew, the word is *barak* (or since technically Hebrew does not use vowels, some scholars write *brk*).

A blessing was a declaration of favor. In the Old Testament, wealth or power was considered a sign of blessing from God. For example, Genesis 26:12 says, "Isaac planted crops in that land and the same year reaped a hundredfold, because the LORD blessed him." Likewise, Abraham's servant, when searching for a wife for Isaac, tells Rebekah's family, "The LORD has blessed my master abundantly, and he has become wealthy. He has given him sheep and cattle, silver and gold, menservants and maidservants, and camels and donkeys" (Gen. 24:35).

We can bless God, God can bless us, we can bless one another. One dictionary notes that blessing implies relationship: "*Brk* is most often a relational marker, signifying the existence of some sacral, legal, or social relationship. God, angels, and humanity may bless; God, humanity, animals, and inanimate objects may be blessed."[1]

God gives blessings to people, land, animals, the Sabbath, and more. People can bless each other or ask God to bless another person. Scripture records several instances of fathers blessing their children or grandchildren. This was more than a sentimental well-wishing. Blessings named both character strengths and weaknesses, and had a prophetic element that told how those character traits would ultimately play out (see Gen. 48–49). "In every instance, praise and blessing are given to God because of who he is and what he has done. God's character is always evident in his actions, and his actions are always consistent with his character."[2]

In Deuteronomy 16, God commands his people to bring an offering to each of the three festivals he has ordained. The offering should be commensurate with the person's wealth, which is attributed to God's blessing: "No man should appear before the LORD empty-handed: Each of you must bring a gift in proportion to the way the LORD your God has blessed you" (Deut. 16:16–17).

A recurring theme is the choice between blessings and curses. Because of the Fall, man is cursed, but God chooses to bless Abraham and all humanity through him. As God gives his people the law, he asks people to choose to obey, because obedience will bring blessings:

> See, I am setting before you today a blessing and a curse—the blessing if you obey the commands of the LORD your God that I am giving you today; the curse if you disobey the commands of the LORD your God and turn from the way that I command you today by following other gods, which you have not known. (Deut. 11:26–28; see also Deut. 30)

Deuteronomy 28 paints a picture of those who are blessed and those who are not. God is not capricious, but rather, blesses obedience. He withholds his blessing from those who don't obey him, leaving them vulnerable to difficulties.

## BLOOD

The Old Testament is a bloody book, full of stories of war, blood rituals, and violence. But its stories and laws, despite their visceral imagery, convey a respect for life. Abel's "blood cries out" (Gen. 4:10) to God, and so God calls Cain to accountability for his brother's murder. Specific prohibitions and punishments for killing, whether accidentally or intentionally, fill the pages of the Pentateuch.

Blood is a symbol of life. The Hebrew word *dam*, which occurs more than three hundred times in the Old Testament, means not only the fluid that runs through the veins of people and animals, but the very life-force within each being.

God taught his people (who lived in a violent pagan culture) that blood and life are sacred. He wanted his people to be different, set apart—so he told them not to kill one another. He also prohibits the escalating revenge that was common in that day by placing limits (an eye for an eye).

The law also prohibited eating or drinking blood—again to stand in sharp contrast to pagan rituals around them, and perhaps, though they didn't know it at the time, for health reasons (Gen. 9:4; Lev. 7:27; 17).

Blood played a huge role in the worship rituals of God's people—they were to sacrifice animals as atonement for sin. Aaron and his sons were consecrated as priests in Exodus 29 with an elaborate blood ritual, involving the slaughter of one bull and two rams. The blood of the bull was to be smeared on the horns of the altar and poured out around the base of the altar. The blood of the rams was sprinkled on the sides of the altar, but God gives this instruction for the second ram: "Slaughter it, take some of its blood and put it on the lobes of the right ears of Aaron and his sons, on the thumbs of their right hands, and on the big toes of their right feet. Then sprinkle blood against the altar on all sides" (Ex. 29:20). After that, the priests were to sprinkle some of the blood from the altar, and some oil, onto their clothes.

The word for "right hand" is *y'maniy*. The hand, especially the right hand, "represents the ownership, power, or control that its possessor (either an individual or a people) exercises . . . a symbol of divine power and salvation." In several places, significant events or laws are to be remembered as "a sign on your hand" (Ex. 13:9).[1]

These elaborate consecration rituals reminded the people that sin had a price. One cannot come into the presence of God lightly or flippantly. Consecration sets someone apart, makes them able to serve God, to enter the holy of holies. (See also Lev. 4, for example.)

"In all animal sacrifices blood was the essential element, poured on the altar (Lev. 1:5)."[2]

The annual feasts and festivals involved blood as well. Each Passover, for example, the blood of a lamb, smeared around their doors, reminded the Israelites of their past deliverance. Though they did not know it, this ritual foretold in graphic imagery the deliverance Christ, the perfect lamb, would purchase with his blood on the beams of a cross during a Passover week centuries later.

The Israelites were not the only religion that sacrificed animals. In Leviticus 17:7, God tells Moses that the Israelites must bring their sacrifices to the Tent of Meeting and give them only to Yahweh: "They must no longer offer any of their sacrifices to the goat idols to whom they prostitute themselves." Apparently, the Israelites were dabbling in pagan rituals. Their years of wandering in the desert were a time of training in holiness for a people who for four hundred years had been slaves—poor, uneducated, perhaps influenced by the culture to which they were enslaved. And now they were called to be holy. If you read the story of their exodus, you know the process took time, just as it does in our lives. Perhaps the line in the sand between slavery and sanctification had to be drawn with blood.

God patiently explains the "why" behind the sacrifice commands: "For the life of a creature is in the blood, and I have given it to you to make atonement for yourselves on the altar; it is the blood that makes atonement for one's life" (Lev. 17:11).

God's point? The remission of sin requires the shedding of blood. In this way the blood rituals were, of course, pointing prophetically toward the ultimate sacrifice of Christ.

## BREAD

The Hebrew word *lehem* occurs about three hundred times in the Old Testament. It usually means bread, but can be translated "food" or even "meat" in certain verses. It typically referred to a variety of food products made from grain, such as wheat or barley, including not just loaves but porridge, gruel, and cakes. It was a mainstay of the diet at that time. While man does not live by bread alone, bread represented life in many ways.

A second word, *massah*, refers to unleavened bread. Grain offerings required by the law were not allowed to be tainted with yeast. A third word, *hames*, occurs only eleven times and means leavened bread, in contrast to the unleavened *massah*. Because it contained yeast, *hames* was prohibited during Passover and could not be used as a grain offering. (See ***Unleavened***.)

When the Israelites wandered in the desert and complained of hunger, God responded by providing manna. The text says it tasted like wafers with honey (Ex. 16:31), and symbolized God's provision. It was also a prophetic symbol of Jesus, who would someday be the bread of life come down from heaven (John 6:32–41). It was given to the Israelites as they wandered through the dessert, where as nomads they could not cultivate crops. The name literally means "What is it?"

Later, God tells Moses to explain it to the Israelites this way:

> He humbled you, causing you to hunger and then feeding you with manna, which neither you nor your fathers had known, to teach you that man does not live on bread alone but on every word that comes from the mouth of the LORD. (Deut. 8:3)

Jesus quotes this verse when Satan tempts him to turn stones to bread in the desert. In the giving of manna came an important theological and social lesson. Each family was to gather "enough" for the people living in their tent. If they hoarded it, it would rot overnight and become infested with maggots. It is clear that the Israelites, like petulant children, tested this rule. But they began to learn in a very tangible way the principles of God's justice and mercy—that we should not hoard food or possessions but take only as much as we need. Manna was also a foreshadowing of the practices of the early church, which had all things in common and gave so that none would be in need or go hungry.

The prayer of lament in Psalm 80:4–5 says:

> O Lord God Almighty,
> how long will your anger smolder
> against the prayers of your people?
> You have fed them with the bread of tears;
> you have made them drink tears by the bowlful.

This term, *bread of tears* or *bread of affliction,* is a metaphor for God's chastising his people. (See also Deut. 16:3, 1 Kings 22:27.)

> In two passages *lehem* refers to wickedness or moral corruption in the phrases "bread of wickedness" (Prov. 4:17) and "bread of deceit" (cf. Prov. 20:17). Finally, *lehem* refers on one occasion to spiritual wisdom as something of great value to "eat." In Prov. 9:5, Lady Wisdom invites her hearers to come and eat her "bread," which leads to acquiring genuine godly wisdom.[1]

Another important use of the word *lehem* was for what was known as shewbread. Each week, the Israelites were to bake a dozen loaves of bread and place them in the Tent of Meeting.

> Take fine flour and bake twelve loaves of bread, using two-tenths of an ephah for each loaf. Set them in two rows, six in each row, on the table of pure gold before the Lord. Along each row put some pure incense as a memorial portion to represent the bread and to be an offering made to the Lord by fire. This bread is to be set out before the Lord regularly, Sabbath after Sabbath, on behalf of the Israelites, as a lasting covenant. It belongs to Aaron and his sons, who are to eat it in a holy place, because it is a most holy part of their regular share of the offerings made to the Lord by fire. (Lev. 24:5–9)

This was also called the Bread of the Presence (1 Kings 7:48) or the consecrated bread (1 Sam. 21:6). One dictionary says, "The bread of the presence functioned like a grain offering which was sprinkled with frankincense. Aaron would replace the loaves with new ones on a weekly basis. The bread of the presence symbolizes the eternal covenant between God and Israel."[2]

## CHERUBIM

In modern English, the word *cherub* means a sweet, angelic, rosy-cheeked child. In the Bible, however, cherub is the singular of cherubim, which were fierce and mighty warriors assigned to protect the holiness of God. In medieval times, cherubim were considered to be members of the second order of angels (there were nine orders), outranked only by the seraphim.

The first mention of cherubim in the Old Testament is in Genesis 3:24, when God places cherubim with a flaming sword to guard the way to the Tree of Life. What a ridiculous picture comes to mind if we think of an innocent, plump-cheeked toddler protecting the gate of Eden! A cherubim was a warrior, of whom humans would be afraid—they are more like the Navy Seals of the heavenly hosts, the personal bodyguards of the glory of God.

Cherubim are not unique to the Bible; other cultures at that time mentioned similar creatures. *Eerdmans Bible Dictionary* says that cherubim were "Mythological winged creatures, borrowed by the Israelites from ancient Near Eastern traditions." It also notes that huge creatures called *karibati* (gatekeepers) "flanked the entrances of Mesopotamian palaces and temples."[1]

Similarly, forms of cherubim fashioned from gold were a part of the cover of the ark of the covenant, again protecting the holiness of God. In Solomon's temple, where everything from the tabernacle was supersized, giant cherubim made of wood overlaid with gold guarded the ark.

God's instructions for the tabernacle included a tapestry-like curtain. Exodus 26:31 says: "Make a curtain of blue, purple and scarlet yarn and finely twisted linen, with cherubim worked into it by a skilled craftsman." (See ***Tabernacle***.)

Certainly this artwork would have reminded God's people of the story of the Fall, and the cherubim at the gate of Eden. And what was the purpose of this curtain? Verse 33 says, "Hang the curtain from the clasps and place the ark of the Testimony behind the curtain. The curtain will separate the Holy Place from the Most Holy Place." Cherubim are angelic gatekeepers, winged warriors who protect the holiness of God. They represent in many ways the gulf that separates imperfect human beings from a perfect God. (It is of course theologically significant that when Jesus died on the cross, this curtain and its cherubim were ripped asunder, from top to bottom).

Archaeologists have found statues of what they believe were representations of cherubim, which were in the form of a winged lion with a human face. Most scholars believe that the unnamed creatures around the throne of God in Revelation are cherubim.

Psalm 80 describes God as "you who sit enthroned between the cherubim" (v. 1). Ezekiel 1:4–28 paints a fantastic picture of creatures who looked like men but had four wings and four faces (which looked like a man, lion, ox, and eagle), surrounded by whirling wheels. Such apocalyptic imagery again reminds us of the power of the cherubim and their role as protectors.

What do cherubim have to do with us? Even though the temple curtain was torn and we may now approach the throne of grace with confidence, that throne is still flanked by cherubim. The cherubim remind us not to take God or his holiness too lightly, to make grace too cheap. God is love, but he is also perfect, and we are not. The cherubim also teach us to worship God, for they are the ones who cry, "Holy, holy, holy is the Lord God Almighty." We can learn something about respect and reverence from them.

## CLEAN

God's people were to be holy and set apart—and one outward sign of that holiness was physical cleanliness. The theme of cleanliness flows through the Old Testament like water.

The most frequently used Hebrew words for *clean* are *tahor* and *taher*. *Tahor* is used as an adjective to mean pure—physically, morally, ceremonially, or even chemically. When the tabernacle instructions mention "pure gold" for the altar and tools, the word translated "pure" is *tahor*. The verb form, *taher,* means to be clean, to purify or be pure, to cleanse. It appears frequently in the book of Leviticus, which contains several chapters dealing specifically with cleansing and purification.

The first mention of the word *tahor* is in Genesis 7:2, when God tells Noah to put seven pairs of each clean animal and one pair of each unclean animal into the ark. You have to wonder—how did Noah know which animals were which, since the instructions on clean and unclean animals (those that could be eaten or sacrificed, or not) come much later in the biblical narrative? Perhaps God and Noah had a few conversations that were not included in the text. (See ***Unclean***.)

But the scope of meaning for these related words extends much further than the early definitions of what is kosher. The Bible is clear that no human being has been pure since the fall. Proverbs 20:9 asks, "Who can say, 'I have cleansed my heart; I am pure and free from sin'?" (NLT). Obviously no one. (See also Job 4:1.) Purity is not something people can attain by their own efforts, but by the cleansing power of God. He promises in Jeremiah 33:8, "I will cleanse them from all the sin they have committed against me and will forgive all their sins of rebellion against me." (See also Ezek. 37:23.)

And indeed, cleanliness is related to atonement for sin. God is holy and therefore completely clean. People are not, but they could be made clean, temporarily, by sacrifices and ritual washing. The priests went through rigorous purification rituals in order to be cleansed before they could go into the Holy of Holies. And the reason they would even go into this sanctified space is to make atonement for the people, that is, to cleanse them from their sins.

When God tells the Israelites he will appear to them in a cloud, he tells them to consecrate themselves first by washing their clothes (Ex. 19:9–11). The Tent of Meeting included a basin for washing hands and feet. God spends quite a bit of time explaining how to wash clothes that have become mildewed (Lev. 13), and sets up an elaborate ritual for cleansing after one has been healed of an infectious skin disease (Lev. 14).

Uncleanliness was not moral impurity, but had to do with whether a person could approach God or not. A woman was considered "unclean" during her period and after childbirth. Bodily emissions and skin diseases also made people unclean, as did touching a dead person or animal. But cleanliness could be regained by bathing and waiting a prescribed amount of time, often just until the next day. Such rules may seem odd or capricious, but they conveyed an important truth: Sin makes us unclean, yet we can be made clean again.

Why the obsession with cleansing? I would venture that the Israelites washed their clothes much more often than any of the other people in the ancient Middle East. They were likely the cleanest desert nomads ever. But again, they were a people set apart. They were to be different, holy, a shining example. Cleanliness was to reflect their godliness. Indeed, ritual bathing became an important part of the Jewish faith over the centuries, and washing in a *mikvah* is still a part of their faith practice today.

The word for wash is *kabac*, which means literally to trample. Even today in developing countries, they wash clothes by putting them in a large basin with water, climbing in, and stomping on them, which is likely the method the Israelites used.

Psalm 51 puts the cleansing power of God into rich poetry:

> Wash away (*kabac*) all my iniquity
>    and cleanse (*naqah*) me from my sin. (v. 2)
> Cleanse (*chata*) me with hyssop, and I will be clean
>    (*taher*);

> wash (*kabac*) me, and I will be whiter than snow. (v. 7)
> Create in me a pure (*tahor*) heart, O God,
> and renew a steadfast spirit within me. (v. 10)

The word *chata* means both sin and sin purification; in this context, it refers to the effect of making atoning offerings for sin.

The verb *naqah* means to be pure, innocent. The implication, as in Psalm 51:2, is to be guiltless.

While we may think of cleansing as external, it is clear from the context of this psalm that God is more concerned with the cleansing of the heart. Cleansed within, we may approach a holy God.

## COMMAND

Ironically, God's commands are ultimately about our choices. After giving his people his commandments, God tells them:

> See, I set before you today life and prosperity, death and destruction. For I command you today to love the LORD your God, to walk in his ways, and to keep his commands, decrees and laws; then you will live and increase, and the LORD your God will bless you in the land you are entering to possess. . . . This day I call heaven and earth as witnesses against you that I have set before you life and death, blessings and curses. Now choose life, so that you and your children may live and that you may love the LORD your God, listen to his voice, and hold fast to him. (Deut. 30:15–16, 19–20)

Choose life, God urges his people. Well, of course. Who, given the choice between life and prosperity on one hand, and death and destruction on the other, would choose the latter? Yet how often we choose, unwittingly or willfully, ways that are destructive. We choose not to listen, not to love, not to hold fast to the very thing that will give us "life and prosperity." We do not choose life, despite

God's strong urging that we do so. To choose life is to choose obedience, and that's not always easy. But it is the better way.

God wants the best for us. He offers us a way of life that is full of life and blessings, but we must choose it. God's commands spell out clearly what is good. What a gift that is, because when we go our own way, we don't always choose the good.

The Hebrew word *tsavah* is used more than five hundred times in the Old Testament. As a verb, it means to command. It signifies to set up or appoint. Most frequently, God is giving the commands, but the word can be used to describe interaction between people, as in Ruth 3:6. God's commands describe to his people how they are to live in covenant relationship with God.

The Hebrew noun meaning commandment is *peh*. It literally means mouth, commandment—or edge, even edge of a sword, edge of a hole, etc. In a way, the commandments represent God's boundaries, and they come from his mouth.

Another important Hebrew word for commands is *mitsvah*, or *mitzvah*. The plural is a body of laws known as God's word. Keeping the *mitzvah* is how God's people had a relationship with him.

Several synonyms for *commands* are seen in parallel statements in Genesis 26:5, where God tells Isaac he will bless his family because of his father's obedience: "Because that Abraham obeyed my voice, and kept my charge (*mishmeret*), my commandments (*mitzvah*), my statutes (*chuqqah*), and my laws (*torah*)" (KJV).

Apparently, sometimes commands are given because they are a better way to live—e.g., it is better to tell the truth than to lie, we will live lives that are more joyful and less conflicted if we tell the truth. Other commands, though, are given to test us—to see whether we will obey or not.

Deuteronomy 8:1–2 says that the commandments give life, but that some were given "to test you in order to know what was in your heart, whether or not you would keep his commands."

So when God told his people not to wear cotton-poly blends or eat cheeseburgers, when he tells them to wear tassels on their clothing, we have to assume that those were testing commands, symbolic of purity and distinction, not necessarily commonsense commands.

What happens if we choose to disobey God's commands? The consequences are outlined in Deuteronomy 7:9–10:

> Know therefore that the LORD your God is God; he is the faithful God, keeping his covenant of love to a thousand generations of those who love him and keep his commands. But those who hate him he will repay to their face by destruction; he will not be slow to repay to their face those who hate him.

Now, this raises another important issue—the commands were a part of the old covenant. But Christians live under the new covenant. We are not saved by the law. We no longer have to offer sacrifices, for example, because Jesus' sacrifice on the cross was a "once for all" sacrifice. But we do have to discern which of God's commands are for all time and which were for a specific time. While we do not have to keep every Old Testament law, we do have to listen to his voice, hold fast to him, and choose life.

## COURAGE/COURAGEOUS

The word *courage* or *courageous* appears in the Old Testament only twenty-five times, but it is nevertheless an important word, as it often accompanies a phrase seen much more frequently in Scripture: *Do not be afraid.* (See ***Fear***.)

It is significant that this exhortation is an imperative. God does not suggest courage and strength—he commands it. He does not ask us if we'd prefer not to be afraid—he forbids it. *Do not be afraid* is the command most often repeated in the Bible, and arguably, the one most often ignored.

There are several words or phrases that are often used with the word *courage*. One, as we've mentioned, is "Do not be afraid." Another is the word *strong*—in fact, the two words meaning courage can also be translated as "strong," and they're almost always used together. The other idea, whether stated or implied, that is found in the majority of passages about courage is the promise of God's presence.

To be courageous is to be confident, to not let fear have the upper hand. In the Bible, such courage comes not from confidence in human strength, but because of God's presence and help in danger or struggle. As the Israelites were preparing to go in and take over the Promised Land, God told Joshua, who had become their leader after Moses died: "Be strong and courageous. Do not be terrified; do not be discouraged, for the LORD your God will be with you wherever you go" (Josh. 1:9). What was the reason Joshua didn't have to be afraid as he faced the battles in Canaan? His hope was not in the Israelites, who were not exactly trained warriors or a military superpower. But they had God on their side—and that was the sole basis for their courage. Be courageous, God tells him. Why? "For the LORD your God will be with you." That is the foundation for our courage—God's presence and protection.

The Hebrew word, repeated three times in Joshua 1:6–18, is *amats* (or *amas*), which can mean courage or strong. Its root meaning is to be alert. It is typically used in the phrase "Be strong and courageous." The word for strong is *chazaq*, which means to be strong, strengthen, harden, take hold of. Eight times in the Old Testament, the word *chazaq* is translated "courage," showing how closely connected these words are. They are often used together or interchangeably. In fact, *amats* is translated "be strong" about thirty times in the Old Testament, with the implied meaning to be courageous.

For example, Psalm 31 ends with this exhortation: "Be of good courage (*chazaq*), and he shall strengthen (*amats*) your heart" (KJV).

The New International Version reverses the order of the phrases, rendering the verse "be strong and take heart." As they are in English, strength and courage are interconnected.

When the King of Assyria was getting ready to attack Jerusalem, King Hezekiah fortified the city, then rallied his people. Second Chronicles 32 tells the story, and again, the theme is the same:

> [Hezekiah] appointed military officers over the people and assembled them before him in the square at the city gate and encouraged them with these words: "Be strong (*chazaq*) and courageous (*amats*). Do not be afraid or discouraged because of the king of Assyria and the vast army with him, for there is a greater power with us than with him. With him is only the arm of flesh, but with us is the LORD our God to help us and to fight our battles." And the people gained confidence from what Hezekiah the king of Judah said. (vv. 6–8)

We may not have to go into battle against the Girgashites or Amorites (Josh. 3:10) or Assyrians, but we do face struggles every day. Often our work feels like a battle. We're fearful about our family or our finances. We feel *dis*-couraged. That is, we are without courage. So the ancient words are eerily relevant—be strong and courageous, for God is with you. He is with us in our daily lives just as he was with the Israelites in their conquest of Cannan, or in their fight against the Assyrian king. He is with us wherever we go.

## COVENANT

A covenant is a mutual promise to help and not harm another. It goes beyond mere treaty or agreement. A covenant costs something—biblical covenants required, in one way or another, bloodshed. Whether sealed with animal sacrifices or with the cutting of human flesh, a covenant required more than words.

The Hebrew word *berit* is found more than three hundred times in the text and means covenant. The word is sometimes translated "testament," and so the Old Testament is the story of the old covenant between Yahweh and Israel.

The first covenant recorded in Scripture is with Noah (Gen. 6:18). Subsequently, God makes a covenant with Abram, and later it continues with David. In fact, the covenant with David hints that he will have an heir—which means the old covenant will become the new covenant, fulfilled in the person of Jesus (2 Sam. 7).

In the Middle East, when two people made a covenant or agreement, they would often sacrifice an animal, then cut it in half and lay the halves on the ground with an open space between them—a path of sorts. Then they would walk together between the halves, stomping through the blood. The understanding of this ritual was this: Each gave the other the right to do what they'd done to the animal if either broke the covenant, the promises they'd made to each other.

So when God makes a promise to Abram in Genesis 15, and Abram asks how he'll know God will follow through, God answers by telling him to go get some animals. Abram understands immediately. He gets a heifer, a goat, and a ram, cuts them in half (!), and lays the pieces on the ground.

What's amazing is that God does not ask Abram to walk between the halves; only God (in the form of a firepot and torch) walks through. This was a covenant of promise, which unfolds slowly. God promises descendants more numerous than the stars in Genesis 15, but in Genesis 16, Abram jumps ahead of God and has a son with his wife's servant girl. When that boy, Ishmael, is thirteen, God comes back to Abram for the second part of the covenant: Abram and his son are to be circumcised. At this point, God gives Abram a new name—Abraham—which means father of many. This is not a commitment to be taken lightly. A covenant costs.

The covenant with Moses described in Exodus 24 was also sealed with blood—not only the altar, but the people were sprinkled with blood as they would be had they stomped through the blood of animals on the ground. And they declare to God, "We will do everything the Lord has said; we will obey" (v. 7). Which they did—for a short while.

Israel's history might be summed up by this pattern: God makes a covenant, which Israel follows for a while. Then they go their own way, get in trouble, and call on God to rescue them. He does, and they follow him for a while, then they wander astray again. Repent, rescue, go astray, repeat. This happens over and over. God is patient with them, though. It is the thread of grace that runs through the Old Testament.

Covenant is not necessarily about rule keeping. The first and most important commandment in the covenant is to love God fully (Deut. 6:5). And really, that is what God is after—a people who will be his own (Jer. 24:7; Ezek. 11:20; 14:11; 37:27; and elsewhere). His deep desire was for a covenant written on our hearts.

The covenant is not a demand upon us but a loving-kindness of God. However, God asks us to keep that covenant, to choose life, to love his precepts, to meditate on his Word day and night.

The covenant includes all of the laws, some of which may seem arbitrary or odd to us. But Philip Yancey points out:

> When we look back on the covenant between God and the ancient Hebrews themselves, few of them pleaded with God to loosen the dietary restrictions or eliminate some of their religious obligations. They seemed, rather, relieved that their God, unlike the pagan gods around them, had agreed to define a relationship with them.[1]

Jeremiah 31 reminds us that the new covenant will not be like the old:

> "This is the covenant I will make with the house of Israel
> after that time," declares the LORD.

> "I will put my law in their minds
>   and write it on their hearts.
> I will be their God,
>   and they will be my people." (v. 33)

With the yearning of a lover (the verse before this refers to God as a husband), God desires a covenantal relationship with us—one in which his laws, precepts, and loving-kindness are written on our heart.

## CREATE

The Bible begins with the story of creation, and it is a theme that weaves throughout the Scripture. God continually makes all things new. He is the source of life, who made everything out of nothing. He took direction from no one but thought up the intricate web of life and then implemented it in perfect balance and harmony. His work was not drudgery but delight: The creation account pulses with energy and wonder—God takes his time, forming ever-increasingly complex creatures and systems, and each day takes time to stop and proclaim with joy, "It's good!"

Scholars note that compared with ancient creation mythologies, the Genesis account is calm, orderly, and without conflict or struggle. Rather, Yahweh creates via simple spoken imperative: "Let there be . . ." and there is. The story reflects the absolute sovereignty of God, which remains an important theme in other uses of the word *create* in the Old Testament. (See, for example, Isaiah 45, especially verses 8, 12, and 18.)

The Hebrew word *bara* means to create or make. In some contexts it is also translated "creator" (Isaiah 40:28, for example). This particular verb is used to express the idea of making something out of nothing, as in the Genesis creation account, but it also appears repeatedly in Isaiah to communicate a theological concept: God's sovereign power.

We also find it in Psalm 51:10: "Create (*bara*) in me a clean heart, O God" (NLT). The psalmist's prayer is that the creative power of God would be manifest in his heart, making it new. We bring nothing to the table; God creates a heart toward him within us. This verse speaks to the double meaning of *bara*—it refers to both an initial creating and also an ongoing sustaining. God is continually creating a clean heart in us, cleansing us, growing us—just as he is continually creating the world.

In addition to the Genesis narrative, the Old Testament has other descriptions of the creation of the world. Psalm 74 contains a more violent account of God's creation, in which he defeats, rather than simply creates, sea monsters and more.

Proverbs 8 contains beautiful poetry, written from the perspective of Lady Wisdom, about her role in creation. In verse 23 she says, "I was appointed from eternity, from the beginning, before the world began." A few verses later, Wisdom describes God's creation of the world and then declares, "When he marked out the foundations of the earth. Then I was the craftsman at his side. I was filled with delight day after day, rejoicing always in his presence, rejoicing in his whole world and delighting in mankind" (vv. 29–30).

Again, we see the delight and joy that creating brings to the Godhead.

*Qanah* is translated "creator" in Genesis 14:19, 22. Both Abram and the king he is visiting refer to God as the "creator of heaven and earth," but *qanah* means to get or acquire (and is sometimes translated "possessor").

*Asah* means to create, make, or do. It is sometimes parallel to *bara*. You have to look at the context to determine its meaning.

God created the cosmos out of nothing, but a second major theme in the Old Testament is God's ongoing work of creation, his continuing creation care. He did not create and then abandon the world, but continues to maintain it. Psalm 8, for example, talks about God's creation of the world and seems to imply that it is an ongoing project that human beings are meant to be stewards of (v. 6). The psalmist puts in beautiful poetry the sustaining work of God:

> He makes grass grow for the cattle,
> and plants for people to cultivate—
> bringing forth food from the earth:
> wine that gladdens the heart of man,
> oil to make his face shine,
> and bread that sustains his heart.
> How many are your works, O LORD!
> In wisdom you made them all;
> the earth is full of your creatures.
> When you send your Spirit,
> they are created (*bara*),
> and you renew the face of the earth. (Ps. 104:14–15, 24, 30)

This ongoing renewal is an important aspect of God's creative nature. He is both maker and sustainer of the physical world and our spirits. Being created in his image, we too are to care for creation and be creative—finding ways to innovate and create, and remembering to stop and say, "It's good!"

## DEATH

Our culture, despite its violence, lives in a steady denial of death. We have means of keeping people alive artificially when they are sick or even in a coma, and medicine that cures what were once fatal diseases. When people are old and weak, they often die in a nursing home or hospital. Many of us have never seen someone die unless we've been a soldier, firefighter, or police officer, or live in an area plagued by violence.

In the ancient world, death was a much nearer reality. Death was, as it is now, inevitable, but it was much more visible and more common. The threats to the average person—malnutrition, famine, even a common infection—made life tenuous.

One commentary notes: "Death . . . seemed as though it had cords and snares that could pull a person down to the grave (Psalm 18:5)."[1]

People in the Bible sometimes die suddenly, sometimes in an act of God's judgment (2 Sam. 6:6–7).

Stories of God's mercy outnumber stories of his inflicting capital punishment, however. More often the Bible exhorts us to "choose life" in contrast to the ways that lead to death. In spite of the fact that all people will eventually die (Num. 16:29; Heb. 9:27), we can make the choice to follow God and find life to the full. For example, after Moses has given the people the law, God speaks through him to remind the people of this truth: "This day I call heaven and earth as witnesses against you that I have set before you life and death, blessings and curses. Now choose life, so that you and your children may live" (Deut. 30:19).

God is not saying that these people will never die if they obey his laws, but that they will enjoy long life and a higher quality of life. Indeed, they will discover that "the Lord is your life" (v. 20). It seems odd that God would have to remind anyone to choose life over death, blessings over curses. But it is human nature to make poor choices. What seems good at the time may lead us to destruction.

The Hebrew verb *mot* (or *muwth*), means to die, dead, or to kill. The corresponding noun *mawet*, or *maveth*, means death, the end of life, and the opposite of life.

Someone's death, especially of old age, is sometimes described as being "gathered to his people" (Gen. 25:8, for example). This phrase is sometimes thought to be an idiom for burial in a family tomb. Other scholars argue that it is more of a spiritual reality than a physical one.

One dictionary explains that in the times the Old Testament was written,

> People believed a person's physical remains were interred in one place, and that part of the person capable of consciousness and personality went to another location. The gathering to one's people was an event taking place before burial at the time of death.[2]

Another Hebrew word that means to die is *gawa*, to expire or breathe one's last. This is particularly significant because the Hebrew word for *breath* and *spirit* is the same word—*ruawach*. When your breath left your body, so did your spirit.

Some eighteen times, mostly in the books of Job and Psalms, we see the ominous phrase "the shadow of death" a translation of the Hebrew word *tsalmaveth*, a compound comprised of *maveth* with *tsel*, which means shade or shadow. The shadow of death is a metaphor for suffering or the threat of death, from which God protects us.

## DELIVER/DELIVERER

In English, we might talk about delivering a package or letter, or even delivering a person to a specific place. But in the Bible, *to deliver* is most commonly a military term. God delivers people from their enemies, or delivers their enemies to them—meaning he gives them victory.

There are a handful of Hebrew words that can mean deliver. The two most common are *natsal* and *nathan*. *Natsal* literally means to snatch away, whether in a good or bad sense. It is translated "deliver" 179 out of the 213 times it appears in the text. It can also be translated "save" or "rescue," so when it is translated "deliver," it is with that connotation of saving from one's enemies.

The second word, *nathan*, appears much more frequently in the text, but it is most commonly translated "give." Of the 2,008 times it is used in the Old Testament, it means deliver only 174 times. It is often used in a military sense, to give over one's power or control.

Another word, which we see in the Psalms, is *chalats*. It means literally to pull off, strip, depart, deliver, equip. It is translated "deliver" fifteen times. Rather than the idea of delivering an enemy over to someone, *chalats* has an element of mercy toward suffering. In Psalm 50:15, God tells his people: "Call upon me in the day of trouble; I will deliver (*chalats*) you, and you will honor me."

Similarly, in Psalm 119:153, the psalmist's prayer for personal deliverance assumes a loving, covenantal relationship between man and God: "Look upon my suffering and deliver me, for I have not forgotten your law."

The word *deliver* or *deliverer* is used repeatedly in the stories of Israel's ongoing battles with the tribes and nations around them. Even when someone is given a territory, they have to go in and fight for it, and often the text attributes success in these battles to God, saying God delivered the land into their hands.

For example, in 1 Kings 20 we read the story of Israel's battles against Ben-Hadad, the king of Aram, who allies himself with thirty-two other kings and attacks Samaria. The Israelites are vastly outnumbered, and yet God gives them victory—not once, but twice. Both times, he promises deliverance through an unnamed prophet (see vv. 13 and 28), saying, "I will deliver (*nathan*) this vast army into your hands, and you will know that I am the LORD" (v. 28).

*Natsal* appears in several contexts, including the story of God delivering people from Sennacherib, the evil king of Assyria, told in 2 Chronicles 32.

Sennacherib is trash-talking, taunting Israel for believing that God will deliver them as he lays siege to Jerusalem. He notes that other people he's attacked expected their gods to deliver them, but of course they did not. He accuses Israel's king, Hezekiah, of lying to his people when he promises God's protection and intervention—that is, his deliverance. Sennacherib taunts: "No god of any nation or kingdom has been able to deliver (*natsal*) his people from my hand or the hand of my fathers. How much less will your god deliver (*natsal*) you from my hand!" (v. 15).

But Hezekiah's faith in God is unwavering, and God responds by sending an angel to defeat Sennacherib and his armies in a miraculous way. He withdraws in shame, and goes home only to be killed by his own sons! The text then notes: "So the LORD saved (*yasha*) Hezekiah and the people of Jerusalem from the hand of Sennacherib king of Assyria and from the hand of all others. He took care of them on every side" (v. 22).

Here we see another word that means deliver, with the idea of saving or helping: *yasha*. It is used thirty-six times in the Old Testament and is typically translated "salvation" or "save." Its noun form, *yeshua*, means deliverer or deliverance, and almost always refers to God (Deut. 32:15). One dictionary notes, "Many personal names contain a form of the root, such as *Joshua* ('the Lord is help'), *Isaiah* ('the Lord is help'), and *Jesus* (a Greek form of *yeshuah*)."[1]

Because *deliverer* is associated with military conquest, it is no surprise that the Jews of Jesus' day expected the Messiah to overthrow Rome. When a prophet with the name *Yeshua* shows up, that just fuels the fire. But *Yeshua* had a different kind of deliverance in mind—a spiritual deliverance from the power of sin. In our daily battle against addictions, anger, fear, greed, or bitterness (just to name a few), we can look to God, who is able to deliver us and help us to live victoriously.

## DUST

Paradox clings to the word *dust* in the Old Testament like, well, dust. It is a miraculous substance, of which God formed human beings (Gen. 2:7). It is a metaphor for abundance, as God promises Abraham that his descendants will be as numerous as dust particles on the earth (Gen. 13:16).

But dust also has strong negative connotations—the serpent's curse is that he will forever crawl on the ground and eat dust. It's a metaphor for our frailty and finiteness—as it says in Genesis 3:19: "By the sweat of your brow you will eat your food until you return to the ground, since from it you were taken; for dust you are and to dust you will return."

In Deuteronomy 28, God lays out for his people the consequences of obedience and sin. Basically, he promises that those who follow his laws will be blessed in many ways. The first fourteen verses of the chapter tell the many ways in which God will bless the obedient. Verse 12 paints a picture of this abundance: "The LORD will open the heavens, the storehouse of his bounty, to send rain on your land in season and to bless all the work of your hands. You will lend to many nations but will borrow from none."

Verses 15–68 detail the consequences of failing to follow God's rules, the results of disobedience and rebellion. The parallel opposite of verse 12 is in verse 24: "The LORD will turn the rain of your country into dust and powder; it will come down from the skies until you are destroyed." God clearly spelled out the consequences of not following him—and in a dry land like Israel, the threat of no rain was a threat of starvation.

Dust was also a sign of repentance. For example, in Nehemiah 9, we read of the Israelites fasting, wearing sackcloth, and putting dust or earth on their heads. The noun in Nehemiah 9:1 is *admah*, meaning earth or ground or soil. In other verses, we read of people mourning by sitting in the dust and throwing it on their heads (Job 16:15). In this verse, the Hebrew word for dust is *aphar*, or *apar*. It is the word most commonly translated "dust" and appears more than one hundred times.

*Apar* is a rich and varied word, which can mean dust, clods (of dirt), plaster, ashes. We see it first used in the Old Testament to describe the loose topsoil from which God scoops out the first human being, Adam (whose very name means dirt or earth, see ***Earth***).

The word can also mean plaster or ashes. In Leviticus chapter 14, *apar* is used to describe both dry plaster or mortar (v. 41), and in the very next verse, wet plaster (v. 42). It is sometimes used to describe the ashes or rubble of a city that has been completely destroyed (2 Kings 23:4; 1 Kings 20:10).

Another word, *abaq*, appears just six times. It connotes fine particles. We see it in verses like Isaiah 29:5, where God, through the prophet, tells the Israelite city of Ariel that it will be destroyed. Its enemies will be very numerous and will seem to be everywhere: "But your many enemies will become like fine dust, the ruthless hordes like blown chaff." This verse illustrates why context is so important. On its own, it might sound like a curse against the enemies, saying they would be ground down into dust or scattered like dust or chaff. But when we read the text, we see that this metaphor is meant to paint a picture of enemies too numerous to count, surrounding and overwhelming God's disobedient city.

We are finite; we're made from a scoop of dust in God's hand. Yet within that handful of dirt is the very breath of God. The word *dust* has varied and even opposite meanings; it reminds us of the humility of our position as creatures, and the awe and wonder that we are deeply loved, created in God's very image. While we are imperfect, we are his precious children and are called to make our influence in this world as pervasive as the dust.

## DWELL/DWELLING PLACE

The children of Israel were descended from Abraham, who, at God's command, traveled to dwell in a foreign land. For many years, they were nomads. They dwelt in tents, which is the literal meaning of one Hebrew word that is translated "dwell."

The Hebrew word *yashab* first appears in Genesis 4:16: "Then Cain went out from the presence of the Lord and dwelt in the land of Nod on the east of Eden" (NKJV). Other versions translate the word *yashab* as "live in" or "settled in."

While this is the primary meaning of *yashab*, it can also mean to sit, or to abide. It describes people sitting or even God dwelling among the people. It often describes people dwelling with one another.

Psalm 23:6 says, "I will dwell (*yashab*) in the house of the Lord forever." This and other similar verses (Ps. 27:4, for example) do not mean we sequester ourselves in church or a monastery but rather paint a picture of spiritual connection with God no matter where we go.

Despite the fact that the Israelites were former slaves, wandering homeless in the wilderness, God initiated dwelling with them. He also made them two promises related to dwelling. First, he would give them a land in which they could live and prosper, a place they could dwell.

This promise was conditional—if the people kept Torah (which ultimately, one does by walking with God, living in his presence), then they would have a land to live in: "So you shall observe My statutes and keep My judgments, and perform them; and you will dwell (*yashab*) in the land in safety" (Lev. 25:18 NKJV).

And second, God promised to dwell among them. More often, when speaking of the dwelling presence of God, we see a second key word: *shakan*. It literally means to dwell or live in a tent. But God uses it to speak of himself and his desire to dwell among his people. (Perhaps yet another prophetic hint of the coming Incarnation.)

Numbers 35:34 says, "Therefore do not defile the land which you inhabit, in the midst of which I dwell (*shakan*); for I the LORD dwell (*shakan*) among the children of Israel" (NKJV).

Even as they wandered the desert, God made his presence obvious as he went before the people as a pillar of fire or cloud (Ex. 13:20–22).

*Shakan* is closely related to the Hebrew word *shaken*, which means neighbor. This makes perfect sense: Your neighbors are the people you dwell beside.

*Shakan*'s noun form is *mishkan*, which means dwelling place or tent, and is often translated "tabernacle." The *mishkan* represented the presence of God among his people. Where they went, he dwelt with them, no matter what. (See ***Tabernacle***.)

God gave elaborate instructions (Ex. 25–30) for making the *mishkan*, the tabernacle, a symbolic home for his presence. He tells them: "Then have them make a sanctuary (*miqqdash*) for me, and I will dwell (*shakan*) among them. Make this tabernacle (*mishkan*) and all its furnishings exactly like the pattern I will show you" (Ex. 25:8–9).

Also called the Tent of Meeting, and later the Temple, the *mishkan* was a physical reminder of God's longing to dwell intimately with his people. It was, of course, a foreshadowing of Jesus, who came to dwell among us, and the Holy Spirit, who now dwells in human hearts. Centuries later Paul wrote, "Do you not know that your body is a temple of the Holy Spirit, who is in you, whom you have received from God?" (1 Cor. 6:19).

The word *shakan* communicates the presence of God, who is always with us. He dwells within us. From that word, we derive the word *shekhina*, the presence or glory of God.

This theme runs through the Old Testament, especially in the poetry of the Psalms. For example, Psalm 16 describes God as a refuge, one who is always near, who has put the boundary lines in pleasant places. *Shakan* can also be translated "rest," so it's not surprising that the psalmist chooses the word *shakan* for the ninth verse: "Therefore my heart is glad and my tongue rejoices; my body also will rest secure." In God's presence, we can rest or dwell without worry.

## EARTH

Just as the word *earth* in English can refer to both the planet and the dirt that coats its surface, the word *erets* is used to describe what God created in the beginning, and also the ground from which mankind tries to scratch a living.

The word *erets* is contained in the very first verse of the Bible: "In the beginning, God created the heavens and the earth," and it is repeated twenty-one times in the first chapter of Genesis alone. In that chapter, we find the first definition for *erets*: "God called the dry land Earth" (Gen. 1:10 NRSV). "Dry land" is a translation of the Hebrew word *yabbashah*. This word can mean dry, but also dry land. It comes from the word *yabesh*, which means to be dried up or withered. The root of *yabesh* means to be ashamed or disappointed—think of a plant that has dried up and withered, or a soul that feels dry because of disappointment.

With a word from God, dry land becomes earth, *erets*. God named things by speaking them into existence in one flourishing, creative act—the utterance both creates the earth and names it.

The second verse in the Bible describes this *yabbashah* earth before God turns it into something productive: "The earth (*erets*) was formless and empty" (Gen. 1:2). This is the testimony of the earth—before God's word touched and transformed it, the earth was *yabbashah*—dry, withered, formless, void. But it became *erets*, and life sprung forth from it (Gen. 1:11). So it is with our hearts, which without God are dry and lifeless, but with God, are fruitful and alive.

Psalm 24:1 notes, "The earth is the Lord's, and everything in it."

Psalm 148 exhorts the earth and its creatures, even its weather, to worship the creator: "Praise the LORD from the earth, you great sea creatures and all ocean depths, lightning and hail, snow and clouds, stormy winds that do his bidding" (vv. 7–8).

After describing the wonders of the created earth, the psalmist concludes: "Let them praise the name of the LORD, for his name alone is exalted; his splendor is above the earth and the heavens" (v. 13).

Vine's Bible dictionary notes: "The Hebrew word *erets* also occurs frequently in the phrase 'heaven and earth' or 'earth and heaven.' In other words, the Scriptures teach that our terrestrial planet is part of an all-embracing cosmological framework which we call the universe."[1]

The word *erets* is also translated "land" or "soil." God commanded his people about how they should care for the land—by allowing it to rest from planting every seven years. *Erets* also describes countries, used in phrases like "the land of Canaan" or "the land of Egypt"—specific places occupied by specific people, or places God tells his people to go.

So when God tells his people to enter the land he is giving them, is he only speaking of a territory, Canaan, or is he speaking of the earth? We must rely on context to determine the intended meaning, or to figure out if specific words are in the text because of their other meanings, which lie below the surface—underground, so to speak.

As the Israelites enter the Promised Land, and God tells them that it is the *erets* that he is giving them, might it evoke memories of Eden, when God gave human beings the entire world (*erets*) to fill, subdue, and steward?

A second word translated "earth" is *adamah*, often translated "ground." The first human being received his name from it. The Hebrew word for man is *adam*, which is related to the verb *adom*, which means to be red, and of course related to *adamah*. The color of a ruddy complexion, the color of the red soil from which man was formed, all tie together. In the opening pages of Genesis, *adam* is used both in the generic sense, meaning people or human beings, and the specific man, Adam, whom God created.

The *Tyndale Bible Dictionary* notes: "One Hebrew word translated 'earth' is also used generically for 'man,' or Adam (Gn 2:7, 19). That word refers to reddish soil from which Adam's body was made."[2] Again, we are reminded of how fragile we are, that we are little more than dust—and yet so much more.

## ELDER/ELDERS

In English, *elder* can be an adjective or a noun. In the Bible, the two different parts of speech are two different Hebrew words. The biblical words for *elder* refer to someone who is older than another, like an elder brother, or someone advanced in age as well as wisdom or authority. When *elder* is used as an adjective to describe the oldest child in a family, the word is *gadol*, which much more frequently means great. When someone is an elder, the word is *zaqen,* which can also simply mean "old"—again, the meaning depends on the context.

In addition, those known as elders (*zaqen*) were also formally recognized leaders of the community. This more formal office was typical among both the Israelites and their heathen neighbors. The first mention of elders in the Bible is actually the elders of the house of Pharaoh and of Egypt (Gen. 50:7). Some versions translate the word "dignitaries"—which provides a clue about the role of elders in that culture.

However, an elder within the nation of Israel was a person

who held a position of authority. Elders were an important part of the power structure within the Mosaic system. The *Tyndale Bible Dictionary* defines *zaqen* as the "person who, by virtue of position in the family, clan, or tribe; or by reasons of personality, prowess, stature, or influence; or through a process of appointment and ordination, exercised leadership and judicial functions in both religious and secular spheres in the ancient world, both among biblical and nonbiblical peoples."[1] In other words, someone who was a leader in the community.

The first official elders were designated by Moses at the suggestion of his father-in-law. People had been coming to Moses to ask for his wisdom to settle disputes—they saw him as someone wise who could offer judicial insights. For a long time, Moses did all of this work himself. But eventually he realized he would have to share the load, or he would burn out.

This story points to an important truth—we all have limits, especially when it comes to giving care to people. We cannot take care of everyone, all the time, especially when those people are in conflict. We need limits. Each person can care for some, but not all. And each who gives care or leads others also needs someone to lead them, to care for them.

Within the cultural context of patriarchy, elders were men, typically the father of a family. Often, a clan consisting of several families would be ruled by the patriarch of each of those families, who made up a council of elders.

The word *elder* has to do with leadership, specifically with the role of serving as judges or enforcers of the Law. Many churches today are governed by a board of elders, a tradition that stems from the days of the Exodus, when elders governed Israel.

> Supervision of the life of the community was placed in the hands of a group of elders, not in the hands of a single elder. . . . The elders were members of the community; their judgments would flow not only from knowledge of the law and custom but

> also from intimate knowledge of the persons who might stand before them.[2]

Each city, tribe, and nation had elders to rule it (Judg. 8:14; 11:5). The elders of the nation of Israel served as a model for church government in the early church. They provided guidance, discipline, and order. Elders were a necessary part of a covenantal community, as they are today in many churches. God uses people to carry out his will, to impart wisdom to the community.

## ENEMY/ENEMIES

Several Hebrew words are translated "enemy." The most common, *oyeb*, can describe a person or a nation. It appears some 282 times in the text. It comes from the word *ayab*, meaning to hate. It conveys active hating.

The second, *tsar*, is essentially a synonym, but is more often used to describe an enemy nation. *Tsar* is general; *oyeb* is specific. *Tsar* literally means narrow, as in being in a tight place. It comes from the word *tsarar*, which means to wrap, tie up, be narrow, be in the pangs of birth, etc. Literally it means to cramp. *Tsarar* can also mean adversary or trouble.

Another word we often find translated "enemy" and other times with a phrase like "someone who hates you" is *sane*. It means to hate someone personally, or to feel jealous.

In Joshua 6, we read of the miraculous taking of Jericho, where marching and a shout bring the walls tumbling down. Verse 21 (the part left out of the Sunday school song) tells us that the Israelites went in and killed everyone in the city—men, women, and even animals. In Joshua 8, we read of further conquests to take over the Promised Land, and in verses 24–25 the text says, "When Israel had finished killing all the men of Ai in the fields and in the desert where they had chased them, and when every one of them had been put to the sword, all the Israelites returned to Ai and killed those who were in it. Twelve thousand men and women fell that day—all the people of Ai."

The book of Joshua and other Old Testament books that chronicle the military exploits of Israel make it quite clear that God leads his people into battle and directs them to kill their enemies.

Think of how countercultural Jesus' message to love your enemies was to a people with more than a half-dozen words that mean enemy! (And another half-dozen or so that mean oppressor.) Here they are, living under the rule of enemies that oppress and hate them, and Jesus tells them to love those very enemies!

The Old Testament is a rich tapestry that contains threads of both violence and mercy. We see hints, perhaps prophetic, of the coming kingdom in verses like Exodus 23:4–5: "If you come across your enemy's (*oyeb*) ox or donkey wandering off, be sure to take it back to him. If you see the donkey of someone who hates you (*sane*) fallen down under its load, do not leave it there; be sure you help him with it."

Similarly, in Proverbs 25:21–22, we read: "If your enemy is hungry, give him food to eat; if he is thirsty, give him water to drink. In doing this, you will heap burning coals on his head, and the LORD will reward you."

Scholars argue about the meaning of the idiom "heap burning coals on his head." Some say it means making him feel embarrassed or shamed; others suggest that it is a way of blessing your enemy as you would if you were generous to him.[1] While it is worthwhile to investigate various idioms and cultural context, we can often use Scripture to interpret Scripture. So we could look to Romans 12, where Paul quotes this verse:

> Do not take revenge, my friends, but leave room for God's wrath, for it is written: "It is mine to avenge; I will repay," says the Lord. On the contrary: "If your enemy is hungry, feed him; if

> he is thirsty, give him something to drink. In doing this, you will heap burning coals on his head." Do not be overcome by evil, but overcome evil with good. (vv. 19–21)

The context makes it clear that we are to leave revenge to God. And also that we are to overcome evil with good—when we are kind to our enemies, we show them Christlike love. Our motive is to not make our enemy feel guilty, but they may end up feeling that way. We aren't trying to change our enemy, but they may be changed. Our motive is simply to love, out of obedience to God. By being kind to our enemies, we show that love is stronger than hate, we overcome evil with good, and perhaps God will change their hearts.

## EPHOD

The word *ephod*, a transliteration of the Hebrew word, typically describes an elaborate priestly garment, first custom-designed for Aaron and his sons to wear while ministering before the ark of the covenant.

The ephod was made of linen, with the colors of gold, blue, purple, and scarlet interwoven into its intricate design. It was decorated with precious gems.

Exodus 28 describes the clothing the priests were to wear. God said to Moses, "Make sacred garments for your brother Aaron, to give him dignity and honor" (v. 2). Part of the priest's uniform was the ephod. Quality mattered to God, as the words "fine linen" and "skillfully made" appear several times in its description (see vv. 6–8). The ephod was apparently worn over the tunic and robe of the priests.

The ephod had two onyx stones, each inscribed with the names of six of the twelve tribes, attached to its shoulder straps.

One dictionary says the ephod was a thigh-length vest, part of the elaborate dress of the priest: "The 'ephod' of the high priest was fastened with a beautifully woven girdle (Ex. 28:27–28) and had shoulder straps set in onyx stones."[1]

To make such a garment would have been a costly undertaking. Why would God command such a design for priests? These vestments communicated that approaching God was not to be taken lightly—that he was worthy of our best.

This colorful garment was worn over the robe. It was made in the same colors and materials as the veil of the tabernacle. A breastplate, adorned with twelve colorful precious stones set in gold filigree, in a three-by-four square, attached to the front of the ephod with gold chains held by gold rings. Each gem was inscribed with the name of one of the twelve tribes. This colorful square of fabric was called the "breastpiece of decision" or the "breastplate of judgment." Verse 30 elaborates: "Also put the Urim and the Thummim in the breastpiece, so they may be over Aaron's heart whenever he enters the presence of the LORD. Thus Aaron will always bear the means of making decisions for the Israelites over his heart before the LORD." There is some debate as to what Urim and Thummim actually are—it is likely that they were some sort of objects used for casting lots, to determine God's will. They're also known as the lots of divination and were carried in a pocket of the ephod's breastplate.

The *Tyndale Bible Dictionary* adds: "Prior to the Babylonian exile, the ephod served as a means of revelation from God, especially concerning military operations. Abiathar the priest brought the ephod into David's camp on one occasion for consulting the Lord (1 Sm 23:6–9; 30:7)."[2]

The robe of the ephod (see vv. 31–35) was to be made of blue cloth with blue, purple, and scarlet "pomegranates" and gold bells hanging from its hem.

The ephod was held in place with a richly embroidered wide

belt or, as the King James Version puts it, "the curious girdle of the ephod." (See verses 8:27–28, and elsewhere). The Hebrew word translated "curious girdle" (or "skillfully woven waistband") is *chesheb*, which means a belt or strap.

Think of how such finery would have stood in contrast to the dusty, threadbare clothing normally worn by desert nomads.

The ephod was highly symbolic. It was inscribed in two different ways with the names of the twelve tribes, reminding God's people of their national identity and unity as a people. The ephod communicated to the people that they were precious to him. It also reminded the people that although the Levites were the tribe who served as priests, they approached the altar of God as representatives of all twelve tribes, not just their own tribe. Imagine a member of the tribe of Benjamin or Reuben, watching the priest perform his sacred duties, seeing their family name inscribed on a precious gem.

A linen ephod can also be a simple garment, like the one Samuel wore when he served in the temple with the priest Eli, or the one King David stripped down to when he was dancing before the ark of the covenant in 2 Samuel 6.

## EVIL

The Hebrew word *ra*, which means evil, wicked or wickedness, mischief, bad, hurt, or trouble (along with other meanings), appears in the Old Testament 663 times.

Evil is of course related to sin. The first sin was to ignore God's prohibition of eating fruit from the tree of the knowledge of good and evil (Gen. 2:9). The phrase "good and evil (*ra*)" points to the fact that sin is a choice. We don't know just evil, we know good. We know better. Once human beings had gained the knowledge of good and evil, they sometimes continued to choose evil. To choose to do evil is to sin. Evil is a more general reality; sin is a specific action or a propensity toward evil actions.

*Strong's Hebrew Dictionary* says the noun *ra* "combines together in one the wicked deed and its consequences. . . . While the prominent characteristic of the godly is lovingkindness, one of the most marked features of the ungodly man is that his course is an injury both to himself and to everyone around him."[1]

As God gives his people the law, he often cites as a reason, "you must purge the evil (*ra*) from Israel" (Deut. 17:12; 19:19). Evil must be avoided if God's people are to be holy, set apart. In order to instruct his people in what is right, God must spell out, by way of contrast, what is wrong. Many of the Bible's rules seem morally reasonable to us because our morality is shaped significantly by our Judeo-Christian culture. Evil is not merely what is harmful to society, but what God has declared to be prohibited. His commands are the moral standard of the Bible, rather than "the good of society."

*The New International Encyclopedia of Bible Words* states:

> A single family of Hebrew words focuses on the Old Testament concept of evil. *Ra'a* is the verb, which means "to be evil, or bad," or more often, "to act wickedly," "to do harm." The masculine noun *ra'* means "evil" or "bad." The feminine noun *ra'ah* means "evil," "misery," or "distress" and includes every kind of calamity and wickedness.[2]

In Exodus 5:22–23, Moses complains to God that he has "brought trouble upon this people" (other versions use "evil" or "harm") and wonders aloud when he will rescue them. The word in Hebrew is *ra'a,* meaning to spoil, or literally to break into pieces. It connotes doing evil to people.

In an article from *Baker's Evangelical Dictionary*, William C. Williams makes a distinction between moral evil and natural evil. Natural or physical evil happens when nonrational beings cause suffering—say a lion attacks a man; or when something like a tornado or hurricane strikes. He notes that moral evil can be social sins (murder or theft), or what he calls "cultic evil"—sins against God such as idolatry or blasphemy. While some theologians feel that sins against God are somehow worse than sins against society, Williams argues that in God's economy, social and cultic evil are equally bad, because God forbids them both. While the distinction can be helpful, he notes that evil is defined not by its effect on people or society, but by God. Anything he's forbidden is evil.[3]

The Bible implies that we are created with an internal moral compass by which we can know right and wrong. However, our selfishness often overrides our conscience. We must, therefore, submit our will to God's if we are to resist the temptation of evil.

In the face of evil in our world, many question why evil happens at all. The Bible, however, is strangely silent on this question. It states that there is evil in the world, then simply says we should avoid it by following God and obeying his precepts.

## EXALT/EXALTED

When we exalt someone or something, we praise them, we make note of their virtues and speak highly of them. Over and over, the Bible reminds us to exalt the Lord, to praise him.

During worship services, I love it when we sing the Twila Paris chorus "We exalt thee" over and over, letting it wash through our congregation. It's moving, yet disturbing: It puts me in my proper place.

The word *exalt* is found most frequently in the Old Testament in the book of Psalms. While there are seven Hebrew words that can be translated "exalt" or "exalted," the one that appears most frequently is *ruwm*. This word is often used as a call to worship, as it is in Psalm 34:1–3:

> I will extol the LORD at all times;
> his praise will always be on my lips.
> My soul will boast in the LORD;
> let the afflicted hear and rejoice.
> Glorify the LORD with me;
> let us exalt (*ruwm*) his name together.

Here we see two typical Hebrew poetic conventions—first, stating something in parallel form for emphasis. Each of the three verses is saying something quite similar. Second, these three verses create a triad, essentially repeating the idea three times. Repeating something three times emphasizes perfection in the Hebrew mind (think of "holy, holy, holy is the Lord"). The word *extol* in the first verse is translated in other versions as "bless"—the Hebrew is *barak*. The idea of blessing God is quite similar to exalting him. We are not giving him something he does not have, but recognizing his worthiness. To exalt is to recognize what is true and name it with the intent to worship and honor.

*Ruwm* means up or to raise. *Ruwm* connotes something that is already on a higher level, or is moving toward that higher plane. In the case of this and many other psalms, it means to honor and hold in high regard, to lift up by praising.

A prophecy in Daniel 11 tells of the "king of the North" who will exalt (*ruwm*) himself in a misguided attempt to convince others he is greater than God, although he ultimately falls.

This odd prophecy, outlining the coming exploits of the kings of the north and south, reminds us that we are not to exalt ourselves. Self-exultation leads us to the sin of pride, which leads to destruction. In fact, exalting God is an antidote for pride. We gain a proper perspective on our own position compared with God. Most often, *exalt* is used as an imperative, directing us toward worship not of an earthly king, but of God.

The same Hebrew word can communicate the idea of God lifting up the weary:

> But you, LORD, are a shield around me,
> my glory, the One who lifts (*ruwm*) my head high. (Ps. 3:3 NIV)

There are several other words that can be translated "exalt."

Proverbs 4:8 says this of wisdom: "Cherish her, and she will exalt you" (NIV). The word in this verse is *calal*, which means to exalt or raise up.

The word *gabahh* usually means to soar or be lofty, and is found in verses like Ezekiel 21:26: "The lowly will be exalted and the exalted will be brought low."

The Hebrew words *sagab*, *ramam,* and *alah* can also mean exalted.

The word *nacah*, which most typically means up, or to bear, can also mean exalted. It is the same word translated "bear," meaning to carry, in Exodus 28:12, describing the stones on the ephod that Aaron bears on his shoulders, that he carries or lifts up before God. The connotation is of substitutionary atonement, which means that one person (or in the Old Testament, sometimes an innocent animal) took the punishment or responsibility for the sins of another.

Knowing that usage and connotation, it's significant that the prophet Isaiah makes an interesting word choice for this messianic prophesy:

> Prepare the way of the LORD;
> Make straight in the desert
> A highway for our God.
> Every valley shall be exalted (*nacah*)
> And every mountain and hill brought low. (Isa. 40:3–4 NJKV)

Certainly those hearing the prophecy would realize that God was speaking not of leveling the hilly countryside of Palestine, but of righting wrongs and correcting injustice, and that it would be accomplished by one who would bear our names into the Holy of Holies.

## EXILE

As we have explored previously, the Old Testament is the story of a covenantal people. Unfortunately, sometimes God's people violated that covenant. God warns them through prophets not to go astray, but when they ignore his warnings, he allows their enemies to overthrow them and take them into captivity, that is, to be exiled.

Deportation and resettlement was a common occurrence in the ancient Middle East. Nations would frequently attack one another, and the victors in these conflicts would often take prisoners and force them to relocate to become slaves or to serve in worship of their gods. It's likely that even in their own military conquests, Israel took prisoners to be slaves.

But after King Solomon died, the nation of Israel split into two kingdoms: Israel to the north and Judah to the south. Judah was captured by the Babylonians and was exiled, along with all the treasures of the temple (Jer. 25–30).

The northern kingdom was led by a series of sinful kings. They fell away from God (see 2 Kings 15 and following). Eventually, God got fed up with them and allowed the kings of Assyria to capture and exile the Israelites. Second Kings 17:6 says, "In the ninth year of Hoshea, the king of Assyria captured Samaria and deported the Israelites to Assyria. He settled them in Halah, in Gozan on the Habor River and in the towns of the Medes."

The word translated "deported" in this verse is *galah*, sometimes translated "carried away" or "exile." It is a word with a variety of meanings, primarily to denude. It is often translated "uncover." But it can also mean to go into exile (perhaps because prisoners were often stripped of all their possessions and clothing).

The chapter backtracks a bit to explain how that happened, how God's people refused to obey him and followed false gods: "They rejected his decrees and the covenant he had made with their fathers and the warnings he had given them. They followed worthless idols and themselves became worthless" (2 Kings 17:15).

The text says repeatedly that the Lord removed them from his presence or thrust them from his presence, and concludes in verse 23: "So the people of Israel were taken from their homeland into exile in Assyria, and they are still there." Again, the Hebrew word conveying the idea of being carried off into exile is *galah*.

In fact, when the Jews were deported from Samaria, the king of Assyria relocated some of his own people to live there. They didn't like it when God sent some lions in to eat them! (I'm not making that up—read it for yourself in 2 Kings 17.)

One dictionary states:

> There is nothing in the history of Israel as devastating as the Exile. It destroyed the holy city, the temple and the historic ritual of worship; it removed kingship and priesthood from their place in society; it drove the bulk of the people from the land; and it brought an end to Israel's existence as an autonomous nation. Such a devastation brought the people of God to a major crisis in their faith.[1]

The Septuagint (the Greek version of the Old Testament) refers to the various exiles of the Jewish people from their homeland as the *diaspora*, a Greek word meaning "sowing" or "scattering."

Another Hebrew word that means to transport into captivity is *shabah*. We find it in Jeremiah 41:10 ("Ishmael made captives of all the rest of the people who were in Mizpah. . . . Ishmael son of Nethaniah took them captive and set out to cross over to the Ammonites") and several other verses.

What does the exile teach us? That when we reject God's way to follow our own whims, or stop serving him in order to follow other gods (in our culture, we're tempted by "gods" like money, comfort, or success), we will not end up where we want to be. We may not be captured by a foreign army, but we will displace our souls and find that we are no longer at home in God's love.

## FACE

The face of God is a mystery. The Scriptures tell us to seek God's face, but that no one may actually see it and live. While it is possible to be in relationship with God and to know him, we continually seek to know God more. We never stop seeking his face, and yet we never fully attain (in this life, anyway) all knowledge of an infinite God.

Psalm 27:8–9 says:

> My heart says of you, "Seek his face!"
> Your face, LORD, I will seek.
> Do not hide your face from me,
> do not turn your servant away in anger;
> you have been my helper."

Human hearts are hard-wired to search for God. This poetic language expresses the psalmist's desire for God, his commitment to pursue God. His prayer that God not hide his face is explained by the next line in the poem—to hide one's face is to be angry.

Other psalms entreat God to make his face shine upon us (Psalm 80, for example). This prayer is obviously a metaphor. In English, a shining face usually is an idiom for someone who is smiling or happy. In Hebrew, this expression means showing favor. It is a prayer asking for blessing. The Hebrew word *paniym* is the most common word used for face, even though it can also be translated "before," and in fact is much more often used to mean that (as in someone standing before another, i.e., facing them).

One Bible dictionary notes, "The intimacy of a right relationship with God is expressed by God's turning his face toward people, or being seen."[1] (See Psalm 17:15, for example.)

We also find the word *paniym* in the description of the tabernacle. The table in the Holy Place of the tabernacle contained several items, including twelve loaves of bread, which were eaten by the priests after seven days and then replaced. This bread, called the "bread of the Presence" or in some versions of the Bible, the shewbread, is in Hebrew *lechem paniym* or literally, "the bread of the face" (Ex. 25:30; 35:13; Lev. 24:4–6). These loaves were a reminder of God's provision and his presence with the people.

Exodus 33 describes Moses's intimacy with God. Even before the tabernacle was built, Moses would pitch a tent a short way outside the camp, and there he would meet with God (vv. 7–10). In fact, their easy companionship is captured in verse 11: "The LORD would speak to Moses face to face, as one speaks to a friend" (NIV).

And yet, a few verses later, the text tells us that Moses boldly asks to see God's glory, and God says to Moses that seeing his back will have to suffice: "You cannot see my face, for no one may see me and live" (v. 20). The next three verses contain beautiful imagery of Moses in the cleft of a rock, and God approaching and holding up his hand to block Moses's view, so that he will only glimpse God's back.

This apparent contradiction shows us that the word *paniym* is used idiomatically in both these verses. The phrase "face to face" in verse 11 is a metaphor that paints a picture of Moses's intimacy with God—ongoing conversations and even banter mark their interactions.

Likewise, in verses 20 and 23, when God says no one can see his face, or his glory, the idea conveyed is that God is too holy and perfect for us to behold. We cannot see his face, that is, know him fully, because we are finite and he is infinite; we are imperfect and he is perfect. God is, in fact, beyond our limited comprehension. He's not really saying, "Don't peek, Moses." Even Moses, who talked with God like a friend would, was limited in what he was able to comprehend.

Two other words that are sometimes translated "face" are words that literally mean a specific part of the face: *aph,* which can mean nose, nostrils, face, or anger; and *ayin*, which means eye, but sometimes face or presence.

## FATHER

When Jesus taught his disciples to pray, he told them to call God "Abba, Father." The Aramaic term of endearment, *Abba*, was similar to the English *Da-Da* or *Papa*, words that even a babbling baby can manage. Such a name for God is scandalously intimate, yet reminds us that we are small and vulnerable:

*Abba* derives from the Aramaic word *ab*, meaning Father. The Hebrew word happens to have the same English transliteration.

Jesus' direction to speak to God in such intimate, familiar terms may have jarred the sensibilities of some of his listeners. While the Old Testament refers on several occasions to God as a Father, they also thought of him as Yahweh—all-powerful, too glorious and fearsome to approach. After all, God had ordained that the priests approach him on behalf of the people, and ordinary people never ventured into the Holy of Holies. He was a Father of authority and power.

The Old Testament makes much of genealogy, and so we find the word *father* there often, referring to human parents. The Hebrew word *ab* can be used to refer to not only a father but a grandfather or even an ancestor, as well as God. It appears in the text more than twelve hundred times.

God is called by a variety of names, such as *Elohim* or *Adonai*, each expressing different aspects of his character. The Old Testament refers to God as a father both directly and indirectly, and also as a mother (Isa. 66:12–13). The phrase "the shadow of your wings," used to describe God's protection, is a maternal image of a mother hen protecting her chicks with her wings.

While the New Testament refers much more frequently to God as Father, there are a number of verses that do so in the Old Testament. For example:

> Is he not your Father, your Creator, who made you and formed you? (Deut. 32:6)

> Do we not all have one Father? Did not one God create us? (Mal. 2:10 TNIV)

> Yet you, LORD, are our Father.
> We are the clay, you are the potter;
> We are all the work of your hand. (Isa. 64:8 TNIV)

These three verses, and many others, place the words (or ideas) *Father* and *Creator* in parallel. The term *Father* acknowledges him as the source of our life.

*Father* also has a connotation of protection and redemption, as well as authority:

> A father to the fatherless, a defender of widows, is God in his holy dwelling. (Ps. 68:5)

> But you are our Father,
> though Abraham does not know us
> or Israel acknowledge us;
> you, O LORD, are our Father,
> our Redeemer from of old is your name. (Isa. 63:16)

In Jeremiah 3:19, God speaks through the prophet to his people and longingly refers to himself as Father and them as children, saying he wanted to give them an inheritance, but they turned away.

The Messianic prophecy in Isaiah 9:6 refers to Jesus by a list of names including "everlasting Father," acknowledging his oneness with the first person of the Trinity.

The image of God as Father can be troubling. Those abused, neglected, or abandoned by their earthly fathers, or mothers for that matter, struggle to embrace a Father God metaphor. But when we try to put God into terms our finite minds can understand, we must remember that the biblical writers were trying to describe the indescribable. What they are saying is not "God is like YOUR father" but "God is like the perfect ideal of the concept of Father." However, God is not a concept, idea, or vague force, but a person, which is another reason the Bible refers to him as a father.

Any anthropomorphic image of God is, by definition, incomplete. And certainly God, though father-like, is a being who is beyond gender—neither male nor female—yet the two genders both reflect the image of God (Gen. 1:26–27). And yet, to simply say God is love, or God is power, does not give us a complete picture either. But these two approaches complement one another. As C. S. Lewis wrote,

> Never . . . let us think that while anthropomorphic images are a concession to our weakness, the abstractions [metaphysical and theological] are the literal truth. Both are equally concessions; each singly misleading, and the two together mutually corrective.[1]

What Lewis is saying is that when we think of God in abstract terms, we don't get the full picture; yet when we think of him as a Father, we don't get a completely correct view either. But the abstractions and the metaphor of Father balance one another out. While it is helpful to think of God as a perfect Father, he goes far beyond that. We can know him but never completely put him in a box. We must strive to replace the image of our earthly father with one of a perfect Father, all the while realizing that there is more to God than we can ever explain.

## FEAR

God sends his people into battle and tells them not to be afraid. Angels show up and preface their messages with this admonition. Apparently, human response to angelic beings is not just curiosity but terror. Perhaps a careful reading of the text will shatter our illusions of angels being cuddly, feathered, or effeminate. It's also a reminder that God knows us—for all our bravado, we cower inside, especially when faced with the unknown.

Even if you are not visited by Gabriel, there is plenty in this life to fear. And so the most-oft repeated command of Scripture, "Fear not," remains quite relevant to us today. When you walk through the waters or get on an airplane; when you go through the fire, or through your chemotherapy, God promises to be with you, and because of that protective presence, fear is unnecessary (Isa. 43).

But on the other hand, fear is commanded—fear of another kind (Lev. 25:17, 36, 43; Deut. 6:13, 24, etc.). This fear is a respect and awe that recognizes and acknowledges the otherness of God, his power and might.

I don't know about you, but in my church, I don't hear many sermons on this kind of fear. Perhaps our efforts to win converts have inspired us to focus on the friendliness and accessibility of God rather than his power. While he is a God of love, that love becomes all the more amazing when we realize the power that it holds in check. To love God with no fear (as in awe, respect) at all is to love a God far smaller than the one who truly exists, and to limit our experience of him and his power in our lives.

Perhaps that is because if we were to fear the Lord, we would have to admit our own lack of power, that our self-importance is puny next to his glory. If we were to fear him, his love and grace—in light of his power and might—would amaze us more than they do.

There are several Hebrew words that mean fear. The most common is *yare*, which means to be afraid or stand in awe. It refers to the psychological reaction of fear, but also means to acknowledge holiness. This verb is the one typically combined with the negative to express "Fear not." It is the same word that is used in passages where we are commanded to fear the Lord.

The related word *yirah* can describe fear not only of God but also of people. God also can make people afraid of other people. This was, in fact, a primary component of Israel's military strategy as they conquered Canaan. God tells his people: "This very day I will begin to put the terror and fear (*yirah*) of you on all the nations under heaven. They will hear reports of you and will tremble and be in anguish because of you" (Deut. 2:25 NIV). This same word describes fear of the Lord in Isaiah 33:6.

A similar verse is Deuteronomy 11:25: "No one will be able to stand against you. The LORD your God, as he promised you, will put the terror and fear of you on the whole land, wherever you go" (NIV). But in this case, the Hebrew noun that means fear is *morah*. It describes the fear someone feels when they realize they are in the presence of some kind of superior person or being. It could be God, an angel, or even just an enemy who they know is more powerful than they are. Often, it is used to describe the human reaction to the powerful works of God.

Other Hebrew words that mean fear are *pachad*, which can mean a sudden alarm, dread, or terror; *emah*, meaning fright, terror, or fear, deep-seated terror, or dread; and *deagah*, which connotes anxiety or carefulness.

This seeming paradox—we are commanded to fear, but also told we should not be afraid—is resolved when we remember the words of Joshua 1:9: "Have I not commanded you? Be strong and courageous. Do not be terrified; do not be discouraged, for the LORD your God will be with you wherever you go." We are called to be bold and brave, not because of our own power, but because of God's perfect power and strength. His awesome presence is what allows us to face challenges without fear.

## FEAST

The word *feast* (or in some versions *festival*) translates two different ideas. A feast, when it means an elaborate, celebratory, but private meal, is a *mishteh*. The word itself literally means drinking, and it refers to a banquet of celebration. We see it in verses like Genesis 21:8, where Abraham made a great feast, or 1 Kings 3:15, where Solomon makes sacrifices to God and then throws a feast for his entire court.

But the feasts commanded by God are more than just a meal or a party. In these cases, the word translated "festival" or "feast" is *hag* or *chag*, and may or may not involve a lot of food. Often a *hag* requires special symbolic foods, and sometimes it lasts up to seven days. It is a religious ceremony often involving sacrifice. We first encounter this word in Exodus 5:1, where Moses and Aaron ask Pharaoh to let the Israelites go so that they can celebrate a festival to God. Pharaoh, of course, refuses, and so begin the ten plagues on Egypt.

In 2 Chronicles 30:21, Hosea 12:9, and elsewhere, the word *festival* is a translation of the Hebrew word *mo'ed*, which literally means a season or appointment. It is most often translated "congregation," the idea is a place of meeting.

Traditionally, there were seven major feasts in the Hebrew calendar. In the spring, all within one month, were, in this order: Passover (remembering their deliverance from Egypt), the Feast of Unleavened Bread (remembering the Exodus), and the Feast of Firstfruits, an offering of the first sheaf of barley. Fifty days after the Feast of Firstfruits (also called the Feast of Harvest) came Pentecost, also called the Festival of Weeks. This day celebrated the birth of the nation of Israel and Moses coming down from Mount Sinai with the Law (Ex. 23).

Many believe that it is no accident that Jesus was crucified on Passover (probably as the lambs were being slaughtered for the festival in the temple), was buried on the Feast of Unleavened Bread, and resurrected on the day of First Fruits. Fifty days later, on the day of Pentecost, the Holy Spirit arrived. On a day celebrating the birth of the Jewish faith, the church was born.

Later in the year, in the fall, the feasts of Rosh Hashanah (the feast of trumpets), Yom Kippur (the Day of Atonement), and the Feast of Tabernacles or Booths were held. These three sacred autumn festivals were all within a month of each other. The scholars who see significance in the correspondence between the spring festivals and Christ's suffering predict that the fall festivals will somehow coincide with his triumphant return.[1]

Other feasts and festivals include the feast of Dedication (Hanukkah) and Purim. Both are remembrances of God's assistance in saving his people (through Judas Maccabeas and Esther, respectively). The weekly Sabbath was also considered a feast to the Lord, as was the monthly New Moon celebration (Num. 28:11–15). A key element of the feasts is their communal aspect.

> Each festival places great emphasis on community participation and on the community of social or religious tradition. . . . Such shared memory has a cohesive effect upon a cooperating community, large or small, and serves to establish the traditions by which the group lives.[2]

Often, God commanded his people to be joyful, enjoy food and drink, rest from their labor, and enjoy fellowship with one another. The discipline of celebration is woven through the text.

These were to be inclusive events, where even slaves and the poor would be invited to participate. Deuteronomy 16 reviews several festivals or feasts. God reminds his people to be radically inclusive in their celebrations:

> Be joyful at your Feast—you, your sons and daughters, your menservants and maidservants, and the Levites, the aliens, the fatherless and the widows who live in your towns. For seven

> days celebrate the Feast to the LORD your God at the place the LORD will choose. For the LORD your God will bless you in all your harvest and in all the work of your hands, and your joy will be complete. (vv. 14–15)

The feasts were times to celebrate, but also to bring sacrifices to commemorate how God had blessed them. God told them not to show up empty-handed at his feasts, but to bring sacrifices (Deut. 16:16–17).

While we may not celebrate all of the feasts of ancient Israel, we are commanded to live sacrificially and joyfully, and to recognize the blessings of God and thank him for those—not just on special occasions but each day of our lives.

## FIGHT

In an MTV world, following Jesus sometimes feels like a battle. In fact, ever since the Fall, human existence has always had an element of struggle. Philo of Alexandria said, "Be kind, for everyone you meet is fighting a great battle." As Paul wrote in 2 Timothy 4:7, "I have fought the good fight, I have finished the race, I have kept the faith."

Fighting is a metaphor for life. Perhaps the Old Testament stories of God's people fighting are to remind us of that truth.

The Old Testament world was not an MTV world. However, war and violence were normal. Pagan religious practices included temple prostitution and sacrifice of infants. Various tribes and nations constantly rose up against each other. Still, we find it somehow disconcerting to think of God commanding his people to fight against and kill their enemies.[1] (See ***Enemy***.)

In 1 Samuel 15, we read that Samuel says to Saul,

> This is what the LORD Almighty says: "I will punish the Amalekites for what they did to Israel when they waylaid them as

they came up from Egypt. Now go, attack the Amalekites and totally destroy everything that belongs to them. Do not spare them; put to death men and women, children and infants, cattle and sheep, camels and donkeys" (vv. 2–3).

Many people stop reading there, wondering why a God who later said "love your enemies" would do such a thing—and not just then, but repeatedly. However, the text tells us that God is meting out justice for wrong done to the Israelites. Just what those wrongs were, we don't always know.

The story has an odd blend, though, of justice and mercy. We read that Saul musters an army of 210,000 men and plots his attack. But before he does, he warns the Kenites, an apparent ally living near the Amalekites, to flee, because they had shown kindness to Israel. They escape the bloodshed (v. 6).

The story that unfolds in 1 Samuel 15 is full of twists and some interesting thoughts on what it means to obey God. We get an idea of what type of person the king of the Amalekites was when he finally dies. Samuel accuses him of being a baby killer: "As your sword has made women childless, so will your mother be childless among women" (v. 33).

As the Israelites stand on the border of the land God had promised them, they are too afraid to go in and take over the land. Their enemies the Amorites and Anakites are there, and they're terrified. Moses tells them, "The Lord your God, who is going before you, will fight for you, as he did for you in Egypt, before your very eyes" (Deut. 1:30).

The word translated "fight" is *lacham*, which means literally to feed on, to consume. By implication, it means to battle. It is translated "fight" 149 times. It first appears in Exodus 1:10, when Pharaoh fears his Hebrew slaves will join forces with his enemies and fight him. It is used to describe armies fighting in battle, which happens quite often in the Old Testament. It's used in the verses that talk about Israel fighting their enemies, David fighting Goliath, and so forth. God often tells his people to fight other nations in order to take over territory that he is "giving" them—they must engage in battle in order to receive this gift.

A related word is *milchamah*. It appears in the text 319 times and most often means war or battle. It is translated "fight" only five times. Its frequency reflects the reality that war and military conquest and defense were part of life of the ancient world—just as they are in ours.

## FILL

The words *fill* and *fullness* have both literal and figurative meanings, both in English and Hebrew. God declares through the prophet, "Do not I fill heaven and earth?" (Jer. 23:24). Declarations like this, of God's omniscience, are of obvious theological importance, and occur throughout the text.

The Hebrew word in this verse and more than two hundred others is *male'*, and it means to fill or to be full, to fill up a space like water in a cup.

Throughout the Old Testament, we find verses that draw a picture of God's presence by describing a cloud or smoke that fills a space completely. For example, Exodus 40:34, 1 Kings 8, and 2 Chronicles 5 describe the temple being filled with the glory of the Lord, or with a cloud that represents the glory. The word for *filled* in these verses is *male'*. It can sometimes mean filled to overflowing. In these verses, it means filling to capacity.

The opening verses of Isaiah 6 describe a vision the prophet has:

> In the year that King Uzziah died, I saw the Lord seated on a throne, high and exalted, and the train of his robe filled (*male'*) the temple. Above him were seraphs, each with six wings: With two wings they covered their faces, with two they covered their feet, and with two they were flying. And they were calling to one another:

> "Holy, holy, holy is the LORD Almighty;
> the whole earth is full (*melo*) of his glory."

> At the sound of their voices the doorposts and thresholds shook and the temple was filled (*male'*) with smoke. (vv. 1–4)

Isaiah is undone by this vision. Notice the repeated idea of fullness—God's train, his glory, smoke. God does not recline in the corner, waiting for his prophet to notice him. He's unavoidable and uncontainable—the whole earth is completely full of his glory.

The temple or tabernacle is often considered a type, or symbol, of the human heart. In the same way that he fills the temple, he wants to inhabit our souls—utterly and completely, unmistakably. His presence is unavoidable, but in a good way.

*Male'* is also sometimes translated "fulfill," typically to express the idea of fulfillment of prophesy, as it is in 2 Chronicles 36:21: "The land enjoyed its sabbath rests; all the time of its desolation it rested, until the seventy years were completed in fulfillment of the word of the LORD spoken by Jeremiah." This verse also hints at another use of *male'*, which is to express the fulfillment of a set amount of time (in this version, translated "completed").

A second word group that is translated "fill" or "fulfill" is *sabea'*, which means to be satisfied, as with food. The related *soba* is typically translated "fullness." It is often used to describe God's generous provision for us, both physically and spiritually. We are fully satisfied in our relationship with God.

This beautiful word expresses the abundance of God's goodness, the fullness with which he meets our needs. It reminds us that there is more than enough of God and his goodness to go around—that his goodness, love, mercy, and indeed his whole self cannot be contained. There are no shortages when it comes to his glory, nor to his love for us. *Sabea'* is often translated "satisfies."

"Blessed are those you choose and bring near to live in your courts! We are filled with the good things of your house, of your holy temple" (Ps. 65:4). (See also Ps. 103:5.)

Many seek fulfillment. These words remind us that what will truly fulfill us is the fullness of God's presence and his goodness.

## FIRSTFRUITS

The Bible is more than a list of rules—we must read the text with discernment to discover how to apply it to our lives today. For example, we no longer have to sacrifice bulls and goats (see the book of Hebrews). But how can we live with a biblical mindset? What does that mean?

God's people believed that everything belonged to God, and that any wealth they had was the result of his blessings. Rather than make the jump of logic to a prosperity gospel (if I'm good, God will make me rich—which is neither true nor biblical), perhaps we should consider this question: What if I were to see everything in the world, including things I label "mine," as gifts on loan from a generous God?

If we look for a rule for giving, we can extract one from the text: Give ten percent—tithe. And if we can manage that, after paying the mortgage and the light bill, we see ourselves as generous. We take our old clothes and beat-up furniture and donate them to charity. Even in our generosity, we view it as giving God something that belongs to us. But consider the possibility that this practice is essentially giving God the leftovers. The Bible asks that we give God the best—the first portion, not the last.

The Hebrews believed that everything belongs to God, and we are simply stewards of it—a truth the New Testament teaches as well. Any steward's goal is to manage and use his master's resources in a way that will support and protect the master's interests, not his own.

The practice of giving God the firstfruits tangibly acknowledged this reality. Throughout the year, various crops came into season. The Hebrew calendar was tied to these harvests. As each crop ripened, the first portion went to God. It was as if they were saying, "You first, God." It was an act of both thanks and trust, an affirmation that there was more than enough.

An offering of firstfruits was a way of affirming that God had not only been good, but could be trusted to continue to be so. By giving rather than hoarding the first part of a harvest, God's people took the risk of trusting him to provide more, to replenish their supply.

Firstfruits offerings were "waved" before God and then could be eaten by the priests, because they did not have any means to grow their own food. They were a celebratory offering.

The concept of firstfruits connects with the festivals. The Festival of the Harvest, also known as the Feast of Firstfuits, less than a week after Passover, is held in the spring and celebrates the first of the barley harvest: "Celebrate the Feast of Harvest with the firstfruits of the crops you sow in your field" (Ex. 23:16).

Fifty days later was the feast of Pentecost, also known as the Festival of Weeks, when the next crop, the wheat, was harvested. Later crops were celebrated with later festivals—again to acknowledge God's goodness. Exodus 34:22 says, "Celebrate the Feast of Weeks with the firstfruits of the wheat harvest, and the Feast of Ingathering at the turn of the year." The year was punctuated with gratitude, expressed as feasts and festivals.

Two Hebrew words are translated "firstfruits." Both words occur in Leviticus 23, which outlines all of the festivals. In verse 10, we read, "Speak to the people of Israel and say to them, When you come into the land that I give you and reap its harvest, you shall bring the sheaf of the firstfruits of your harvest to the priest" (ESV). The word for firstfruits is *reshiyth*.

In Leviticus verse 17, just seven verses later, the word translated "firstfruits" is *bikkuwr*.

*Reshiyth* means not just the first harvest of a crop, but the first in place, time, order, or rank. *Reshiyth* is often translated "beginning." We find this word in the opening sentence of Scripture, "In the beginning . . ."

It also means the first thing, or it can be used in a comparative sense to mean the choicest or best (Dan. 11:41).

The second word, *bikkuwr*, means specifically the first harvest of a crop. It is a word that recognizes God's ownership of the land. It is the word used to name the festival of firstfruits, which occurred right after Passover and fifty days before Pentecost (Num. 28:26; Lev. 23:15–16). Both firstfruits and Pentecost included a firstfruits offering.

While we may not keep these festivals, we should make their attitude part of our faith. God does not want our leftovers, but the first and best of our resources, our efforts, and our love.

## FOOL

In English, the word *fool* means someone who is silly or intellectually inept. A fool is stupid, someone who is perhaps headstrong and makes dumb choices, with the implication that he doesn't know better. But in an apparent attempt to remain politically correct, we have extracted the moral component of foolishness—and this is the heart of the definition of this biblical word. We don't blame foolish people for their foolishness, or see it as a moral failure—they are, as the saying goes, "just plain stupid."

A fool in the Old Testament is not merely stupid or intellectually challenged. The Bible fearlessly links foolish behavior with corrupted morals—someone acts wrongly or foolishly because they are not following God, because they are being selfish or sinful.

Foolishness in its various forms is the outcome of sin, a moral rather than intellectual shortcoming. The terms *fool* and *foolish* occur most frequently in the wisdom literature, especially Proverbs. Wisdom and foolishness are opposites, but again, they do not have to do only with intellect, but with morality, which stems from a person's connection to God.

The words *fool, folly,* and *foolishness* are translations of three Hebrew words (and their derivatives): *iwwelet, kesil,* and *nabal.*

*Iwwelet* refers to a rebel, a person who makes destructive choices. For example, "Folly (*iwwelet*) is bound up in the heart of a child, but the rod of discipline will drive it far from him" (Prov. 22:15).

The idea here is not that children are stupid, but that they have within them the propensity to sin. While children are in some ways innocent (in the sense that they are naïve), anyone who has spent time with a two-year-old knows that they are also capable of rage, deceit, and selfishness. In other words, they are sinners. Human nature has a sin component. No parent has to teach their child to shriek "Mine!" but they all do it. *Iwwelet* reflects that reality of human nature.

We don't outgrow this tendency. Proverbs 14:1 uses this same word: "The wise woman builds her house, but with her own hands the foolish (*iwwelet*) one tears hers down." *House* is used metaphorically to describe a woman's life and family.

Our culture tends to see foolishness as mental incapacity, but the Old Testament words connote moral deficiency. A fool is not just lacking intelligence; he or she is rebellious. This is key because if someone is merely stupid, it is easy to excuse them for their behavior. The Bible makes no such excuses.

*Iwwelet* comes from the same root as *eviyl*, which is used to describe a person who despises wisdom or is quarrelsome or licentious. *Eviyl* appears twenty-six times; nineteen of those are in the book of Proverbs, in verses like this one: "Wisdom is too high for a fool (*eviyl*); in the assembly at the gate he has nothing to say" (Prov. 24:7).

The second word, *kesil*, refers to fools who are stubborn, who continue to make bad choices despite the consequences. This type of fool doesn't really care what is right or wrong, even when he is injured by his own actions. It's typified by this verse: "As a dog returns to its vomit, so a fool (*kesil*) repeats his folly (*iwwelet*)" (Prov. 26:11).

This term, which occurs seventy times, most often in Proverbs, describes those who "have knowledge of God but do not properly evaluate and understand what they know."[1]

In 1 Samuel 26, we read of Saul trying to win back David's trust. He says, "Surely I have acted like a fool and have erred greatly" (v. 21). The Hebrew word is *cakal*, a verb that means done foolishly. This word comes from the same root as *kesil*.

Similarly, in Ecclesiastes 10:3, we read, "Even as he walks along the road, the fool (*cakal*) lacks sense and shows everyone how stupid he is."

The third word, *nabal*, includes more of a sense of stupidity, without absolving the moral failure that caused that stupidity. *Nabal* refers to an inner disposition, foolishness that results in blatant sinful behavior. It means not just foolish but impious, abandoned, wicked. We find this word in the oft-quoted verse: "The fool (*nabal*) says in his heart, 'There is no God' " (Ps. 53:1).

We see this word, in a parallel structure with *kesil*, in verses like this: "To have a fool (*kesil*) for a son brings grief; there is no joy for the father of a fool (*nabal*)" (Prov. 17:21).

Each of us has a choice: to pursue and seek out wisdom (and thus, to gain more wisdom), or to ignore God and live the perilous and unfulfilling life of a fool. If we have even a tiny bit of wisdom, we know which path to walk.

## FOREVER (EVER)

The word *forever* in Scripture does not always literally mean an infinite amount of time. When it describes the reign of God, it does mean eternal, but the word *forever* can also mean a long life, or a continuous action. It can also mean ancient or future times.

*Forever* is often used to describe the blessings God promises, but such blessing is often tied to man's obedience. For example, in Deuteronomy 5:29, we read about the longing of God: "Oh, that their hearts would be inclined to fear me and keep all my commands always, so that it might go well with them and their children forever!"

The word *forever* stresses the eternal nature of God and the eternal nature of his laws and his love. For example, in Exodus 3:15, God tells Moses, "Say to the Israelites, 'The LORD, the God of your fathers—the God of Abraham, the God of Isaac and the God of Jacob—has sent me to you.' This is my name forever, the name by which I am to be remembered from generation to generation."

Likewise, in 1 Chronicles 28, we read that King David tells his royal officials that God has promised him that his son Solomon will continue to reign successfully if Israel follows the Lord. He reports that God told him, "I will establish his kingdom forever if he is unswerving in carrying out my commands and laws, as is being done at this time" (v. 7). It is a conditional promise of sorts because of that little word *if*. And it does not mean that Solomon will literally live forever, but that his offspring and heirs will continue his kingdom. It is also a prophetic word, pointing to the kingdom of God that eventually comes through Jesus.

The most common Hebrew word translated "forever" is *owlam*. It can mean a long duration, antiquity, perpetual, future, and more. It can mean always or for an indefinite future amount of time. It sometimes connotes something the beginning or end of which is not clearly defined. It can also mean a very long life—not necessarily eternity, but rather, "as long as one lives."

> In a few passages the word means "eternity" in the sense of not being limited to the present. Thus, in Eccl. 3:11 we read that God had bound man to time and given him the capacity to live "above time" (i.e., to remember yesterday, plan for tomorrow, and consider abstract principles); yet He has not given him divine knowledge.[1]

Another Hebrew word that means forever, though it is used less frequently, is *tamiyd*. It can mean continuity or continually, perpetually or continuously, or to stretch. In Numbers 28, it is translated "regular" when referring to the "regular burnt offering" that is offered each day.

The word *forever* occurs numerous times in the Psalms, reassuring us of God's eternal nature. Even when things seem bleak, the word *forever* reminds us that in the end, God will prevail.

The word *forever* is repeated numerous times in 2 Samuel 7, where we read of David's concern for the ark of the covenant. In spite of the fact that God had blessed him and his people with a time of peace, he feels upset that he is "living in a palace of cedar, while the ark of God remains in a tent" (v. 2). He discusses this with the prophet Nathan, who then hears from God, telling him that David's son, not David, "is the one who will build a house for my Name, and I will establish the throne of his kingdom forever (*owlam*)" (2 Sam. 7:13).

David responds by praising God, saying things like, "You have established your people Israel as your very own forever (*owlam*), and you, O LORD, have become their God" (v. 24).

We also find *owlam* repeated in the Psalms in phrases like "Save your people and bless your inheritance; be their shepherd and carry them forever" (Ps. 28:9) and "his love endures forever" (Ps. 118:29 and as a repeated refrain in Ps. 136).

In other psalms we find other Hebrew words translated "forever." For example, the word *ad*, which comes from the word *adah,* to advance or continue. *Ad* means duration, in the sense of advance or perpetuity. We find it in verses like "The fear of the LORD is pure, enduring forever" (Ps. 19:9).

Both words are found in Psalm 10:16, showing that they are synonyms: "The LORD is King for ever (*owlam*) and ever (*ad*)."

Because we belong to God, we are also eternal beings who will live forever. The struggles of this life will not last forever, but our relationship with God will. Do we live our lives as if we really believe this is true? Do we fully grasp the truth that even our toughest trials are "light and momentary troubles" in view of eternity?

## FORTY

*Forty* is a word, but of course, a word that means a number. It is one of several numbers in the Bible that is symbolic and highly significant. We almost always find the word *forty* associated with periods of either forty days or forty years.

Some ancient calendars were set up in forty-day cycles, even though the lunar cycle is twenty-eight days. So it makes sense that, especially in the historical books, this was used as a mark of time. Where we might say "a month," many ancient people, both biblical and extra-biblical, might refer to forty-day increments. The Bible even mentions that the Egyptian process of embalming took forty days (Gen. 50:3).

In the New Testament, Jesus begins his ministry with a forty-day time of solitude, fasting, and prayer, in which he is tested. This would have made perfect sense to the people of Jesus' day, who understood that the number forty often signified testing or trials. Forty sometimes can refer to a period of time (whether days or years) in which people experience the chastisement or judgment of God. Whether forty years of peace or forty years of struggle, both are seen as consequences from the hand of God. This is rarely explained directly in Scripture because it is assumed that the original readers would understand it, so we must rely on extra-biblical sources to discern its significance.

The Hebrew word is *arbaiym*, a multiple of *arbaah*, which is four. The word *forty* appears in the text 136 times.

The first important period of forty in the Bible is in the story of Noah. God floods the earth with forty days and nights of rain, rescuing only Noah and his family because of their obedience, along with selected animals.

We may remember Sunday school stories indicating there were two of each species, but the text actually points out that there were seven pairs of clean animals and birds, and two of each unclean animal (Gen. 7:2). Seven was another significant number indicating perfection.

The story of Moses and the children of Israel is loaded with references to the number forty. Moses spent his first forty years living as a prince in Pharaoh's palace, then fled to work as a shepherd in Midian for forty years, then spent the final forty years of his life leading the children of Israel to the Promised Land. Both his trips onto Mount Sinai lasted forty days, and when he came down, his face continued to glow for forty days.

After forty years in the desert, Moses sent spies into the Promised Land. They explored Canaan for forty days, then reported back to the Israelites of the land's riches, but also its strong armies. For their cowardice in refusing to go into the Promised Land, God told them they would have to wander the desert for another forty years, one year for each day (Num. 14:34).

Goliath taunted Saul's army twice a day for forty days until David showed up and put him in his place (1 Sam. 17:16). When Jonah went to Nineveh, he gave them forty days' warning about God's wrath, during which time they repented.

The history of Israel is studded with important forty-year periods, although it cannot be neatly divided into only forty-year increments. One notable exception is the Exile, which lasted seventy years (2 Chron. 36:21).

During the period of the judges, Israel would sometimes be at war with its neighbors, but then a good leader would arise, and several times the text says that the land or its people "had peace for forty years" (Judg. 3:11; 5:31; 8:28).

Many of Israel's great kings, including David and Solomon, each reigned for forty years—although Asa, David's son, who followed God, reigned forty-one years (1 Kings 15:9–11). Israel was under Philistine occupation for forty years (Judg. 13:1). Both Isaac and Esau were forty years old when they married (Gen. 25:20; 26:34).

One website, www.biblestudy.org, points out that these forty-year increments, whether of prosperity and peace or of struggle, were each probationary in their own way. Moses's forty years in Midian and Israel's forty years in the desert were each a probation in which they waited for God.[1]

The number forty reminds us that both times of peace and times of wandering in the desert do not last forever. Sometimes we must endure testing or struggle, but those struggles are only for a season.

## FRUIT/FRUITFUL

The word *fruit* appears in the opening paragraphs of the Old Testament. On the third day of creation, God commands the land to produce vegetation, including fruit trees, and it quickly complies: "The land produced vegetation: plants bearing seed according to their kinds and trees bearing fruit with seed in it according to their kinds" (Gen. 1:12). The words *fruit* and *fruitful* are connected with the themes of abundance and productivity in the Old Testament.

A few verses later, Genesis 1:22 says, "And God blessed them, saying, 'Be fruitful and multiply'" (NKJV). This verse is the first instance of the word *fruitful* in the Bible. If you look at the context, you'll see this first blessing was decreed not to human beings (who, according to the narrative, had not yet been formed), but to the animals, birds, and fish. It sounds like a command, but the verse says it was a blessing, along the lines of "May you be fruitful." It's the only instructions he gives to the animals, who apparently were happy to obey.

A few verses later, God repeats this blessing, this time to the humans he's made in his own image. This is how it was before the Fall—God's first priority included something that would be enjoyable for everyone involved. The world in all its magnificence, and the gift of sexual relations (which are a necessary part of being fruitful), and of children, were given to people as a blessing.

The most common Hebrew word for fruitful is *parah*, meaning to bear fruit. It can refer to trees that bear fruit or beings having young. It occurs twenty-nine times in the text. The word for fruit, *p'riy*, comes from *parah*, and means both fruit of plants and offspring of human beings and animals. It is found more than one hundred times in the Old Testament. Children are referred to figuratively as the "fruit of the womb" of their mother or "fruit of the loins" of their father.

The metaphor is rich: A child is not merely a physical reproduction of his parents, but continues to carry the image of God within himself that his parents did.

In the books of the prophets, we see a second word appearing occasionally, *karmel*, which means a planted field or garden. It can mean a fruitful field or, in just a couple of references, a full ear of corn. We see it in Isaiah 29:17, where the prophet warns of coming chaos: "In a very short time, will not Lebanon be turned into a fertile field (*karmel*) and the fertile field seem like a forest?" (See also Isa. 32:15–16.)

Fruit (*p'riy*) can also mean the product or result, as it does in

Proverbs 31, which speaks of a woman who buys a vineyard with the "fruit of her hands," i.e., income she's earned by working. Similarly, many passages use fruit as a metaphor for the result of God's work in the world. For example, Psalm 104:13 says, "He waters the mountains from his upper chambers; the land is satisfied by the fruit (*p'riy*) of his work."

God's blessing command to "be fruitful" means more than simply having children, but also includes productivity in general. It underscores this important theological point: We were created to work and be productive.

Work is not a part of the curse; before the Fall, Adam worked in the garden. The Fall made work much more difficult, but the ability to work itself was part of how we are created in God's image. Just as God is at work in the world, so are we to be working in the world—furthering his kingdom, providing for our families, exercising our creativity, doing the things he has called us to do. These are part of what it means to be fruitful. And being fruitful is part of what gives life meaning, what gives us joy and satisfaction.

Rather than seeing work as drudgery, what if you could see your work, whatever it is, as a way of obeying God's command to "be fruitful"?

## GLEAN

For a few years now, my father, who is retired, has participated in an early morning group called The Gleaners. These men visit orange and avocado orchards near my parents' home in Southern California and pick leftover fruit that the farmers cannot sell. The fruit is then donated to food banks and shelters in the area so that the poor may have orange juice and, apparently, guacamole.

The word *gleaner* comes from the Old Testament word *glean*, which means the practice of going over a field a second time to pick up leftovers of the harvest. God told his people not to glean their own fields, not even to harvest all the way to the edges, but to leave some grain or fruit behind so that the poor could glean there—that is, gather up the leftovers. Gleaning was the ancient Middle Eastern equivalent of the cardboard sign reading "Will work for food."

While the words *glean, gleaned,* and *gleaning* appear fewer than two dozen times in the Old Testament (and of those, a dozen of the references are in one chapter, Ruth 2), it still represents an important theme, because it reflects God's heart of compassion for the poor.

There are two Hebrew words that are translated "glean" or "gleaning." One is negative, the other positive.

The first, *alal*, means to affect thoroughly, to deal with severely. It can also mean to glean, but implies overdoing or abuse. One dictionary listed this colorful definition: "to be saucy to."

Judges 20 describes a battle between Israel and the tribe of Benjamin. After Israel defeats Benjamin, their soldiers pursue and "cut down" (*alal*) five thousand more men of the tribe of Benjamin (v. 45). The King James Version says, "They gleaned of them in the highways," that is, went back to kill those who had escaped the first battle.

The second word, which is used a dozen times in Ruth 2, is *laqat*, which means to pick up, to gather, to glean. The related *leget* means gleaning. The words are often translated "gather." In the book of Ruth, two widows find a kinsman-redeemer by going to a field and gleaning.

The word is not used but implied in verses like Deuteronomy 24:19–21 (NIV):

> When you are harvesting in your field and you overlook a sheaf, do not go back to get it. Leave it for the foreigner, the fatherless and the widow, so that the LORD your God may bless you in all the work of your hands. When you beat the olives from your

> trees, do not go over the branches a second time. Leave what remains for the foreigner, the fatherless and the widow. When you harvest the grapes in your vineyard, do not go over the vines again. Leave what remains for the foreigner, the fatherless and the widow.

Unlike the pagan gods of the ancient world, Yahweh is concerned for the poor. He also wants his people to be humble, to remember that they too were slaves and they know what it is to be poor. God is quite thorough, telling them not to glean their grain, olives, or grapes. All of it should be harvested in such a way that some is left—reflecting the abundance of God and the heart of generosity God wants his people to have.

Leviticus 19:9–10 says, "When you reap the harvest of your land, do not reap to the very edges of your field or gather the gleanings (*leqet*) of your harvest. Do not go over (*alal*) your vineyard a second time or pick up the grapes that have fallen. Leave them for the poor and the foreigner. I am the LORD your God" (TNIV).

A similar verse just four chapters later says the same thing: "When you reap the harvest of your land, do not reap to the very edges of your field or gather the gleanings (*leqet*) of your harvest. Leave them for the poor and for the foreigner residing among you. I am the LORD your God" (Lev. 23:22 TNIV).

This second reminder comes as a seeming interruption—Leviticus 23 is a list of the annual festivals and feasts the Israelites are to keep. It's as if God, in the middle of reminding them of the feasts, says, "Oh, did I mention—don't forget about the poor." It's a poignant look at the heart of God, who even as he tells his people to feast, reminds them to feed the poor. What good would feasting be if his people forgot the hungry? What good would remembering and celebrating God's deliverance be if they ignored the disenfranchised among them?

## GLORY

Depending on our faith tradition, we may sing choruses that pray, "Let the glory of the Lord rise among us," or recite liturgy that says, "Glory to you, Lord Christ." But do we really understand glory?

God's glory is an attribute he possesses, but it's also something we are to give him. His glory is sometimes shown in a very localized situation, and yet it is also something that the whole earth is full of and the universe declares. In others words, it is a mysterious word, not easily pinned down. It can mean renown or honor, brilliance.

The *Tyndale Bible Dictionary* says glory is "indefinable" but gives this attempt to explain the mystery of God's glory: "All the attributes of God are summarized in Scripture's references to the glory of God. The majesty, splendor, beauty, and brilliance of God who dwells in unapproachable light are expressed by this indefinable term."[1]

The Hebrew word most frequently translated "glory" is *kavod*. The word connotes weight or worthiness, significance. It was often used to describe a person who is impressive or significant.

In Exodus 14 and 15, we read of the miraculous escape of the Israelite slaves from Pharaoh of Egypt. He commands them to go to the edge of the sea, where they will appear to be trapped when Pharaoh pursues them. God's military strategy of having his people seem confused so that Pharaoh will pursue them was unconventional, to say the least. His people fear they will die. But God assures them, "The Egyptians will know that I am the LORD when I gain glory through Pharaoh, his chariots and horsemen" (Ex. 14:18). The purpose of parting the seas, allowing Pharaoh to pursue, and so on is for God to show his power, to "gain glory."

After the Israelites march through the sea on dry land, and then turn to watch as God drowns the Egyptian army, the text says, "And when the Israelites saw the great power the LORD displayed against the Egyptians, the people feared the Lord and put their trust in him and in Moses his servant" (Ex. 14:31). And then Moses leads them in a song of worship, honoring God for what he has done. Part of that song says, "Who among the gods is like you, O Lord? Who is like you—majestic in holiness, awesome in glory, working wonders?" (Ex. 15:11).

God is awesome in glory whether we notice it or not, and yet, when we respond with reverence and praise to his marvelous and miraculous acts, we give him glory, or as the text says, he "gains glory."

In Numbers 14:10, it says that the glory of the Lord rather suddenly appears at the tent of meeting, and God speaks directly to Moses. What did that glory look like? Was it like the cloud, or the pillar of fire?

The word *glory* (*kavod*) is related to both of these things—it is the power and majesty of God, yet also his love. It is God's self-revelation, through nature and human hearts. Glory is the aspect of God that fills us with awe, wonder, and worship—not out of obligation, but because it is our natural response when we see it.

For example, we read in Psalm 19:1: "The heavens declare the glory of God; the skies proclaim the work of his hands." The parallel phrasing of the poetry aligns God's glory with his works. Those works testify to his power and glory.

Isaiah 6 describes a vision of angels who continually declare, "Holy, holy, holy is the Lord Almighty; the whole earth is full of his glory" (v. 3).

Rob Bell writes about *kavod*:

> The whole earth is full of the weight and significance of who God is. The prophets were deeply influenced by this understanding that the earth is drenched with the presence of God. . . . According to the ancient Jewish worldview, God is not somewhere else. God is right here. It is God's world and God made it and God owns it and God is present everywhere in it. . . . But

God is always present. We're the ones who show up. For the ancient Jew, the world is soaked in the presence of God. The whole earth is full of the *kavod* of God.[2]

## HARVEST

In her book *Animal, Vegetable, Miracle*, author Barbara Kingsolver tells a story of her husband harvesting vegetables from his suburban garden, and the neighbor children gathering curiously to watch. When he pulls a carrot from the dirt, they stare at it in wonder. One child demands to know how he got that carrot into the dirt! Our culture separates us from the land. We think food comes from a grocery store, wrapped in cellophane. We eat things that are made mostly of chemicals and a bit of genetically altered oil, and call them treats.

However, the Old Testament was written to a people who did not eat Twinkies and who farmed the land or gathered from woods and fields. Their idea of "processed food" was olive oil, flour, and wine.

In an agrarian society, the harvest is the focus. It's the whole point. If the harvest goes well, you eat. If it doesn't go well, you could starve. So it's not surprising that *harvest* is an important word, and that the weather that provided a good harvest was seen as God's blessing. Harvest was not just a time of gathering in the crops, but one of celebration. Several of the feasts had to do with the harvest of various crops (see ***Feast***) and, as we have seen, making sacrifices from them (see ***Firstfruits***).

Even the Hebrew calendar was based on the cycle of planting and harvesting crops. Throughout the long growing season, harvests of various crops were celebrated, often by sacrificing a part of the harvest to God.

In Hebrew, the word for harvest is *qatsiyr*. We also see the word *aciyph*, which means ingathering, a synonym for harvest—the crops that are gathered in.

Exodus 23:16, for example, says, "Celebrate the Feast of Harvest (*qatsiyr*) with the firstfruits of the crops you sow in your field. Celebrate the Feast of Ingathering (*aciyph*) at the end of the year, when you gather in your crops from the field."

Palestine had two growing seasons. Grain grew through the winter and was harvested in the spring, while fruits like grapes and olives grew through the summer and were harvested in the fall. The grain was planted after the fall rains (also known as the "former rains") had softened the earth. The Feast of Passover was tied to the Festival of the Harvest (or Firstfruits) and was at the beginning of the year, in the spring, when the barley crop that had been growing through the winter first ripened. Fifty days later, the feast of Pentecost celebrated the harvest of wheat (Ex. 34:22). As the grain was ripening and being harvested (in the spring), the other crops were sowed and began to mature through the long, hot summer.

One website adds,

> The grapes begin to ripen in August, but the gathering in for making wine and molasses (*dibs*), and the storing of the dried figs and raisins, is at the end of September. Between the barley harvest in April and the wheat harvest, only a few showers fall, which are welcomed because they increase the yield of wheat (compare Am 4:7).[1]

Three festivals in the fall—Rosh Hashanah, Yom Kippur (the Day of Atonement), and the Feast of Tabernacles (also called the Feast of the Ingathering)—celebrate the fall harvest of fruit. As that harvest is gathered in, the grain is planted again, and the cycle repeats.

The word *harvest* is also used metaphorically.

> The "time of harvest," in the Old Testament frequently meant the day of destruction (Jer 51:33; Hos 6:11; Joel 3:13). "Joy in harvest" typified great joy (Isa 9:3); "harvest of the Nile," an

> abundant harvest (Isa 23:3). "The harvest is past" meant that the appointed time was gone (Jer 8:20). Yahweh chose the most promising time to cut off the wicked, namely, "when there is a cloud of dew in the heat of harvest" (Isa 18:4, 5). This occurrence of hot misty days just before the ripening of the grapes is still common. They are welcome because they are supposed to hasten the harvest. The Syrian farmers in some districts call it *et-tabbakh el'ainib wa tin* ("the fireplace of the grapes and figs").[2]

*Qatsiyr*, like many Old Testament words, is also a prophetic image. When Jesus comes, he says things like, "The harvest is plentiful but the workers are few" (Matt. 9:37), using *harvest* as a metaphor for saving souls.

## HEART

The psalmist pleads, "Create in me a clean heart, O God" (Ps. 51:10 KJV).

A clean heart, according to Hebrew thinking, would influence all of life. (See ***Clean***.) And according to the next line of the psalm, a clean heart is parallel to a "right spirit." The word for spirit is *ruwach*, which can mean breath, spirit, or even wind. It is the essence of a person and is sometimes used to describe a person's disposition or temper.

Because our culture is more influenced by Greek and Latin roots, we need to recalibrate our thinking in order to understand the Old Testament. Hebrew thinking did not focus on the dichotomy of body and soul, but rather the contrast between the inner self and the outer appearance. The heart, soul, or spirit were inner; one's name, reputation, and how others perceived you was outer.

The Bible tells us, "For the LORD does not see as mortals see; they look on the outward appearance, but the LORD looks on the heart" (1 Sam. 16:7 NRSV).

To the Hebrew way of thinking, the goal of the life of faith was to bring the inner and outer self into alignment. And because one's actions flowed from the heart, that was the place for transformation to begin.

The Hebrews also didn't even talk about a distinction between "the heart and the head" as modern-day Western thinkers do, separating the emotional from the rational self. The ancient Hebrews saw the heart as the seat of emotion and motive, but also of human understanding. When the Old Testament mentions knowing something in one's heart, it can be considered to be a synonym of "mind," a person's knowledge and wisdom (or lack thereof).

The first two mentions of the word *heart* in the Bible come one right after the other, in Genesis 6, where we read: "The Lord saw how great man's wickedness on the earth had become, and that every inclination of the thoughts of his heart was only evil all the time. The Lord was grieved that he had made man on the earth, and his heart was filled with pain" (vv. 5–6).

These two verses establish that man's propensity to sin is based in his heart, and that God also has a heart, which is broken by that sin. The good news is that God can change a person's heart, and thereby transform them completely, as promised in Ezekiel 11:19: "I will give them an undivided heart and put a new spirit in them; I will remove from them their heart of stone and give them a heart of flesh."

When Moses asks Pharaoh to let the Israelites go, Pharaoh's refusal is described in a strange way. In some verses, it says Pharaoh hardened his heart and refused. Obviously, as it is in English, a hardened heart is an idiom for stubbornness.

But some verses make Pharaoh seem like a puppet of sorts: they say that God hardens his heart. Scholars argue about what this means. Some say God actually hardened Pharaoh's heart, and who are we to judge what God does? Others say the use is idiomatic, because the text also says Pharaoh hardened his own heart, and in fact was a hardhearted person who ordered babies killed and kept a whole nation in slavery. His heart was already like a stone. God could have softened it but chose not to because Pharaoh was unrepentant.

The Hebrew words translated "heart" most often are *leb* and a synonym, *lebab*. Both mean heart, mind, or midst. "Often means the inner person, with a focus on the psychological aspects of the mind and heart, which also includes decision making ability."[1] *Lebab* can also mean mind or understanding, or courage.

Another word that is translated "heart" about a dozen times is *nephesh*. This is an important word in Scripture, appearing some 753 times. In the vast majority of those instances, it is translated "soul" or "life." It again refers to the inner vitality or life of a person or animal, the very heart of a person—emphasizing the inner person from which thoughts and actions flow. (See ***Soul***.)

As noted above, God's people aimed to bring their outer and inner life into consistent alignment, which was why they prayed for a "clean heart." This single-mindedness is a theme throughout Scripture and a prayer we'd do well to pray fervently. We should care as much about the purity of our hearts as we do about how we appear to others.

## HELP/HELPER

The word *help* in English can have various connotations, depending on context. *Help* can be a verb meaning to assist, or it can be a noun describing servants—as in, "the help." It can also describe the actions of a parent or superior reaching down to help someone who cannot function alone, who "needs help."

In Genesis 2:18, God notices that Adam is alone. Everything else in creation up to that point has been declared good, but God says that aloneness is not a good thing. So he creates a helper or help suitable for Adam.

The word translated "helper" or "help" is *ezer*. Many dictionaries define *ezer* simply as "one who helps." But how does an *ezer* help? As a child helps a parent, or as a parent helps a child? As a secretary or administrative assistant helps the boss (this was the meaning I was taught growing up in the church)? Or as a shepherd helps his sheep?

One way to determine the meaning of the word is to look at the way it is used in other verses. In almost every other occurrence, the word *ezer* is used to describe the help we receive from God. And this is not the gentle, nurturing side of God (although that obviously exists). Rather, it is the strong, warrior side of God. For example, in Deuteronomy 33:29, we read, "Blessed are you, O Israel! Who is like you, a people saved by the Lord? He is your shield and helper (*ezer*) and your glorious sword." This military imagery gives us a clue to the meaning of *ezer*: a strong warrior who aids and protects.

This is the word God used to describe Eve—a warrior to stand beside Adam. In almost every other instance, *ezer* refers to God. In Exodus 18:4, Moses names his son *Eliezer*, which means God is my helper; in 1 Samuel 7:12, Samuel sets up a stone for an altar and names it *Ebenezer*, which means stone of help. In these and all of those other instances, it describes the help God gives to his people.

Carolyn Custis James, in her book *Lost Women of the Bible*, writes:

> Thinking regarding the *ezer* began to change when scholars pointed out that the word *ezer* is used most often (sixteen of twenty-one occurrences) in the Old Testament to refer to God as Israel's helper in times of trouble. That's when *ezer* was upgraded to "*strong* helper," leaving Christians debating among themselves over the meaning of "strong" and whether this affects a woman's rank with respect to the man. Further research indicates *ezer* is a powerful Hebrew military word whose significance we have barely begun to unpack. The *ezer* is a warrior, and this has far-reaching implications for women, not only in marriage, but in *every* relationship, season, and walk of life.[1]

The Bible has other words that are also translated "help." The word *azar*, which *ezer* comes from, appears eighty-two times and can mean help or helper, again often describing the help of God or the help of one king or city to another. The word *ezrah* or *ezrath* is the feminine form of *ezer* and means help or helpers. We find it especially in the Psalms, such as Psalm 40: "Be pleased to save me, LORD; come quickly, LORD, to help me. . . . But as for me, I am poor and needy; may the Lord think of me. You are my help and my deliverer; you are my God, do not delay" (vv. 13, 17 NIV). Again, the word is a picture of strength and comfort, emphasizing the kindness of God and his sufficiency.

The word *teshu'ah* means deliverance or salvation, and in some verses is translated "help." The word *yasha* means to save or deliver, and also to help. It has a connotation of freedom and safety, of rescue.

Another word that is sometimes translated "help" is the word *y'shuwah*, which is most often translated "salvation" or "deliverance." Of course, this word sounds familiar, as the name *Jesus* is the Greek form of *y'shuwah*. (The names *Joshua* and *Isaiah* also contain this root, and both mean the Lord is help.) (See ***Deliver***.)

We all need God's help, and we must be humble enough to ask for it. We are, as the psalm says, poor and needy. To fully appreciate the help of God, we must humble ourselves before him. And our ultimate help (not just for temporal problems but for eternal ones) comes from *Y'shuwah*.

## HID/HIDDEN/HIDE

In Genesis 3, God extracts this terrible confession from Adam: "I heard you in the garden, and I was afraid because I was naked; so I hid" (v. 10). The word in Hebrew is *chaba*. It means to hide yourself, with an implication of secrecy. It is found thirty-three times in the Old Testament—Adam was not the only one who tried to hide. God was obviously not pleased—he knew immediately that because Adam had something to hide, sin had entered the world.

That is a huge part of what it means to sin—to do wrong and to try to hide it. Perhaps not coincidentally, the Hebrew word for sin, *chata*, is similar to the word for hid, *chaba*. In Hebrew they are both three-letter words whose first and last letters are the same.

Satan is the father of lies and wants us to believe that we must hide our sin, for if God knew of it, he would not forgive us. But of course, God knows about it. And the only path to forgiveness is disclosure.

One cannot hide from God (see Ps. 139). Our lives and in fact our very souls are laid bare before him. This is both good news and bad—that he knows all. Yet the story of redemption is one that includes hiding—the hiding we must come out of when we trust God (see again Ps. 139, esp. vv. 23–24).

A number of other words are translated "hide," "hid," or "hidden."

The word *cathar* (sometimes transliterated *satar*) appears eighty-two times in the text. It means to hide by covering, to conceal, hide, shelter. Sometimes it implies protection, as in Jeremiah 36:26, when God hides his people from an enemy. But it can also be a consequence of sin, as it was for Cain. His sin caused him to be hidden from God's presence (Gen. 4:14). Similarly, in Micah 3:4 it is used to describe God hiding his face from his people because of their sin.

Hide can have a positive connotation, as it does in Psalm 119:11, which says, "I have hidden your word in my heart that I might not sin against you." The word in this passage is *tsaphan*. It appears thirty-three times in the text, and it means to hide or treasure up, as it does in Proverbs 10:14: "The wise store up (*tsaphan*) knowledge, but the mouth of a fool invites ruin" (NIV). *Tsaphan* can also have a less positive connotation when it means to lurk or lie in wait (Prov. 1:18).

A word that appears frequently in the text but is only translated "hide" a handful of times is *kacah*. Of the 152 times it appears in the text, it most often means to cover. It literally means to plump or fill up, by implication to cover, that is, to hide or conceal. It is found in verses like Psalm 143:9: "Rescue me from my enemies, O Lord, for I hide myself in you."

The word *taman*, which means to hide by covering over, appears thirty-two times in passages like Exodus 2:12, where Moses hides the body of the Egyptian he killed by burying it in the sand. From this root we get another word, *matmun*, which appears only five times and means a secret storehouse, hidden treasure.

Other words that are also translated "hide" or "hidden" are *alam* (to veil from sight), *kachad* (to destroy or conceal), and *ta'alummah* (a thing that is hid, a secret).

The Bible has many different words to describe hiding. This again points to the fact that our nature is to try to cover up our wrongdoing, to keep secrets. When we hide, we remain in unresolved pain and guilt. But as it says in John 3:20–21, "Everyone who does evil hates the light, and will not come into the light for fear that their deeds will be exposed. But whoever lives by the truth comes into the light, so that it may be seen plainly that what they have done has been done in the sight of God" (NIV).

What we eventually see is that we cannot hide from God. We feel as Adam did, fearful and exposed. But when we realize that there is really no place to hide, we give up. We stop trying, and in that coming out of hiding, coming into the light, we find freedom. In the light of God's love we are fully known and forgiven.

## HOLY

The word *holy* is first used in the Old Testament by God himself, to describe the ground where he meets Moses in front of the burning bush. He tells Moses to take off his shoes, "for the place where you are standing is holy ground" (Ex. 3:5).

In his video *Breathe*, Rob Bell comments on this passage:

> Moses has been walking this land for forty years. I mean, it isn't as if the ground all of a sudden became holy. The ground didn't just change. It's that Moses becomes aware of it. Which raises the question for us, "Are we standing on holy ground, all the time?" Passing burning bushes on the left and the right, and because we're moving too fast and we're distracted, we miss them. What do you believe it means "to be standing on holy ground"? Are we standing on holy ground all of the time, but are not aware of it?[1]

What does this word *holy* actually mean? The Hebrew word in this verse and hundreds of others is *qodesh*. If a thing is *qodesh*, holy, it is set apart, sanctified, other.

Pagans in ancient times also believed their gods were holy, that is, they were different and set apart from mortals. The differences between the pagan and Hebrew definition of holy are subtle but critical to our understanding, not just of the Bible but of the very nature of God.

Scholar M. William Ury notes:

> Through revelatory instruction Moses taught Israel that their conception of the holy affirmed an essential difference between themselves and deity. Pagan worshipers in that region could not have reflected on the nature of the holy with that sort of clarity. What was "other" than the normal for them was distinct in Israel as a personal "Other."[2]

Ury points out that the pagan understanding that their gods were "holy" meant that they were filled with absolute terror of those gods, and their various sacrifices and rituals were attempts to guess at what would appease the anger of those gods. Different religious rituals developed among followers of the various gods.

Yahweh radically differs from pagan gods because, Ury posits, "Yahweh is looking for those who are willing to 'walk' with him rather than cower in fear alone."[3] (See ***Walk***.)

This information puts verses like Micah 6:8 in a whole new light: "What does the Lord require of you? To act justly and to love mercy and to walk humbly with your God." No other god in ancient days spelled out what he required, and none invited people to walk with him.

When Isaiah encounters the holiness of God (Isa. 6), his first response is one of realizing his own unholiness. "Woe to me!" he cries. "I am a man of unclean lips!" (v. 5). But God purifies Isaiah's lips and makes him a holy messenger. Again, the otherness of God becomes an invitation into relationship.

R. C. Sproul writes:

> The Bible says that God is holy, holy, holy. Not that He is merely holy, or even holy, holy. He is holy, holy, holy. The Bible never says that God is love, love, love, or mercy, mercy, mercy, or wrath, wrath, wrath, or justice, justice, justice. It does say that He is holy, holy, holy, the whole earth is full of His glory.[4]

Holiness is arguably God's most important characteristic, but one we focus very little on in today's culture. We'd prefer to focus on his love and mercy, loving-kindness and patience. We think of him as the God next door, which is, in a way, what Jesus modeled. But he is still holy and deserving of our respect.

Sproul writes:

> The primary meaning of *holy* is "separate." It comes from an ancient word that meant "to cut" or "to separate." Perhaps even more accurate would be the phrase "a cut above something." When we find a garment or another piece of merchandise that is outstanding, that has a superior excellence, we use the expression that it is "a cut above the rest."[5]

Exodus 15:11 says:

> Who among the gods
> is like you, O LORD?
> Who is like you—
> majestic in holiness,
> awesome in glory,
> working wonders?

The parallel phrasing gives us clues about what holiness is: a holy God is majestic, powerful. He's awesome, he works wonders, his very nature is glorious. (See ***Glory***.)

## HONEY

My friend Sandy's mother is known to Sandy's kids as Grandma Honey. She got that name from her eldest grandchild, because she would say to him, "Bring that book to Grandma, honey, and I'll read you a story," or "Give a kiss to Grandma, honey." So, in that irrefutable logic of children, he assumed her name was Grandma Honey. The name, pardon the pun, stuck, and now all three grandkids, even though they are teenagers, call her that—which she loves.

We use honey as a sweetener and as a term of endearment. Honey is medicinal, being an effective cough suppressant, for example.

Ancient people used honey as a sweetener, but also to treat everything from rashes to sore throats. There's some evidence the Egyptians used it for embalming. It is mentioned in the Quran as a gift from Allah, and in sacred writings of other faiths as well.

Archeologists believe that ancient Egyptians kept bees, but these insects were also plentiful in woods and fields, so that anyone could harvest wild honey.

The Hebrew word for honey is *debash* (or sometimes transliterated *devash*). It appears fifty-four times in the text—of those, twenty-one times in the phrase "milk and honey," a phrase used to describe the Promised Land.

The word *debash* can mean honey (from bees) but also syrup, or to be gummy. Some scholars believe that honey referred not only to honey from bees but also to the syrup made from dates. Dates grow on date palm trees, which grow in the desert. It can also refer to the syrup left after wine is made from grapes.

Milk in ancient times came mostly from goats and sheep. The phrase "flowing with milk and honey" describes a land that is fertile—where rain is sufficient and soil is rich enough that flowers and pastures can grow, so that bees can make honey, and milk-producing animals can graze.

The word *flowing* is an interesting one. It can mean to flow, gush, issue, discharge. The same word is used in Leviticus 15 and elsewhere to describe a bodily discharge or "issue."

The idea is that this land is just oozing with abundant provision of food. Some scholars claim that the idea of flowing with milk and honey has a sensuous or even sexual connotation of abundant fertility.

The phrase refers to the blessings God will give to his people. But he warns them to not become complacent and predicts that their newfound wealth will cause them to forget God (Deut. 31:20).

Some of the oddest Bible stories involve honey. In Judges 14, Samson kills a lion, then later finds that bees have built a hive in its carcass, which makes him think up a riddle to share at his wedding feast. It's an odd story. An even odder one is found in 1 Samuel 14, where the word *debash* is combined with another word, *ya'arah*. Together the words describe a honeycomb in a forest that is literally dripping honey. Saul had commanded the people to fast, even as they walked through a wood where there was honey everywhere, even on the ground. Saul's son Jonathan had not heard this decree, so when he finds honey dripping from the trees, he eats some. The text says "his eyes brightened" (v. 27), meaning most likely that his strength was renewed. This later gets him in trouble with his father. Again, it's a strange story.

In Deuteronomy 32, Moses speaks of Jacob, as a way of talking about God's people Israel, saying that God provided: "He nourished him with honey from the rock, and with oil from the flinty crag" (v. 13). Psalm 81:16 echoes the phrase, which speaks of the miraculous provision of God. It may seem strange to think of honey coming from a rock, but before people cultivated bees, bees would often nest in rocks, trees, or anyplace they could find a crevice to build a nest.

The image of milk and honey is another prophetic image, this time of God's grace—something wonderful we've been given without earning it.

There are other words that mean honey or honeycomb. The word *tsuwph* means honeycomb. The word *nopheth* is translated "honeycomb" but refers to shaking a honeycomb to release the honey from it.

We see these words in Psalm 19:10, which says of God's judgments:

> They are more precious than gold,
> than much pure gold;
> they are sweeter than honey (*debash*),
> than honey (*nopeth*) from the honeycomb (*tsuwph*).

## HOPE

There's something ironic and, well, hopeful, about the fact that the two books of the Bible that the word *hope* appears in most frequently are the Psalms (primarily the Psalms of Lament) and the book of Job.

There are several words that are translated "hope" in the Old Testament. Most frequently, it is the word *yachal*, which means to wait or to be patient. For that is what hope is—not just a vague longing but a confident expectation, a patient waiting. To hope in God is to trust him.

We find *yachal* often in the Psalms and prophets in the phrase "hope in the LORD" or "hope in God" in verses like Psalm 31:24: "Be strong and take heart, all you who hope in the LORD." Hope, in some ways, connects the present to the future. Hope does not ignore the struggles of life, but acknowledges them. Biblical hope is not mere wishful thinking; it has an object: God himself. As Psalm 42:5 says:

> Why, my soul, are you downcast?
> Why so disturbed within me?
> Put your hope (*yachal*) in God,
> for I will yet praise him,
> my Savior and my God. (NIV)

Another Hebrew word that is frequently translated "hope" is *tiqvah*, which appears thirty-four times and is also translated "expectation." The word literally means a cord, conveying the idea of an attachment. It figuratively means expectancy. We find it several times in the book of Job, in verses like this: "Should not your piety be your confidence and your blameless ways your hope?" (Job 4:6).

*Tiqvah* also appears in an oft-quoted verse about hope, Jeremiah 29:11, in which God tells his people, "'For I know the plans I have for you,' declares the LORD, 'plans to prosper you and not to harm you, plans to give you hope and a future.'" The phrase "a hope and a future" is translated in the King James Version simply "an expected end," the rendering of two Hebrew words, *tiqvah* (hope or expectation, expected) and *achariyth* (end, latter, posterity).

There are several other words meaning hope or expectation that appear infrequently in the text: *towcheleth*, meaning expectation or hope; *batach* and *betach,* which convey the ideas of trust, safety, security; *bittachown,* meaning confidence; *shabar*, meaning hope, tarry, wait; *seber*, meaning expectation; and *mibtach*, which occurs fifteen times but typically means security, assurance, or trust and is translated "hope" only one time.

A very interesting word that has a variety of meanings, including hope, is the word *miqve* (also transliterated *miqveh or mikvah*). This word occurs twelve times in the Old Testament. It comes from the same root as *tiqvah*: the word *qawah*. This root and its derivatives focus on what is in the future. We find it in Ezra 10:2: "Then Shekaniah son of Jehiel, one of the descendants of Elam, said to Ezra, 'We have been unfaithful to our God by marrying foreign women from the peoples around us. But in spite of this, there is still hope (*miqve*) for Israel.' "

*Miqveh* can also mean something waited for, confidence, a collection, pond, caravan or drove, gathering together, hope, linen yarn, or a pool. These meanings are not as diverse as they may seem. Modern Jews are very familiar with the term *mikvah*, used to describe a ritual bath for cleansing. It is a pool in which a "collection" of water was "gathered together." In ancient days it was used by priests before entering the Holy of Holies, and by women who would bathe after their monthly cycle was completed. Because Jewish couples do not have relations during a woman's period, but are encouraged to do so after she has bathed in the *mikvah*, it is also something "waited for."

The Jewish *mikvah* was a precursor to Christian baptism, a symbol of renewal and hope. One website notes:

> The "mikvah" was the immersion pool used by God's people in ancient times for purposes of purification. Each morning, before beginning their priestly service at the Temple, the priests and Levites would immerse themselves in a mikvah bath at the Temple, to purify and cleanse themselves, so they were physically and ritually pure, before performing their priestly duties.

> Also, each worshipper at the Temple was required to undergo a mikvah bath of immersion before coming onto the sacred Temple Mount.[1]

The connection between baptism and hope becomes obvious in the New Testament. As it says in Ephesians 4:4–6: "There is one body and one Spirit—just as you were called to one hope when you were called—one Lord, one faith, one baptism; one God and Father of all, who is over all and through all and in all."

## HORN

The first time that the children of Israel heard the voice of God, it sounded to them like a horn or trumpet. In Exodus 19, we read:

> On the morning of the third day there was thunder and lightning, with a thick cloud over the mountain, and a very loud trumpet blast. Everyone in the camp trembled. Then Moses led the people out of the camp to meet with God, and they stood at the foot of the mountain. Mount Sinai was covered with smoke, because the LORD descended on it in fire. The smoke billowed up from it like smoke from a furnace, and the whole mountain trembled violently. As the sound of the trumpet grew louder and louder, Moses spoke and the voice of God answered him. (vv. 16–19 NIV)

The word for trumpet is *shophar* or *shofar*, which is a trumpet crafted from a hollowed-out ram's horn that has been heated and shaped. Because they heard this sound when they were given the Torah, the *shofar* became a sacred instrument. The *shophar* is still sounded at the beginning of Rosh Hashanah, the Jewish New Year. It is meant to be a blast that awakens God's people to repentance, to return to God.

In the Bible, the word *horn* is primarily an Old Testament

word, occurring only one time in the New Testament (Luke 1:69) and thirty-five in the Old Testament. The plural *horns* occurs sixty-seven times, again mostly in the Old Testament. The only place it is found in the New Testament is in the book of Revelation, where it occurs ten times. The word *shophar* occurs seventy-two times in the Old Testament.

The Hebrew word typically translated "horn" or "horns" is *qeren*. This word means the horn of a ram or other animal, something that projects, a flask, a cornet. The word *horn* has a figurative meaning of power and strength—as a ram's power is in its horns.

As it does in English, a horn can mean the bony projection that grows from the head of an animal, or a musical instrument like a trumpet. In fact, it's clear that ancient people made musical instruments from animal horns. Joshua's famous knocking down the walls of Jericho was accomplished by the blowing of the *shophar*, trumpets made from rams' horns (Josh. 6).

The story in Joshua uses the words *shophar*, *qeren*, and another Hebrew word, *yobel*. This word literally means the signal, blast, or sound coming from a horn and refers specifically to the horn blown to assemble the people for sacred holidays and festivals. Even more specifically, *yobel* means jubilee—the celebration held every fifty years in which slaves were set free and land was returned to its original owners. This celebration was heralded with silver trumpets rather than the cruder trumpets fashioned from rams' horns.

The word *qeren* can mean the horn of an animal, or something constructed to look like a horn. The elaborate instructions for the tabernacle contained in the book of Exodus describe in painstaking detail the specifications for the altar. The altar was where atonement was made, centered in the Holy of Holies. It is a rectangular box made of gold, which is not surprising. However, the instructions note very clearly that it is to be embellished with horns: "Make a horn at each of the four corners, so that the horns and the altar are of one piece, and overlay the altar with bronze" (Ex. 27:2).

Two chapters later, God tells the priests how to incorporate the horns into the sacrifice ritual: "Take some of the bull's blood and put it on the horns of the altar with your finger, and pour out the rest of it at the base of the altar" (Ex. 29:12). The horns were the specific part of the altar where atonement was made: "Do not offer on this altar any other incense or any burnt offering or grain offering, and do not pour a drink offering on it. Once a year Aaron shall make atonement *on its horns*" (Ex. 30:9–10, emphasis mine).

Throughout the Bible, the word *horn* is a symbol of power. Daniel's apocalyptic vision (Dan. 7) includes beasts with horns, and also disembodied horns with eyes—again this is a symbol of the power of God.

The phrase "horn of salvation" is a metaphor for God's power and strength: "The LORD is my rock, my fortress and my deliverer; my God is my rock, in whom I take refuge. He is my shield and the horn of my salvation, my stronghold" (Ps. 18:2; see also 2 Sam. 22:3). God defends us like a charging bull; he breaks down the strongholds that hinder us or hold us back. His is not a self-serving power but one that works for our salvation, for our good.

## HOUSE

The Hebrew word *bayith* is found at least once in every book of the Old Testament except Jonah, occurring 2,055 times in the text. The word primarily means house, household, or home. It can also mean family, temple, palace, prison, or place.

*Bayith* is a rich tapestry of a word, and obviously an important one. Of course, like *house* in English, *bayith*'s primary meaning is a permanent physical structure where people live. Its second meaning is expressed in the phrase "the house of the Lord," in which case it can mean the temple or a place of worship.

It's also used to describe a household, with the connotation of family or descendants, in phrases like the "house of David" or the "house of Judah." This is referring to a large extended family or tribe. The Psalms often exhort the "house of Aaron" or the "house of Jacob" to follow after God.

We see both of these uses in Psalm 122:

> I rejoiced with those who said to me,
> "Let us go to the house of the LORD." (v. 1)

This is a reference to the temple, with the idea of going to the house of the Lord for the purpose of worshiping him.

Another word that reminds us of the idea of *bayith* is found in verse 4:

> That is where the tribes go up—
> the tribes of the LORD—

This is a reference to the people of God, the twelve tribes of Israel, who together are known as the house of Israel. The following verse uses *bayith* again:

> There the thrones of judgment stand,
> the thrones of the house of David. (v. 5)

*Bayith* can also be used to refer to immediate family, or those living within a household, which in Old Testament times often meant more than one generation. We see this use in Joshua's declaration to the children of Israel after they have taken possession of the Promised Land:

> But if serving the LORD seems undesirable to you, then choose for yourselves this day whom you will serve, whether the gods your forefathers served beyond the River, or the gods of the Amorites, in whose land you are living. But as for me and my household, we will serve the LORD. (Josh. 24:15)

In 1 Kings 6, which describes Solomon's temple, the word *bayith* is found thirty-four times in just thirty-eight verses. In modern translations of this chapter, *bayith* is rendered "temple," but in the King James Version and other older translations, it is translated "house." While *temple* is certainly accurate, *house* conveys the idea not only of a building but of a family and a legacy—which are an integral part of the meaning of *bayith*. Solomon's moral struggle—was he building a house for himself, or for God—should inspire us to reflect on our own similar question: Are our lives about building God's kingdom, or advancing our own agenda?

Psalm 127:1 reminds us, "Unless the Lord builds the house, its builders labor in vain." Here we see *bayith* being used metaphorically. God does not come down with hammer and nails to construct a building (although he did, eventually, in the person of Jesus, come to think of it). Rather, in this verse, *house* is a metaphor for a person's goals and desires, the very structure of their life. Jesus echoed this teaching when he talked about building a house on shifting sand instead of a firm foundation.

The word *house* appears many times in the historical books, often to speak of the houses of various kings and rulers. Some houses were blessed because of obedience; others were destroyed because of sin. In the peculiar story of Ahab the king of Samaria and his wife, Jezebel, found in 1 Kings 21, we see *bayith* used both literally and metaphorically.

Ahab wants a vineyard owned by Naboth, because it is near his palace (*bayith*). Naboth refuses to sell the vineyard, so King Ahab goes back to his house (*bayith*) to pout.

His wife, Jezebel, takes matters into her own hands, and has Naboth killed. God's punishment of Ahab and Jezebel is swift and will last for generations: "I will make your house (*bayith*) like that of Jeroboam son of Nebat and that of Baasha son of Ahijah, because you have aroused my anger and have caused Israel to sin" (1 Kings 21:22).

In our culture, we often focus on the physical house we live in but neglect the house of our legacy and family. The Old Testament calls us to a richer understanding of this word and its implications for our lives: What sort of house are we building?

## ISRAEL

The word *Israel* occurs more than 2,500 times in the Old Testament. In Hebrew the word is nearly the same as English: *Yisrael*. The word is the name given to Jacob after he spends the night wrestling with God, in the form of a man. The story is recorded in Genesis 32: "Then the man said, 'Your name will no longer be Jacob, but Israel, because you have struggled with God and with men and have overcome' " (v. 28).

The name *Israel* means struggles with God or he strives with God. It can also mean "he will rule (as) God."[1] *Yisrael* is rooted in two Hebrew words: *sarah*, which means to prevail or power, and *El*, meaning God. The name is rich with meaning—it means not just to wrestle (as in a struggle against), but also to cling wholeheartedly to God. It also contains overtones of being able to overcome or prevail.

Jacob's new name comes with a blessing and is confirmed a few chapters later. By confirming his name, God is reiterating his covenant, which was begun with Jacob's grandfather, Abraham. One commentary notes that this name signified "God's confirming of his covenant with Jacob. . . . The name spoke of his being bound with a bond of life and love to God."[2]

Israel is not just Jacob's new name; it becomes the name of all of his descendants, who are known as the children of Israel, or the Israelites. This phrase is the predominant usage of this word in the Old Testament.

The Old Testament is essentially the story of the children of Israel. Jacob had twelve sons, and their story is told in the closing chapters of Genesis. The narrative focuses on his second to youngest boy, Joseph, whose brothers' jealousy leads them to sell him into slavery. God continues to watch over and bless Joseph, and he is eventually reunited with his father and brothers.

Jacob/Israel's family continues to grow, and in the opening pages of Exodus, we read of their oppression and slavery by the leaders of Egypt, where they were living because Joseph had brought them there when he was in power. After Joseph dies, a new king comes to power, "to whom Joseph meant nothing" (Ex. 1:8 NIV), and he decides to make them slaves.

Thus begins four hundred years of slavery, in which God's chosen people toil until God sends Moses and Aaron to lead them out of Egypt.

Their miraculous escape from Pharaoh and wanderings through the desert for forty years are recorded in Exodus. The rest of the Old Testament includes the details of their covenant with God, their history, and their poetry. While they are God's chosen people, they often turn against him or do not follow his laws. They are described as "stiff-necked people," stubborn, rebellious, and willful (see Ex. 33:3–5 for example). "Children" seems an apt moniker for them—their behavior often seems immature. They turn away from God, get into trouble, then call on him for help. This push and pull continues throughout the Old Testament. Truly they are a people who wrestle with God.

And yet, despite their fickleness, God loves them deeply. He longs for them to turn toward him, to be his people. He desires not only to seek them out, but that they would seek him out and follow him. (See, for example, Jer. 29:12–14.)

Israel is the root of the Christian faith. The New Testament tells us that non-Jewish believers are a branch grafted in to that root (Rom. 11). The history of the children of Israel is the history of God's people, and therefore the history of the church and anyone who believes.

When God comes to earth in the form of Jesus, he is born into a family within Israel, but he says that he comes to preach to both Jews and Gentiles. Luke 2:32 says that Simeon prophesied about Jesus when he was only a baby, calling him "a light for revelation to the Gentiles and for glory to your people Israel."

## JUBILEE

The word *jubilee* in English sounds celebratory, rolling off the tongue in a joyful sort of way: jubilee! And yet it is a word we don't use much, certainly not with its biblical meaning. It is one of the most interesting and provocative words in the Old Testament. The Hebrew is *yobel*, which means a ram's horn as well as a Jubilee year. (The ram's horn was blown to announce the year of Jubilee.) (See ***Horn***.)

Jubilee is first mentioned in Leviticus 25, which outlines God's economic principles. Crops were to be cultivated for six years, then the land was to lie fallow for a year.

> But in the seventh year the land is to have a sabbath of rest, a sabbath to the LORD. Do not sow your fields or prune your vineyards. Do not reap what grows of itself or harvest the grapes of your untended vines. The land is to have a year of rest. Whatever the land yields during the sabbath year will be food for you—for yourself, your manservant and maidservant, and the hired worker and temporary resident who live among you, as well as for your livestock and the wild animals in your land. Whatever the land produces may be eaten. (vv. 4–7)

Notice that what grew was to be shared among landowners and slaves, livestock, and even wild animals. God's provision was literally for everyone!

The text goes on to say that after seven Sabbath years—which would equal forty-nine years—the fiftieth year was to be proclaimed a Jubilee. In that year, three things happened: Land returned to its original owners, debts were cancelled, and slaves were set free. (Debt and slavery often went hand in hand, as people would sell themselves into slavery to pay off debt.)

The Jubilee year was to be announced on the Day of Atonement with a sounding of the ram's horn (*yobel*).

God's economic laws feel foreign to us. But University of Missouri professor Michael Hudson writes that throughout the ancient world, similar "clean slate" traditions were common and considered necessary. The first such laws were implemented around 2400 BC. He writes:

> Radical as the idea of the Jubilee seems to modern eyes, these "restorations of order" were a conservative tradition in Bronze Age Mesopotamia for 2,000 years. What was conserved was self-sufficiency for the rural family-heads who made up the infantry as well as the productive base of Near Eastern economies. . . . The clean-slate tradition was so central to Israelite moral values that it framed the composition of both the Old and New Testaments.[1]

Modern farmers know that allowing land to lie fallow occasionally will boost its productivity. This law makes sense agriculturally, but for many of us, it does not make sense in any other way. Our culture is one of grabbing what you can and hanging on to it, of fiercely defending what we believe is ours.

The ancients did not think this way. Even pagans in the ancient Middle East believed that land was owned by gods, and that people who inhabited land had to worship the god whose land it was. (See ***Exile***, also 2 Kings 17.)

So even though the Jubilee command says that the land is to revert to the original owner, it actually is an affirmation that the "original owner" has the land on loan from God, who is the ultimate land LORD.

Theologian Ched Meyers writes,

> The prescribed periodic rest for the land and for human labor goes beyond the agricultural good sense of letting land lie fallow. It functions to disrupt human attempts to control nature and "maximize" the forces of production. Because the earth belongs to God and its fruits are a gift, the people should justly distribute those fruits, instead of seeking to own and hoard them.[2]

The Jubilee law, then, is a call to justice and compassion and a reminder that the earth and all that is in it belongs to God. It is also a prophetic picture of the ultimate freedom that we have in Christ, and the clean slate that cancels our debt of sin when we put our trust in him.

## JUDGE

Our tolerant society sometimes recoils at the word *judge*, especially when used as a verb. We say to anyone who questions our behavior, "Don't judge me," in a self-righteous attempt to deflect criticism of our bad behavior.

Nevertheless, judges maintain orderly society. Without judges, criminals would not be punished, unjustly accused people might suffer, chaos would ensue. Laws must be enforced, and the weak protected—which is, ideally, what a judge does. Ironically, shows featuring judges, from Judge Judy to Simon Cowell, are immensely popular.

In ancient times, lawlessness was common. Nations warred, and even people within a kingdom argued, of course. It's human nature. But it is also part of human nature to long for justice—a sense of fairness is built into us, and if that justice is violated by wrongdoing, we want someone to pay, to be punished for their injustice.

The Old Testament book of Judges records the history of Israel after they came into the land of Canaan under Joshua's leadership. Their allegiance to Yahweh was tenuous at best. They would follow him, then go astray, then plead for mercy. God would rescue them, only to have them go astray again. It was not a highlight on the résumé of God's people.

The Middle East at the time of the judges was in a state of flux, with various tribes and peoples attacking each other, vying for land rights and so forth. And the children of Israel, within a generation of Joshua's death, had fallen away from God and were not keeping his covenant. God attempts to restore them, we read in Judges 2:16–17:

> Then the LORD raised up judges, who saved them out of the hands of these raiders. Yet they would not listen to their judges but prostituted themselves to other gods and worshiped them. Unlike their ancestors, they quickly turned from the way in which their fathers had walked, the way of obedience to the LORD's commands.

The little phrase "raised up judges" shows us an important theological truth. When God has an important task to do, he raises up leaders—people. He does not hurl thunderbolts or send hurricanes; he sends a person, spiritually gifted to lead and organize, someone who could help rally a defense against Israel's enemies.

The Hebrew word in this passage is *shaphat*, which means to judge, deliver, or rule. It can be a verb, meaning to govern, or a noun, meaning a judge or a leader. Vine's dictionary says, "*Shaphat* refers to the activity of a third party who sits over two parties at odds with one another."[1]

We find this word in Exodus 18, which tells a wonderful story of Moses and his father-in-law, Jethro. On a visit, Jethro saw that Moses's job of judging the people's disputes was too overwhelming. He provided him a model of government so that the load was shared, and thus saved Moses from sure burnout. Moses appointed other leaders (the Hebrew word is *sar*, meaning ruler or chief) to take on some of the judging responsibilities. Again, God's method for imparting his wisdom is by raising up leaders—people who will be his instruments.

The word *shaphat* sometimes means deliverance and is translated "vindicate" in some versions. For example, Psalm 43 begins: "Vindicate me, my God, and plead my cause against an unfaithful nation" (NIV). Some older versions say "Judge me"—the idea is that God is both our judge and our advocate, because when he judges impartially, he will see that we have been mistreated and deliver us. In this and other verses, *shaphat* means to deliver from injustice or oppression. (See also 1 Sam. 24:15.)

A second Hebrew word, used somewhat less frequently, is *diyn* or *duwn*, meaning to rule, to judge, or to strive.

There is a subtle difference between the two words: "*Diyn* implies a settlement of what is right where there is a charge upon a person. *Diyn* is a judicial word marking the act whereby men's position and destiny are decided. *Shaphath* is an administrative word pointing to the mode in which men are to be governed and their affairs administered."[2]

A third word, *mishpat*, means judgment or rights. It can mean the act of sitting as judge or the rights belonging to a person.

## JUST/JUSTICE

The Bible describes God as just, meaning that he is fair, righteous, unbiased. He will not punish unjustly, nor will he allow sin to go unaccounted for. The Bible also calls us to act justly, to use just weights and measures (that is, to act fairly in our commerce), to make sure that courts and laws are unbiased.

The Bible also calls us clearly to fight injustice, to defend the cause of the fatherless, the widowed, the orphaned and oppressed.

There are several related words that mean just or justice. They are also related in some ways to the previous word, *judge*: "Appoint judges (*shaphat*) and officials for each of your tribes in every town the LORD your God is giving you, and they shall judge (*shaphat*) the people fairly" (Deut. 16:18).

The word *fairly* gives us a hint of what it means to be just. *Fairly* is how the New International Version renders two Hebrew words: *tseqed* and *mishpat*. The King James Version renders the end of this verse "they shall judge the people with just (*tseqed*) judgment (*mishpat*)."

*Mishpat* also means justly:

> He has shown all you people what is good.
> And what does the LORD require of you?
> To act justly (*mishpat*) and to love mercy
> and to walk humbly with your God. (Micah 6:8 TNIV)

*Mishpat* means judgment or rights, as we discussed in the previous entry. How does one "act *mishpat*"? These three exhortations are each facets of the same idea: When we love mercy, not just for ourselves but others, when we walk humbly, not considering ourselves to be more important than we are, then we will act in such a way that protects the rights of others, that shields them from injustice—just as God would do. When we are walking with God, we will act in ways that are consistent with his character, we will remain in step with him—thus being both fair and merciful.

The Hebrew word *tsaddiyq* means both righteous and just. It is sometimes used to describe God, as it is in Deuteronomy 32:4, where the parallelism helps us understand its meaning:

> He is the Rock; his deeds are perfect.
> Everything he does is just and fair.
> He is a faithful God who does no wrong;
> how just (*tsaddiyq*) and upright he is! (NLT)

The closely related *tsadaq* means to be or make right, justify, righteous, just, justice. It originally meant to be stiff or straight. This word is used to describe a person who has been set free or delivered from affliction or condemnation. Thus, it is used to describe someone who has received justice. Nearly half of the forty-one times it occurs are in the book of Job. We also find it in verses like this:

> Do not deny justice (*tsadaq*) to your poor people in their lawsuits. Have nothing to do with a false charge and do not put an innocent or honest person to death, for I will not acquit the guilty. (Ex. 23:6–7)

> Defend the weak and the fatherless; uphold the cause (*tsadaq*) of the poor and the oppressed. (Ps. 82:3 NIV)

Some older versions, including the New American Standard Version and the King James Version, translate *tsadaq* as "do justice." The prevailing idea behind *tsadaq* is that we would not simply avoid doing injustice, but rather, that we would be advocates of justice for those who need our help. It is an active rather than a passive word.

Biblical justice is both relational and legal, both dynamic and static. It refers to just standards of conduct that do not change, but also justice that is based on compassion and love, which cannot be legislated but only practiced as we imitate God.

Ronald J. Sider points out that there is a strong connection between the words *love* and *justice* (Hos. 10:12; Deut. 10:18). He argues that many Christians ignore the plight of the poor, and that doing so is unjust. Sider writes, "Biblical justice does not mean we should merely help victims cope with oppression; it teaches us to remove it. Biblical justice does not merely require fair procedures for the poor; it demands new opportunity!"[1]

## KING

The word *king* appears thousands of times in the Old Testament, in part because so much of it is devoted to the history of God's people, particularly their leaders.

The Hebrew words translated "king" or "ruler" are *malak*, which means at its root to reign or ascend to the throne, and its derivative *melek*, meaning a king or royal. In that society, the function of the king was to be commander in chief of the army, chief executive of the people, and an important religious figure. Even pagan kings were seen as representatives of the gods they followed.

As the children of Israel were moving into the Promised Land, God told them through Moses that someday they would likely want to have a king, as the nations around them did. He set up rules for kingly behavior, most of which we now read with a sense of irony and sadness because so many kings flagrantly disregarded these rules, which included prohibitions against having too many horses, chariots, wives, or too much silver and gold (Deut. 17:14–20).

Unlike judges, who ruled for a season, kings would stay in power their entire lives, then pass the throne on to their sons. The potential for corruption was far greater.

One website offers these insights:

> In and of itself, the desire to have a king was not bad. . . . A king was in God's plan for Israel. Yet, the *reason* Israel wanted a king was wrong. "Like all the nations" is no reason at all. . . . We may also get into trouble when we want the right things for the wrong reasons. In those situations, God may give us what we want, and then deal with us regarding the reasons.[1]

Despite God's warning and reluctance to give them a king, the people insist (1 Sam. 8:4). In the period of the judges, which preceded the monarchy, the people often did not listen to the man God had raised up as a judge. It seems inevitable that they would also not pay attention to a king. The book of 1 Samuel tells the complicated story of how the monarchy was established in Israel.

The temptation for the subjects of any king is to make the king more important than God, rather than seeing him as a representative of God. In 1 Samuel 12 we read of God's response to the request for a king through the prophet Samuel. He tells the people:

> Now here is the king you have chosen, the one you asked for; see, the LORD has set a king over you. If you fear the LORD and serve and obey him and do not rebel against his commands, and if both you and the king who reigns over you follow the LORD your God—good! But if you do not obey the LORD, and if you rebel against his commands, his hand will be against you, as it was against your fathers. (vv. 13–15)

To illustrate his point and show God's power, Samuel calls on God to send a thunderstorm that day, which was during the wheat harvest, thus ruining their crop, reminding the people of God's power.

Even so, God is merciful. He tells them simply to follow him, and that he will care for them if they do, but if they don't he'll destroy both them and their king.

Israel had good kings and bad kings. The first king in the Old Testament is Saul, who is most striking for his inconsistency—sometimes following God, but at other times wandering far from God's will (1 Sam. 28).

The king who takes over next is David, who is known as a good king despite his making several huge errors in judgment. He was known as a man after God's own heart, despite the fact that he committed both adultery and murder!

Evil kings were worse. King Jehoram, son of Jehoshaphat, once he took over, killed all eight of his brothers so that none could take over his throne! (2 Chron. 21).

Solomon was known for wisdom as king, but also for his

financial excesses. He built the temple his father David had envisioned, but he also built a huge palace for himself, succumbing to the corruption God had predicted back in Deuteronomy.

The kings of Israel, even the good ones, illustrated with their lives the frailty of human kingdoms. They pointed to the ultimate king, Jesus, who would reign not on an earthly throne, but in our hearts.

## LAMENT

M. Scott Peck famously declared, "Life is difficult. This is a great truth, one of the greatest truths. It is a great truth because once we truly see this truth, we transcend it. Once we truly know that life is difficult—once we truly understand and accept it—then life is no longer difficult."[1]

Even if we accept that life is difficult, there are times we need to vent about it. We need to cry, moan, maybe even have a small tantrum. It is for this very thing that the Psalms of Lament were written. But the poetry is more sophisticated than just angst. The poems of lament provide instruction in how to mourn and how to turn toward God rather than away from him with our sorrows and burdens.

A lament is a prayer, a "cry for help" (Ps. 5). The word often translated "lament" in the Psalms is *hagiyg,* which means a murmur or complaint. Oddly, the King James Version translates this word "meditation."

The *Dictionary of the Old Testament Wisdom, Poetry, and Writings* notes:

> The central aim of this genre is to appeal to God for something. They endeavor to present the psalmist's case or argument as to why God should intervene. . . . The concluding vows of

> praise testify that obtaining something from God is not to be viewed as an end in itself. Another aim of lament psalms is to have something to praise God about. Praise should have the last word.[2]

Psalms of Lament (see especially Psalm 22, which Jesus quotes from the cross) were written as "models of prayer composed for the generic needs of God's people. In this respect, a lament psalm is not a mirror reflecting the composer's experience; rather, it provides worshipers a framework to interpret their own experiences and to guide their expressions of prayer."[3]

The book of Lamentations, written by the woeful prophet Jeremiah, is five poems, all but one an acrostic with each line beginning with successive letters of the Hebrew alphabet. They were used to bemoan the exile, to cry and be upset about the results of sin in the communal life of Israel. Unlike the Psalms, the poems of Lamentations don't resolve with praise. The book begs for mercy, but in a rather pessimistic way: "Restore us to yourself, O LORD, that we may return; renew our days as of old unless you have utterly rejected us and are angry with us beyond measure" (Lam. 5:21–22).

One commentary notes,

> The book of Lamentations is a compilation of corporate laments written in response to the destruction of Jerusalem by the Neo-Babylonians in 587/6 B.C. Many interpreters have suggested these laments were recited annually during the days of fasting held at the ruined temple site throughout the time of exile.[4]

In Jeremiah 22:18, we see the phrase "they shall not lament for him" in the King James Version, in other versions "mourn for him." The Hebrew word in this and similar verses is *caphad*. It means to tear the hair and beat the breast, i.e., to lament, wail, or mourn.

The word *qiynah* (a dirge or lamentation) and its root *quwn* (to strike a musical note, to chat or wail at a funeral, to lament) are found in verses like Ezekiel 32:16: "This is the lament (*qiynah*) they will chant (*quwn*) for her. The daughters of the nations will chant (*quwn*) it; for Egypt and all her hordes they will chant (*quwn*) it, declares the Sovereign LORD."

The biblical laments give us permission to mourn and are a model for bringing our sadness to God in prayer. If Jesus used them as a framework for prayer in his darkest hour, shouldn't we?

## LAMP

Growing up in church, we sang a Sunday school song that said, "Give me oil in my lamp, keep me burning, burning, burning . . ."

Most of us had never seen an oil lamp and had no idea what the song meant, except that we wanted to burn with fervent faith. We also made up other verses for the song, one of which went "give me wax on my board, keep me surfin' for the Lord . . ."

The traditional lyrics of that song came from the commandments given in Exodus 27:20–21 (and repeated in Leviticus 24):

> Command the Israelites to bring you clear oil of pressed olives for the light so that the lamps may be kept burning. In the Tent of Meeting, outside the curtain that is in front of the Testimony, Aaron and his sons are to keep the lamps burning before the LORD from evening till morning.

The Hebrew word translated "lamp" in these verses is *nerah* (alternately transliterated *niyr, nir, neyr*, or *ner*), and means candle, lamp, or light. Many of the Psalms also mention keeping one's lamp burning, an idiomatic use of this phrase that means to continue one's life. (See also 1 Kings 11:36.) "The expression 'his lamp' is used often in Scripture to symbolize life."[1]

The word *lamp* is indeed connected to the word *oil*—a precious commodity, a symbol of blessing.

So the request in our little song to God for oil in our lamps had many levels of meaning—that our life would continue, that our faith would stay strong, that we would shine with God's love to the people around us, that God would anoint us and bless us.

In English, we refer to people "finally seeing the light," or how a person can "illuminate" us with a clear explanation. Light is a metaphor for understanding. The word *nerah* is also a metaphor for God's guidance and direction. We find it in the Psalms in verses like "Your word is a lamp to my feet and a light for my path" (Ps. 119:105), or "You, O Lord, keep my lamp burning; my God turns my darkness into light" (Ps. 18:28).

Lamps shine forth as a symbol of God's covenant. The first mention of a lamp in the Old Testament is in Genesis 15:17, where God makes his covenant with Abram and appears as a smoking firepot and a torch. The word for torch (in older translations, lamp), is *lappid*, meaning to shine, a lamp or flame, burning, or firebrand.

This same word appears fourteen times in the text, often used metaphorically, as it is in Isaiah 62:1:

> For Zion's sake I will not keep silent,
> for Jerusalem's sake I will not remain quiet,
> till her vindication shines out like the dawn,
> her salvation like a blazing torch (*lappid*).

Lamps and a lampstand were key pieces of furnishings in the tabernacle. Exodus 25 spells out in detail how these pieces are to be designed and arranged. We find two important Hebrew words in this chapter. The word often translated "lamp" is *nerah* or *niyr*, which we saw above. The lamps in the tabernacle were made of pure gold and were to be always kept burning. Their fuel was olive oil. To keep a lamp burning 24/7 would be costly—it was, in some ways, a perpetual sacrifice. The idea of having a light in the tabernacle symbolized the wisdom and power of God, and also the preciousness of God's presence.

The second word for lamp, often translated "lampstand," is *menorah*. Exodus 25:33–34 describes its elaborate design:

> Three cups shaped like almond flowers with buds and blossoms are to be on one branch, three on the next branch, and the same for all six branches extending from the lampstand. And on the lampstand there are to be four cups shaped like almond flowers with buds and blossoms.

The modern descendant of the *menorah* is of course the candelabra used to celebrate Hanukah, the festival of lights.

*Nerah* is often used metaphorically for preserving someone's life or his race. In 2 Chronicles 21, we read of Jehoram taking the throne of his father, and his evil and corrupt reign. Yet God does not destroy this evil king, because "He had promised to maintain a lamp for him and his descendants forever" (v. 7). Similarly, 1 Kings 15:4 tells of God's mercy toward evil kings in David's line in this way: "For David's sake the LORD his God gave him a lamp in Jerusalem by raising up a son to succeed him."

## LAW

A large portion of the Old Testament is devoted to the law—God's instructions for his people. The law tells people how to live. Many of God's rules or laws make sense from a moral or even health standpoint. Others are simply ways in which God's people were set apart from the people around them, so that their pagan neighbors would know that they were holy, different, unique.

Some laws, such as not wearing two different kinds of cloth at the same time or sowing two kinds of seed together, are symbolic of the purity God wanted his people to have (Lev. 19:19). Many of the laws are God's way of driving home the truth that sin has consequences and prescribe sacrifices to be made to atone for various sins.

The New Testament wrestles with the dichotomy between the law and grace, and even declares that the law does not justify us to God (Gal. 3). But when the law was first given, it was indeed a way to life. Unfortunately, legalism crept in, so the focus was not on God but on the rules.

The word almost always translated "law" is the familiar word *torah*. It means law, direction, or instruction. It refers in general to all of God's teachings and instruction, and even to the teachings wise teachers pass on. It also refers specifically to the law as given in the Pentateuch.

"Torah is life" is a well-known Jewish expression derived from a refrain that runs throughout the Old Testament, including this verse in Proverbs: "The teaching (*torah*) of the wise is a fountain of life, turning a person from the snares of death" (13:14). *"Etz Chaim,"* another popular Jewish expression, means Tree of Life and is often used to refer to the Torah, meaning that Torah is a tree of life to those who cling to it. God's people saw the Torah as a gift, a means by which they could access God and the abundant life he offered them.

Through Moses, God told his people:

> Now, Israel, hear the decrees and laws I am about to teach you. Follow them so that you may live and may go in and take possession of the land the LORD, the God of your ancestors, is giving you. . . . And what other nation is so great as to have such righteous decrees and laws as this body of laws I am setting before you today? (Deut. 4:1, 8 NIV)

While the law may seem restrictive to us, God's people welcomed it because it clearly defined the covenant. Followers of other ancient religions had to guess what would appease their gods and lived in fear of their capricious anger. God's law was not arbitrary rules but the parameters for a relationship. It is woven with love and mercy. Obedience brought life.

For example, in Deuteronomy 30:9–10, 15–16, God tells the people:

> The LORD will again delight in you and make you prosperous, just as he delighted in your ancestors, if you obey the LORD your God and keep his commands and decrees that are written in this Book of the Law (*torah*) and turn to the LORD your God with all your heart and with all your soul. . . . See, I set before you today life and prosperity, death and destruction. For I command you today to love the LORD your God, to walk in obedience to him, and to keep his commands, decrees and laws; then you will live and increase, and the LORD your God will bless you in the land you are entering to possess. (NIV)

The word *laws* is found often in an important triad: "These are the commands, decrees and laws the LORD your God directed me to teach you to observe in the land that you are crossing the Jordan to possess" (Deut. 6:1).

In some versions, the three words are commandments (*mitzvah*), statutes (*chuqqah*), and judgments (*mishpat*). Together, the *mitzvah*, *chuqqah*, and *mishpat* make up the Torah.

Ultimately, all of these point to the new covenant, in which God's law will be written on his people's hearts.

> "This is the covenant I will make with the people of
>   Israel
> after that time," declares the LORD.
> "I will put my law in their minds
> and write it on their hearts.
> I will be their God,
> and they will be my people." (Jer. 31:33 NIV)

## LIFT

In English, we think of the word *lift* to describe picking something up. In Britain, it can refer to an elevator. But the biblical word is sometimes more similar to our English word *uplifting*. It has to do with honor and praise. Other times, it describes conflict—when someone lifts his hand against another.

The word *lift* (or *lifted*) appears more than two hundred times in the text, frequently as the phrase "lift up" or "lifted up." The two Hebrew words most often translated "lift up," we've studied previously: *ruwm*, which means to be high, to rise or raise up; and *nacah*, which has a variety of meanings, including up, bear, take, carry, or lift. Both of these words, particularly *ruwm*, are often translated "exalt." (See ***Exalt***.)

We often find either word used in the expression "lift up the head." This biblical phrase can mean to restore someone to honor in a relational way, or even in a judicial sense of declaring someone innocent of a crime. It contains a sense of triumph, of justice finally prevailing. It can also mean be bold or confident, as it does in Psalm 24:9, which says,

> Lift up (*nacah*) your heads, O you gates;
> lift them up (*nacah*), you ancient doors,
> that the King of glory may come in.

The word *nacah* is also found in the odd story of Joseph in prison in Genesis 40. Two of the Pharaoh's officials have dreams that Joseph accurately interprets. One, the cupbearer, is restored to his position—his head is lifted up. But the other, the baker, has his head lifted *off*—which means he is gruesomely executed by being impaled on a pole.

In Judges 8:28, *nacah* is used in a military context. It can describe utter defeat of an enemy: "Thus Midian was subdued before the Israelites and did not raise (*nacah*) its head again. During Gideon's lifetime, the land enjoyed peace forty years."

It is also used to describe conflict: "Then Ahimaaz called out to the king, 'All is well!' He bowed down before the king with his face to the ground and said, 'Praise be to the LORD your God! He has delivered up those who lifted (*nacah*) their hands against my lord the king'" (2 Sam. 18:28).

Conversely, *nacah* is used to describe lifting our hands up to God in praise, or lifting our soul to him, lifting our eyes to seek him, lifting our voices to glorify God. For example: "Lift up (*nacah*) your hands in the sanctuary and praise the LORD" (Ps. 134:2). (See also Ps. 121 and 134.)

*Nacah* also hints at the idea of carrying or taking responsibility for another's sins—pointing to Christ. In such contexts, it is often translated "to bear" or "to carry," as it is in Leviticus 16:22, which describes the release of the scapegoat on the Day of Atonement: "The goat shall bear (*nacah*) on itself all their iniquities to an uninhabited land; and he shall release the goat in the wilderness" (NKJV). (See also Ex. 28:12.) This meaning is used to prophesy of the coming Christ, who will be "lifted up" for our transgressions, and "bore (*nacah*) the sin of many" (Isa. 53:12).

The word *ruwm*, as we have said, is often translated "exalt" in verses that exhort us to exalt and honor God. One of the most amazing descriptions of God in the Bible is found in Psalm 3:3, which says, "But thou, O LORD, art a shield for me; my glory, and the lifter up of mine head" (KJV). The verb again is *ruwm*, a word that we often use to speak of exalting God. There is a beautiful paradox in these words—when we exalt God (which means humbling ourselves and giving honor to him), he lifts up our head, and honors us, restores us.

It is used throughout the Old Testament, especially the Psalms, to describe God's assistance to those who are poor and needy. For example: "He raises the poor from the dust and lifts (*ruwm*) the needy from the ash heap" (Ps. 113:7).

The Bible calls us to lift up God's name, lift up his praises, lift up our hands and our hearts. It also promises that if we do this, God will also lift us up. What an "uplifting" message!

## LION

The only place most of us will ever see a lion is in a zoo, lying in his man-made patch of jungle, looking like a bored, over-sized housecat with a strange haircut. Because our encounters with wild animals, even on an African safari, don't typically put us into real danger, the word *lion* doesn't stir the same kind of awe and fear that it did in the ancient world. Children's television shows that feature puppet or cartoon lions further water down the lion's image. The 1966 movie *Born Free* changed people's view of lions forever, as did the Cowardly Lion in the 1939 film *The Wizard of Oz*.

In C. S. Lewis's classic series The Chronicles of Narnia, Aslan the Lion is the Christ figure. Too often, we remember the gentleness and self-sacrifice of Aslan, not his fierceness. But Aslan is "not a tame lion," as the books remind us. In the story, Aslan kills the White Witch, who represents the power of evil.

The lion is one of the most widely used and recognized symbols. Across cultures and time, a shield stamped with the image of a lion has carried a common meaning of power. The sphinx statues of Egypt (perhaps as slaves, the children of Israel had assisted with their construction) were a mythical creature with the body of a lion and the face of a man. We call the lion the "king of the jungle," and it is often a symbol of royalty or authority. If you've ever heard a lion roar, you don't forget it.

In Old Testament times, marauding lions (and bears, for that matter) were a very real danger to shepherds who watched over flocks of sheep (1 Sam. 17:34). It's possible that sometimes lions wandered into villages or towns (Prov. 26:13). Mention of this wild beast inspired awe and fear.

The most common Hebrew word translated "lion" is *aryeh*, which occurs in the text ninety times, meaning a full-grown lion. However, Hebrew has six distinct words to describe lions in various stages of development—because those stages make lions increasingly more dangerous. The word *gur* means a whelp or lion cub that is still nursing; *shachal* refers to a young lion that has been weaned but still relies on other lions for food (but the word sometimes means fierce lion); and *kepir* describes a young lion that hunts for itself. The word *lebaowth* comes from a word meaning to roar and can mean a lion or lioness, an old lion or a great lion. The word *layish* appears in the text only three times, but it also means lion.

The phrase "Lion of Judah" is found in Revelation, where it refers to the returning and triumphant Christ—although some scholars disagree with translating Revelation 5:5 in this way.[1] But in the Old Testament, a slightly different phrase is found in the words of the prophet Hosea:

> For I will be like a lion (*shachal*) to Ephraim,
> like a great lion (*kepir*) to Judah.
> I will tear them to pieces and go away;
> I will carry them off, with no one to rescue them. (5:14)

A lion *to* Judah, rather than *of* Judah, is a symbol of opposition. In this text, both *shachal* and *kepir* represented God's fierce wrath and punishment. (See also Amos 3:8, which poetically compares God to a lion.)

Another mention of lions and Judah is found in Genesis. Judah is one of Jacob's twelve sons. He is first referred to as a lion in Genesis 49, in a blessing given by Jacob on his deathbed to his sons:

> You are a lion's (*aryeh*) cub (*gur*), O Judah;
> you return from the prey, my son.

> Like a lion (*aryeh*) he crouches and lies down,
> like a lioness (*lebaowth*)—who dares to rouse him? (v. 9)

Jacob goes on to describe the military and political power he predicts Judah will have.

Similarly, in Jeremiah 49, God tells various kingdoms of his coming wrath, and promises, "Like a lion (*aryeh*) coming up from Jordan's thickets to a rich pastureland, I will chase Edom from its land in an instant" (v. 19; see also 50:44).

The book of Daniel also mentions lions—not just the lion's den Daniel was thrown into for praying to God (Dan. 6), but in a key apocalyptic vision and prophecy in Daniel 7.

The frequent mention of lions and the variety of words in Hebrew for *lion* point to the truth that these animals were important both literally and symbolically. Because both God and evildoers are compared in the text to lions, it is especially important that we examine the context of each passage with particular care and caution—which is always prudent when handling lions.

## Lord

In most English Bibles, you will see the word *lord* written three ways in the Old Testament: lord, when it refers to a person who is a master over others or perhaps an official; Lord, when it refers to God as an authority (translating the word *adonay*); and LORD, when translating the name of God that many consider unpronounceable, often represented by four Hebrew letters, or the English letters YHWH. The Hebrew word *adon*, which means lord, i.e., one who is a master or lord over a servant, is most often translated "lord," although sometimes "Lord." It sometimes refers to God as a title of respect, seeing him as master.

In our diverse culture, the word *God* can have a variety of meanings. For some, God is a vague, benevolent presence, or an all-pervasive spirit that they believe resides in all things and people. The God of the Bible is much different from that—he is specific, with a personality, and distinct from his creation.

In Bible times, the word *el* generally meant a god, and while it is sometimes used in the Old Testament to refer to God, it is often combined with other words to tell which God is being referred to, as in *Elohim* or *el shaddai* or *el elyon* (Gen. 14:18–22).

The word *Lord* appears in the Old Testament more than 6,800 times. The English is an approximation of the Hebrew tetragrammaton YHWH, which appears in the text without vowels. It is variously translated and pronounced "Jehovah," "Jahweh," "Yahweh," and so on. The word *Jehovah* comes from combining the consonants of YHWH with the vowels of the name Adonai, as most devout Jews will not read aloud or say the name YHWH, for fear of blaspheming (Lev. 24:16).

Pastor Rob Bell notes that the four letters, when pronounced, sound like "yode, hey, vah, hey"—and points out that the name of God is the sound of breathing.[1]

One dictionary notes, "The name yhwh . . . carries overtones of presence, salvation defined as deliverance and blessing, covenantal bondedness, and integrity."[2]

Another dictionary adds: "Yahweh is a distinctly proper name of God. It is never used to refer to any pagan gods; neither is it used in regard to men."[3]

In Genesis 17:1, God meets up with Abram. We see three of these names in one verse, along with a veiled reference to another name:

> When Abram was ninety-nine years old, the Lord (*Yehovah*) appeared to him and said to him, "I am God (*Shaddai*) Almighty (*el*); walk before me and be blameless."

When God says "I am . . ." that is also a reference to his name. Centuries later when Moses asks God who he should say has sent him, God replies, "'I AM WHO I AM.' And he said, 'Say this to the people of Israel, "I AM has sent me to you."'" (Ex. 3:14 ESV). The Hebrew verb translated "I am" is *hayah*; it means to be or exist. It points to God's self-sufficiency: He is not a created being but has always been. In the verses immediately following this proclamation to Moses, God goes on to refer to himself as the LORD (YHWH, or *Yehovah*) God (*elohim*) (Ex. 3:15–20).

A few chapters later, God and Moses have a further conversation about God's name, and God tells Moses, "I am the LORD (*Yehovah*). I appeared to Abraham, Isaac, and Jacob as God (*Shaddai*) Almighty (*el*), but by my name 'The LORD' (*Yehovah*) I did not make myself known to them" (Ex. 6:2–3 NRSV).

The name Yehovah or YHWH is a picture of God's mysteriousness, his otherness. Psalm 145:3 says: "Great is the LORD (*Yehovah*), and greatly to be praised, and his greatness is unsearchable" (ESV). While the Bible tells us that if we seek God, we will find him, it does not promise that we can know everything about him. We cannot capture and narrowly define him, which is all the more reason to reverence him.

## LOT/LOTS

How do you know God's opinion? Ancient people believed you could discern the will of the gods by casting dice or lots. While we might dismiss this method of hearing from God as superstitious, it was a key component of not only the pagan faiths of the ancient Middle East, but of the Hebrew faith.

For example, Leviticus 16 describes the rituals for the Day of Atonement, which was to be held once a year "on the tenth day of the seventh month" (v. 29). This was the one day a year when Aaron could enter the Holy of Holies to make atonement for the sins of the people. Part of the ritual included choosing two goats—one to be sacrificed on the altar, the other to have the sins of the people symbolically put on its head (often with a scarlet cord—think about the prophetic symbolism of that!) and cast out into the desert to carry away the sins. Which goat got which fate? The text tells us:

> He is to cast lots for the two goats—one lot for the Lord and the other for the scapegoat. Aaron shall bring the goat whose lot falls to the Lord and sacrifice it for a sin offering. But the goat chosen by lot as the scapegoat shall be presented alive before the Lord to be used for making atonement by sending it into the wilderness as a scapegoat. (Lev. 16:8–10)

To cast a lot or lots was similar to flipping a coin or drawing straws. We don't know what the lots looked like—coins, dice, sticks, stones, or even cards are all possibilities. But the point is, the Old Testament seems to indicate that God not only allowed this practice of cleromancy, but instructed his people to use it in specific incidents. He also apparently used it to reveal truth: In the book of Jonah, the sailors on the boat cast lots to determine which passenger had angered the gods, and the lot fell, accurately, to Jonah. When they tossed him overboard, the storm abated, confirming that casting lots did indeed reveal the truth.

The Hebrew word translated "lot" or "lots" is *goral.* It comes from a root word that means to be rough, like a stone or pebble. Often pebbles were used as dice of sorts to cast lots.

Aaron's priestly garments included a pouch or pocket for lots, known specifically as the Urim and the Thummin. They are mentioned only a handful of times in the Old Testament, first in the instructions for the construction of the elaborate breastplate of the priest's garments: "Also put the Urim and the Thummim in the breastpiece, so they may be over Aaron's heart whenever he enters the presence of the Lord. Thus Aaron will always bear the means of making decisions for the Israelites over his heart before the Lord" (Ex. 28:30). (See ***Ephod***.)

This is the first mention in Scripture of these items, so we must assume that they were already used as part of the Israelites' religious practice, or that other religions used them. Urim means lights and Thummin means perfection. These were most likely stones that were used as lots to determine the will of God (Ex. 28:30; Lev. 8:8).

When the Israelites took over the Promised Land, each tribe was given a certain portion of the land (Josh. 14–19). The decision about which portion went to which tribe was decided for the most part by casting lots (Josh. 14:2). A few chapters later, Joshua sends scouts into the land and has them survey it and draw up a map. They cast lots onto the map to determine which tribe gets which portion of land. The text says that "Joshua then cast lots for them in Shiloh in the presence of the LORD, and there he distributed the land to the Israelites according to their tribal divisions" (Josh. 18:10). Each tribe then had a lot, or allotment. This is the reason that even today, a piece of land is sometimes called a lot.

In English usage we talk about a certain situation being one's "lot in life"—the hand they are dealt, so to speak. Again, this comes from the idea of a lot being a seemingly chance thing that is actually ultimately controlled by God. As it says in Proverbs 16:33, "The lot is cast into the lap, but its every decision is from the LORD."

## LOVING-KINDNESS/MERCY

It's been said that justice is getting what you deserve, mercy is not getting what you deserve, and grace is getting what you don't deserve.

Certainly, then, a holy and perfect God who offers forgiveness and extends himself toward human beings who not only make mistakes but reject and forsake his love would have to be described as merciful and gracious.

The Bible is the only sacred text of any major world religion that describes God as loving and merciful. Mercy is not earned. (In Exodus 33:19, God says, "I will have mercy on whom I will have mercy.") We cannot manipulate God into forgiveness, although his wrath is softened by our contrition. God goes looking for the wayward, chooses people not based on their merit but on his love. It is a self-initiating mercy, which, when you compare it to other faiths, is astounding. It seems to be the very hope of God that we would seek his mercy (Jer. 24:7; 29:13; 32:38–40).

There are several words that are translated "mercy" in the Old Testament. The Hebrew word *checed* is used 240 times in the Old Testament. It is translated "mercy" or "kindness" or "loving-kindness" in older translations. More recent translations typically use the word *love* instead. It is found most frequently in the Psalms, and there it nearly always describes an attribute of God.

For example, Psalm 40:10–11: "I have not concealed Your lovingkindness (*checed*) and Your truth from the great congregation. You, O Lord, will not withhold Your compassion from me; Your lovingkindness (*checed*) and Your truth will continually preserve me" (NASB).

We also find this word in the refrain of Psalm 136: "His mercy (*checed*) endures forever." *Checed* is also used to describe the mercy we are to show to one another, as we live in a way that both imitates and seeks after God. For example, an Old Testament teaching later quoted by Jesus says, "For I desire mercy (*checed*), not sacrifice, and acknowledgment of God rather than burnt offerings" (Hosea 6:6). We see a contrast between mercy and loving-kindness on one hand, and rule-keeping on the other. We see a parallel between mercy and "acknowledgment of God." The word translated "acknowledgment" is *da'ath,* which comes from the word *yada,* to know, in an experiential way. When we are merciful and loving, we experience God in a deeper way. (The word *checed* is used in Micah 6:8 in a similar way.)

Although modern translations sometimes translate *checed* as "love" or "unfailing love," it is a different word and different meaning than the word *aheb*, which is often also translated "love" but describes something quite different. *Aheb* (or *ahab*) means emotional attachment, sometimes with a sexual connotation, sometimes to describe love between a man and a woman, parents and children, or loyal friends. *Aheb* is the word used in the commands for us to love God, to love his law, and to love our neighbor, but it is generally not used to describe God's love for us.

Both words are used in verses like Psalm 119:159:

> See how I love (*aheb*) your precepts;
> preserve my life, LORD, in accordance with your love
> (*checed*). (TNIV)

Compare the same verse in the New American Standard Bible, which reads:

> Consider how I love Your precepts;
> Revive me, O LORD, according to Your lovingkindness.

*Checed* is also distinct from *chanan*, which means mercy with the connotation of granting favor or generosity, even forgiveness for wrongdoing, or pity. *Chanan* is often used in verses like Proverbs 14:21 and 31, which talk about showing mercy to the poor, or in verses like Psalm 6:2, in which we acknowledge our spiritual poverty and beg for God's mercy. Another word sometimes translated "mercies" or "compassion" is *racham*, which means a tender, protective sort of compassion.

We find all three words in verses like this:

> Have mercy (*chanan*) on me, O God,
> according to your unfailing love (*checed*);
> according to your great compassion (*racham*)
> blot out my transgressions. (Ps. 51:1)

Mercy in the form of loving-kindness is one of God's defining characteristics, an astounding truth. No wonder this word is the theme of so many psalms of praise.

## MAN

The Bible uses the word *man* to refer to both human beings and to the members of the male gender of human beings. This can create confusion, and sometimes arguments about translation.

When man means human, the Hebrew word is *adam*. In the Genesis account, the first man is given a name that means human. But it can also refer to a specific person—in Genesis, it sometimes refers to that first man, Adam.

The first time we see the word *man* in Genesis, it is being used in the general sense of human beings, people. There can be no mistake in this, simply from the context of the sentence:

> Then God said, "Let us make mankind (*adam*) in our image, in our likeness, so that they may rule over the fish in the sea and the birds in the sky, over the livestock and all the wild animals, and over all the creatures that move along the ground." So God created mankind (*adam*) in his own image, in the image of God he created them; male and female he created them. (Gen. 1:26–27 NIV)

If God created *adam* "male (*zakar*) and female," then in that sentence, *adam* cannot possibly mean only one male person.

Note that the text refers to man as "male and female," and uses the pronoun "them."

However, in Genesis 2, which gives a slightly different version of the creation story, the text still uses the word *adam* to describe the individual he first creates, as it does in Genesis 2:18, "The LORD God said, 'It is not good for the man (*adam*) to be alone.'"

In this sentence, it would seem that *adam* is used to describe one male person. So the meaning depends on the context.

Later in the story, this one male person is given the name Adam. The word *adam* also means red, ruddy, or rosy, perhaps referring to a man's coloring. And the word *adamah*, which comes from the same root, means earth or ground, from which man was formed. (See ***Earth***.) Indeed, the word *adam* also describes the earthy, physical aspect of man.

A few verses later, we find another Hebrew word that is translated "man"—*iysh*, which means a man as an individual or male person. In its feminine form, the word is *ishshah*, which means woman. The pronunciation of the two words is similar, just as man and woman are similar English words. Genesis 2:22–24 says,

> Then the LORD God made a woman (*ishshah*) from the rib he had taken out of the man (*adam*), and he brought her to the man (*adam*).
>
> The man (*adam*) said,
>
> "This is now bone of my bones
> and flesh of my flesh;
> she shall be called 'woman,' (*ishshah*)
> for she was taken out of man (*iysh*)."
>
> For this reason a man (*iysh*) will leave his father and mother and be united to his wife (*ishshah*), and they will become one flesh.

This beautiful mystery points out that *iysh* describes the more soulish, immaterial aspect of man.

Another word translated "man" is *geber*. Essentially a synonym for *iysh*, *geber* appears 689 times in the text and is often used to describe a warrior or strong man. It is also used to express the opposite of *ishshah*, as it does in verses like Jeremiah 44:20: "Then

Jeremiah said to all the people, both men (*geber*) and women (*ishshah*), who were answering him . . ."

In contrast, the word *enosh* describes a weak man, and is used only in the poetic books—especially Job and Psalms—where it contrasts man's frailty with God's strength (Ps. 103:15). It often refers to the frailty of human beings. For example, Psalm 8:4 in the King James Version reads: "What is man (*enosh*), that thou art mindful of him? and the son of man (*adam*), that thou visitest him?"

The New International Version (2011) renders the same verse, "What is mankind that you are mindful of them, human beings that you care for them?"

The Hebrew word *zakar* means male. It can be used as a noun, as it is in Genesis 32:22 in the phrase "that our males be circumcised." It can be used as an adjective to describe a male child, or even a male animal as in Genesis 6:19 or Exodus 12:5.

The word *bachur* means a young man, fully developed and in his prime. (You may recognize the similarity to our English word *bachelor*.)

Each of these words represents an aspect of human beings. We are created in God's image (*adam*). We are strong (*geber*) and yet fragile (*enosh*). We are created male (*isyh*) and female (*ishshah*).

## MANNA

The book of Exodus describes the miraculous flight of the Israelite slaves from Egypt. They march out into the desert, bearing plunder and wealth; cross the Red Sea on dry land; and watch Pharaoh's pursuing armies drown behind them. Still, in very little time at all, the adventure wears thin, and they begin to complain of hunger.

In Exodus 16, we read how God hears their grumbling and responds by feeding them with quail and also with a miraculous "bread from heaven."

> When the dew was gone, thin flakes like frost on the ground appeared on the desert floor. When the Israelites saw it, they said to each other, "What is it?" For they did not know what it was. . . . The people of Israel called the bread manna. It was white like coriander seed and tasted like wafers made with honey. (Ex. 16:14–15, 31)

The word *manna* means "What is it?"

As we have noted in previous chapters, every law and every miracle of the Old Testament has a prophetic significance, but perhaps none are as obvious and profound as the symbolism found in the "bread of heaven," manna. The Bible tells us this manna appeared six days a week, for forty years, until the Israelites settled in Canaan (Josh. 5:12).

Although the word *manna* appears only fourteen times in the text, it is a very important term theologically. The word in Hebrew is *man*.

Manna symbolizes God's provision. The Israelites were commanded to remember this provision by keeping an omer of manna (which never spoiled) in a jar in an honored place in the ark of the covenant, with the tablets of the law. This of course points to the coming of Christ, who called himself the bread of life. (See ***Bread***.)

Manna was more than simple food, some Frosted Flakes for the Israelites to enjoy for breakfast. The way manna was to be gathered provided an important object lesson. Each tent, or household, was to gather "enough" manna for their household. That was defined as one "omer" per person (most scholars think an omer was about three pounds). So each family gathered "as much as they needed."

They were not invited to take as much as they wanted, but only what they needed. In gathering manna, they began to understand the concept of "enough." Some of them had a lot to learn. Despite Moses's strict warning to not hoard or gather too much, some of them did. They woke the next day to find their excess manna completely ruined, smelly and full of maggots (Ex. 16:20).

Manna was also God's method for a primer on Sabbath keeping. On the sixth day of the week, the people were instructed to gather two days' worth of manna. Miraculously, on that day, it would not spoil but stay fresh. And on the seventh day, they ate what they'd gathered the day before, as no manna appeared on the seventh day.

Manna also makes an important theological connection between the idea of "enough" and "rest." We can only truly rest if we trust God will provide enough. Sabbath is connected to loving limits that allow us to be generous and to live in community.

The Jewish traditional Sabbath meal includes two loaves of bread, symbolizing the double portion of manna they were to gather before the Sabbath.

Jesus' teaching and miracles often alluded to manna (John 6). Messianic scholar Avram Yehoshua writes:

> When Yeshua multiplied the loaves for the multitudes (John 6:1–15), the immediate reference was obvious to the Jewish people there. God, through Moses, provided *manna* (bread), for Israel in the wilderness. Yeshua, performing a similar miracle, revealed Himself as the Messiah, the king of Israel, to His Jewish people (Dt. 18:15–18; John 6:14–15). What that also revealed was that in the *Matza* (Bread) of Life, there is more than enough for all of us, just as there was for the Jewish people back there in John 6. . . . We who are alive today are still being fed off of the breaking (crucifixion) of the *Matza* of Life. He continues to "multiply" Himself to feed us.[1]

## NATION/NATIONS

The entire Old Testament is the story of a nation—the promise of it, the birth of it, and its history. Their identity as a covenant people is a national identity. God's people are the descendants of Abraham, whom God promised to make into a great nation. The

Old Testament story includes other nations as well, inasmuch as they interact with the nation of Israel.

Israel's purpose as a nation was, eventually, to give birth to the Messiah, who would be the Savior for all people, for all nations. God's plan was to save not just one nation, but all nations through that nation. (See ***Israel***.) This responsibility was a part of their national identity—to live holy lives that would stand in contrast to the world around them. The purpose of God's covenant with the nation of Israel was not just to police their behavior, of course, but to provide an example to the rest of the world, to show them the kingdom of God.

The Hebrew word most frequently translated "nation" is *goy*. In modern Jewish usage, *goy* is a somewhat derogatory word used to describe a non-Jew, a Gentile. Its original meaning included that connotation—of the 558 times it appears, it is translated "nation" 374 times and "heathen" 143 times. It is also translated "Gentiles" or simply "people." It is sometimes used to describe the inhabitants of Canaan, who lived there before Israel took over. So, depending on the context, it can be a positive, neutral, or negative term. It can be used to describe heathens or Israel herself.

The first time we encounter this word is in Genesis 10, which describes how after the flood, Noah's sons and grandsons moved out to populate the earth: "From these the maritime peoples spread out into their territories by their clans within their nations, each with its own language" (Gen. 10:5). *Goy* here means people or nations distinct from one another because of ancestry.

When God asks Abram to leave his own land and people, he promises him, "I will make you into a great nation (*goy*) and I will bless you; I will make your name great, and you will be a blessing" (Gen. 12:2).

A synonym for *goy* is the word *'am,* which means a people or tribe. It is most frequently translated "people," often meaning relatives or kinsmen. (See ***People***.)

*'Am* often means people with a common ancestor—the nation of Israel was so called because Jacob's covenant name given by God was Israel. And yet many scholars point out that when the Israelites left Egypt, they took with them "a mixed multitude" of people and animals (Ex. 12:38). That chapter also provides rules for assimilating foreigners and sojourners who wanted to convert, to essentially become part of the covenant community (Ex. 12:48). All of these people, whether converts or those born into the race of Abraham, Isaac, and Jacob's lineage, are referred to as *'am*. God's people, then, likely included people of other races who were not linked by blood lineage to Abraham, but because they had converted, were part of the covenantal community.

Both of these words are found in Deuteronomy 4:6: "Observe them carefully, for this will show your wisdom and understanding to the nations (*'am*), who will hear about all these decrees and say, 'Surely this great nation (*goy*) is a wise and understanding people (*'am*).'"

This verse hints at the distinction between these two words. The word *'am*, meaning people or nation, connotes relationship, even family (or in the case of Israel, the relationship founded by their covenant with God). The word *goy*, on the other hand, carries more political overtones, along with the idea of possession of land (Ex. 33:13).

Other words translated "nation" include *leowm*, which usually refers to a race of people; *ummah* (both in Hebrew and Aramaic), and *ezrach*. All of these appear infrequently in the text.

The purpose of a nation or people that belong to God is not exclusivity but example. As God's people, he taught them what it meant to follow him and live in covenantal relationship. They were to be an example to other nations and tribes. Further, their higher purpose was to prepare the way of the coming Messiah. How deeply God loved these people that he would entrust his own son to the care of their community.

## OFFERING

Most biblical scholars believe the children of Israel left Egypt with plenty of plunder—gold, silver, and flocks of animals. They were heading into the unknown and didn't know when they would arrive at the land God said he was going to give to them. How long would their supplies hold out?

We must also consider this truth: Every day, the priests were to offer two one-year-old lambs—one in the morning and the second at night—along with some flour, oil, and wine (Ex. 29:38–41).

The question before them was one of trust. They had to take something of value—two lambs each day—and offer them to God. While we do not offer lambs or bulls any longer, we are still called to offer God our best each day—the best of our treasures, time, and talents.

The complex rules and rituals associated with offerings in the Old Testament may seem strange to us, but in the ancient Middle East, people of various religions made a regular practice of making offerings to their gods. Often, however, their sacrifices and offerings were based on what they guessed or hoped would appease the anger of various deities.

Yahweh was different. He told his people specifically what offerings were to be offered for which offenses. He revealed his will to them, telling them what to offer and how often to do it. He provided very specific rules about what could be eaten, what could not, and what to do with the blood, the fat, and the skins of the animals sacrificed and the grains offered. As a result, we have specific instructions for burnt offerings, sin offerings, grain offerings, guilt offerings, wave offerings, peace offerings, and more. Exodus 29 spells out many of the rituals associated with offerings. Some of the animals offered were to be burned up completely; others could be eaten only by the priests (see, for example, Ex. 29:31–33). Still others could be eaten by ordinary people.

Even before his people received the law, before the priesthood was established, the Bible mentions several important offerings. First, the offerings of Cain and Abel, who each brought an offering. One was accepted, the other was not.

> In the course of time Cain brought some of the fruits of the soil as an offering to the LORD. But Abel brought fat portions from some of the firstborn of his flock. The LORD looked with favor on Abel and his offering, but on Cain and his offering he did not look with favor. (Gen. 4:3–5)

The text tells us that Abel was a shepherd, Cain was a farmer. So each offered God something that represented his vocation. This text is not telling us that God prefers mutton to melons, but rather, that he wants our best. Cain brought "some" fruits—it's notable that it was not his best fruits, or even the firstfruits of his harvest. Abel, by contrast, brought the fat portions—considered a delicacy—from the firstborn of the flock, which was considered the most precious. (See Leviticus 3, which calls specifically for the fat portions as a sacrifice.)

Another important story about offerings is found in Genesis 22, where God tells Abraham to sacrifice his only son, Isaac, as a burnt offering. The Hebrew word is *'olah*, which has the specific meaning of "a whole burnt offering"; the animal was put on the altar whole (not cut into pieces) after it had been skinned. (The same word is used to describe the daily sacrifice prescribed in Exodus 29.) Just in time, God provides a ram to be sacrificed in Isaac's stead. When offering the *'olah*, the person making the sacrifice would lay their hands on the animal's head, signifying that they were transferring their sin onto the innocent animal.

The Hebrew word *qorban* means offering, and can refer to any kind of offering, from animal to grain and even to precious metals. Its root means to come near. The closely related *qurban* refers to the wood offering, where people would provide wood that would help to burn the offerings (Neh. 10:34).

Another type of offering was the sin offering. The Hebrew word is *chattath*, which can mean sin, sin offering, or punishment. The specifics of sin offerings are found in Leviticus 4–6.

A sacrifice given to God but designated as food for the priests was called a *terumah*. The word is translated "heave offering" in older Bible versions, believed to be so named because the priest would lift the offering into the air before placing it on the altar. The New International Version translates *terumah* "fellowship offerings," and other translations use "peace offering." We find this word in verses like Exodus 29:27–28 and Leviticus 10:14–15. It is also used to describe the offerings brought to build the tabernacle, and later, the temple tax.

A *minchah* was a grain offering. It could be offered uncooked, as flour mixed with oil, or cooked (Lev. 2). In some cases, the grain offerings were used as food for the priests. The word *minchah* also sometimes means a gift given by one person to another, or a tribute given to a king or other leader. (See ***Sacrifice***.)

## OVERFLOW

The word *overflow* is used both literally and figuratively in the Bible. In a literal way, it means rivers at flood stage in verses like Joshua 3:15, describing the Jordan river overflowing its banks. The Hebrew word in this verse and others like it is a word that we looked at in an earlier chapter, *male'*. (See ***Fill***.) It means to be filled to overflowing, with the idea of something going beyond its limits.

Another word is found in Deuteronomy 11:4, which describes the Red Sea overflowing the Egyptian army. The word in this verse, *stuwph*, means to flow or overflow.

*Overflow* is used both literally and figuratively in the book of Job, with a variety of words that are translated "overflow." For example, in Job 28:11, we find the word *bekiy*, which is usually translated "weeping": "He bindeth the floods from overflowing (*bekiy*); and the thing that is hid bringeth he forth to light" (KJV).

In Job 6:15, the image of streams that are hit by sudden flash floods and overflow is used as a metaphor for Job's unreliable counselors: "But my brothers are as undependable as intermittent streams, as the streams that overflow." The word in this verse is *'abar*, which can mean to pass over or through, or to overflow.

The word *overflow* is also used metaphorically, to describe both God's judgment and his abundant goodness. The Hebrew word *shataph* means to gush, inundate, or cleanse. It most often describes the inescapable and overwhelming flood of his wrath, or of trouble. For example: "I sink in deep mire, where there is no standing: I am come into deep waters, where the floods overflow (*shataph*) me. . . . Let not the waterflood overflow (*shataph*) me, neither let the deep swallow me up, and let not the pit shut her mouth upon me" (Ps. 69:2, 15 KJV). The New International Version renders the phrase "Do not let the floodwaters engulf me."

*Shataph* is also found in Isaiah 28:17, where God tells his people: "I will make justice the measuring line and righteousness the plumb line; hail will sweep away your refuge, the lie, and water will overflow your hiding place." And in Isaiah 43:2: "When thou passest through the waters, I will be with thee; and through the rivers, they shall not overflow thee: when thou walkest through the fire, thou shalt not be burned; neither shall the flame kindle upon thee" (KJV).

Other words and idioms use *overflow* as a metaphor for abundance. The famous words of Psalm 23 affirm God's goodness and protection, even in difficult situations: "You prepare a table before me in the presence of my enemies. You anoint my head with oil; my cup overflows" (Ps. 23:5). The Hebrew is *revayah*, which comes from the word *ravah*, which means to slake the thirst, or satiate, satisfy. *Revayah* connotes deep satisfaction, a feeling that needs are more than adequately supplied.

Consider this praise to God: "You crown the year with your bounty, and your carts overflow with abundance" (Ps. 65:11). The Hebrew words in this verse rendered "overflow with abundance" are *ra'aph* and *deshen,* which together mean literally to "drop fatness" (KJV), an idiom which means to overflow with abundance.

Another word for overflow is *naba,* which means to flow or gush, bubble up, even "belch forth." The idea is of uncontainable eruption. We find it in verses like this: "May my lips overflow (*naba*) with praise, for you teach me your decrees" (Ps. 119:171) and, "O Israel, hope in the Lord; for with the Lord there is unfailing love. His redemption overflows" (Ps. 130:7 NLT). The King James Version renders the final phrase "plenteous redemption." The word translated "plenteous" is *rabah,* which means to increase or multiply, more, great, abundance. It means to increase numerically, and is used in the phrase "be fruitful and multiply" (Gen. 1:22 NLT).

In some verses we find *male'* combined with the word *saba,* which means abundance or plenty, to describe with hyperbole the uncontainable blessings of God. *Male',* as we mentioned above, means not just full, but filled with more than can be contained. How do we access this abundant overflow of God? The Bible says when we are generous toward God, he will be generous toward us:

> Honor the LORD with your wealth,
> with the firstfruits of all your crops;
> then your barns will be filled (*male'*) to overflowing (*saba*),
> and your vats will brim over with new wine. (Prov. 3:9–10)

Again, we see a picture of glorious abundance, of God's more than adequate provision. But such overflow comes when we are first obedient and generous.

## PEOPLE

In the beginning was God. And yet, God was not alone, if the pronouns tell the story. "Let us make man in our own image," says God (Gen. 1:26). Who is this "us"? God is referred to with a collective noun, because God the Father, Son, and Spirit existed in community from the very beginning.

Likewise, the word *man* in that context is a collective noun, meaning human beings or people, as we saw previously. (See ***Man***.) We were created by community, for community. The Trinity creates a family—not just one person but people.

God's people are a group of men and women who are chosen, despite their flaws, to belong to him. The adjective often preceding the word *people* is *stiff-necked*. They're a stubborn, willful group who keep trying to go their own way. But more often than the negative label, God puts a loving modifier in front of the word *people*: "my."

Some of the most beautiful poetry in the Bible describes the longings of God: "I will be your God and you will be my people" (see Jer. 7:23; 24:7; and elsewhere). The Hebrew in this verse is the word *'am,* which means people or relative.

As we saw when we studied the word *nation*, *'am* sometimes means nation, but most often it is translated "people." This word can be a generic term for human beings, but more often it is preceded by a personal pronoun and describes a familial relationship. Even when the Pentateuch mentions "the people," it is referring to the specific group of God's people, often referred to by their forefather's name, Israel, or "*ben Yisrael*," the children of Israel.

There is an implication of obedience in being God's people: "Obey me, and I will be your God and you will be my people. Walk in obedience to all I command you, that it may go well with you" (Jer. 7:23 NIV).

God keeps repeating this, "You will be my people," as if to remind his rebellious children that he has not given up on them. He even has a nickname for them, a term of endearment: Jeshurun, or in Hebrew *Yeshuruwn*, which comes from the root *yashar*, which means to be straight, right, pleasant, or prosperous. *Yeshuruwn* literally means upright, even though at least one of the three verses where it appears describes their fall from that uprightness (Deut. 32:15).

Of course, there are times where God's patience grows thin. The whole book of Hosea, for example, describes God's frustration with, and judgment of, his people. In Hosea 1, God tells the prophet to give his children names that symbolize God's rejection of his people. His second son is to be named *Lo-Ammi*, which means "not my people."

Because the prevailing social system was patriarchy, the word *'am* often refers to people related to each other by a father or male leader. It can even refer to an entire nation descended from a specific person. In the ancient world, "such a group has strong blood ties and social interrelationships and interactions."[1]

Another word translated "people" is *leom*, which occurs in the text thirty-five times. Three of those occurrences are in one verse, Genesis 25:23, where Isaac's wife, Rebekah, becomes pregnant with twins, who seem very restless within her. So she asks God what's going on, and he replies with this prophetic declaration about Jacob and Esau:

> The LORD said to her,
> "Two nations (*goy*) are in your womb,
> and two peoples (*leom*) from within you will be
> separated;
> one people (*leom*) will be stronger than the other (*leom*),
> and the older will serve the younger."

A similar story happens generations later, when one of those twins, Jacob, is an old man, now called Israel. His son Joseph brings his two sons, Ephraim and Manasseh, to their grandfather for a blessing, and Jacob blesses the younger (Ephraim) instead of the older son. He explains that although Manasseh will "become a people (*'am*)," his younger brother will be greater and become "a multitude of nations (*goy*)" (see ***Nation***). (Gen. 48.)

In Psalm 44, both words occur. *Leom* often describes foreign people, while *'am* describes God's people:

> You sold your people (*'am*) for a pittance,
> gaining nothing from their sale. (v. 12)
> You have made us a byword among the nations;
> the peoples (*leom*) shake their heads at us. (v. 14)

## POOR

One of the more memorable stories in the Old Testament is that of Sodom and Gomorrah, a pair of cities God destroys by raining fire down on them (Gen. 19). Their fate is referenced in dozens of verses following this event, typically as a warning.

We get our English word *sodomy* from the name of this evil city, because one of their many sins was homosexual rape. But that was not their only iniquity. In fact, the Bible later says that Sodom was destroyed for another sin that God apparently considers just as offensive: "Now this was the sin of your sister Sodom: She and her daughters were arrogant, overfed and unconcerned; they did not help the poor and needy" (Ezek. 16:49).

The Hebrew word translated "poor" in this verse is *'aniy*, which appears eighty times in the Old Testament, and means poor, weak, afflicted, humble.

No less than ten Hebrew words can be translated "poor," but *'aniy* is the most common. The culture into which the Bible was written was one in which the vast majority of people were poor. The sheer volume of verses concerned with care of the poor tells us that God's heart is tender toward them.

As in English, *poor* can be an adjective or a noun in Hebrew, although the latter is much more common—God is aware that the poor are *people*, and his concern is for them, not only for "poverty" as a social issue.

*'Aniy* is often used in parallel with *'ebyon* (needy) and *dal* (poor). For example, God tells his people, "Speak up and judge fairly; defend the rights of the poor (*'aniy*) and needy (*'ebyon*)" (Prov. 31:9). *'Aniy* can refer to someone who is physically oppressed, such as a slave.

The word *'ebyon* appears thirty-five times and means needy or poor, often in a material sense. This word is used in parallel phrases with the word *righteous* in Amos 2:6, which points to the moral quality of someone who does not have material possessions.

It appears several times in Exodus 23, which contains commandments about mercy and justice: "Do not deny justice to your poor (*'ebyon*) people in their lawsuits" (Ex. 23:6).

"For six years you are to sow your fields and harvest the crops, but during the seventh year let the land lie unplowed and unused. Then the poor (*'ebyon*) among your people (*'am*) may get food from it" (Ex. 23:10–11). The seventh year was also a time of cancelling debts (Deut. 15), designed specifically to help the poor.

Notice the phrases "*your* poor people," and "the poor among your people" (or KJV, "the poor *of thy* people"). The poor and needy were included in the community of God's people (*'am*—see previous chapter), not excluded, and God does not distain them but commands those with resources to help them.

A third noun, *dal*, appears forty-eight times. It is used to refer to those who are low, poor, reduced, weak; those who appear sickly and weak. The middle class in ancient Israel were physically poor and were known as the *dallim*.

Some of God's commands are direct, nearly impossible to misunderstand: "If you close your ear to the cry of the poor (*dal*), you will cry out and not be heard" (Prov. 21:13 NRSV).

Another phrase found throughout the text is "thou shalt not oppress" (KJV). More modern translations often render it "Do not take advantage." In these directives, God's heart for slaves, strangers, foreigners, and the poor shines through. For example,

> You shall not withhold the wages of poor and needy labourers, whether other Israelites or aliens who reside in your land in one of your towns. You shall pay them their wages daily before sunset, because they are poor and their livelihood depends on them; otherwise they might cry to the LORD against you, and you would incur guilt. (Deut. 24:14–15 NRSV)

Beyond these direct commands, God's compassion for the poor is systemic—it is embedded in many of the laws and practices. (See ***Glean***, and Lev. 19:9–10.)

Even laws like the Sabbath command make provision for the poor. On Sabbath, every person is to rest, even "your maidservant and your manservant." Servants were poor—they were often in slavery because they had sold themselves in order to repay debt.

God is still concerned for the poor and expects his people to care for those in need.

## PORTION

The words *portion* and *portions* are predominantly Old Testament words. Of the 116 times these words are found in the whole Bible, only four are in the New Testament.

In English, the word *portion* is most often associated with food. When people are trying to lose weight, they are often advised to be careful about portion sizes—what they think is a single portion is often too much.

In biblical Hebrew, however, a portion is an allotment or share of not only food but land, or of the spoils of war. Portion is also used poetically to refer to a spiritual possession, grounded in relationship. The word *cheleq*, the most common of several words translated "portion," can mean any of these things.

Several times, especially in the Psalms, the Bible says that God is our portion—that is, he is the provision we are given from a spiritual standpoint:

> My flesh and my heart may fail,
> but God is the strength of my heart and my portion (*cheleq*) forever.
> (Ps. 73:26 NRSV)

> The LORD is my portion (*cheleq*);
> I promise to keep your words. (Ps. 119:57 NRSV)

The word *cheleq* can also mean a chosen pattern or lifestyle. This is obvious in this verse:

> If you see a thief, you are pleased with him, and you keep company (*cheleq*) with adulterers. (Ps. 50:18 ESV)

The word *choq*, which comes from the same root, means an appointment or statute, rule. It often implies a portion assigned to someone (Gen. 47:22, for example). We find it in this passage about sacrifices:

> It shall be for Aaron and his sons as their portion (*choq*) forever from the sons of Israel, for it is a heave offering; and it shall be a heave offering from the sons of Israel from the sacrifices of their peace offerings, even their heave offering to the LORD. (Ex. 29:28 NASB)

Several other words are related to *cheleq*: the Aramaic word *chalaq* (meaning portion); the feminine form of the noun *chelqah*, which has a variety of meanings, including smoothness or flattery (i.e., a smooth tongue).

Another word related to this idea is *chebel*. This word refers to a measuring line, a cord or rope, or the areas marked out by measuring lines—a district or inheritance. It can be translated with a variety of English words depending on context. For example, we see it combined with some of the other words we've already covered in this verse: "For the LORD's portion (*cheleq*) [is] his people (*'am*); Jacob [is] the lot (*chebel*) of his inheritance (*nachalah*—which means property possession or portion)" (Deut. 32:9 KJV). (See ***Lot, People***.)

Another word translated "portion" is *manah*, something weighed out, a division or a ration, especially of food. We see four words that can mean portion in this verse: "The LORD [is] the portion (*manah*) of mine inheritance (*cheleq*) and of my cup (*kowc*): thou maintainest my lot (*goral*)" (Ps. 16:5 KJV).

The word *goral* means lot or destiny. The word *kowc*, translated "cup," can also mean a lot or a portion. The phrase "my portion and my cup" is used several times in Scripture; a person's cup is not a literal drinking vessel but a metaphor for a person's fate. See Psalm 16, and remember Jesus' question to his disciples, "Can you drink the cup?" (Matt. 20:22).

The related *menath* means an allotment by courtesy or law. It is found in verses like Psalm 11:6: "Let him rain coals on the wicked; fire and sulfur and a scorching wind shall be the portion (*menath*) of their cup" (ESV). Other versions simply render "the portion of their cup" as "their lot." The idea is that it is their fate, what God allots to them.

*Manah* is often used to describe the portions of food people would share with one another during the appointed feasts, as in Nehemiah 8: "Then he said to them, 'Go your way, eat the fat, drink the sweet, and send portions to those for whom nothing is prepared; for this day is holy to our Lord. Do not sorrow, for the joy of the LORD is your strength'" (v. 10 NKJV). "Send portions" is commanded several times in the Old Testament as a way of caring for the poor, of extending the generosity that God has shown us to those who are without.

## POWER

Power is a defining attribute of God. In fact, the name *El*, which can mean God or god, also means power. So the term "the power of God" is somewhat redundant to the Hebrew way of thinking, and even the thinking of pagans in the ancient world. People feared the gods because of their power and the unpredictability of how they might wield it.

Finding verses with the word *power* will be a widely varied experience depending on which translation you read. Where some versions might use "power," others will translate with a synonym such as "might" or "strength." The King James Version, for example, uses the word *power* for almost twenty different Hebrew words.

For example, 2 Samuel 22:33 in the King James Version says, "God is my strength and power (*chayil*)." Other versions do not use the word *power* but imply it with wording like: "God is my strong refuge" or "strong fortress" or, as the New International Version puts it, "It is God who arms me with strength." God's power is something he can give to us, which makes it even more awe-inspiring.

*Chayil* is often a term used in military context, so it can mean an army. It can also mean capable or honorable as it does in Ruth 3:11 and Proverbs 31:10, where it is translated "virtuous" or "of noble character."

Additionally, sometimes power is implied in the text but not stated in so many words. For example, "God said let there be light, and there was light" is a strong statement about the power of God, a demonstration of his ultimate power, and yet nowhere in the creation narrative—which clearly displays the awesome power of God—do we find any Hebrew word that can be translated "power."

The most common Hebrew word for power is *kowach*, or *koach*. It is a poetic word meaning the ability to do something. It can describe the power of humans, animals, angels, God, and even soil.

For example, in Daniel 1:4, it is used in the description of Daniel and his companions, who needed to have the ability or competence to handle life in the king's service.

It describes God's power in Exodus 15:6: "Your right hand, O Lord, glorious in power (*kowach*)—your right hand, O Lord, shattered the enemy" (NRSV) and in Deuteronomy 9:29, in Moses' prayer about Israel: "For they are the people of your very own possession, whom you brought out by your great power (*kowach*) and by your outstretched arm" (NRSV).

It can be used to describe the power of people, as in 2 Chronicles 22:9: "So there was no one in the house of Ahaziah powerful enough to retain the kingdom." (Other versions say he "had no power.")

Another interesting Hebrew word is *yad*, which means literally a hand. *Yad* is both figurative and literal, and has a wide variety of meanings depending on the context. It often means a person's rule or reign or dominion. For example, in 1 Chronicles 5:20 and elsewhere, when the text describes enemies delivered into someone's hand, it means coming under their power.

> So the anger of the Lord was kindled against Israel, and he gave them over to plunderers who plundered them, and he sold them into the power (*yad*) of their enemies all around, so that they could no longer withstand their enemies. (Judg. 2:14 NRSV)

The New International Version says "sold them to their enemies," and doesn't mention hand or power. But the word *yad* is in the original text. The King James Version says "hands of their enemies," which is an idiomatic way of expressing that they were under the control or power of their enemies. It is a similar idiom to the English figure of speech, "under his thumb," as a way of saying one person controls or has power over another.

The entire Bible throbs with the power of God, which has many implications. The two perhaps most important are this: God is worthy of our awe and respect because he is all-powerful, and yet God confers that power to us, his servants, enabling us to do far greater things than we could ever possibly do on our own. His power is available to us, to flow through us in order to accomplish the purposes of God.

## PRAISE

The phrase "Great is the LORD and most worthy of praise" (1 Chron. 16:25; Ps. 48:1; 96:4; 145:3; and elsewhere) is found several times in Scripture. The King James Version says "and greatly to be praised." The Hebrew is *meod* (meaning exceedingly or much) *halal*. God is worthy to be praised with much praise because of his greatness.

The most common Hebrew word translated "praise" is *halal*, the root of the word *hallelujah*, which is found 165 times in the text. *Halal* has many nuances. It literally means to be clear (originally of sound, but also of color), but it also means to shine, hence to make a show, to boast, to rave, to celebrate. It is used to describe praise of a person or of God. It is also translated "glory" or "boast" or "shine."

Praise is recognition of God's character and his blessings. When we praise, we affirm and acknowledge that God is good. The Bible exhorts us to praise God, and it also talks about praising people who deserve it. For example, in Proverbs 31's description of an excellent wife, we read that she receives the praise of her husband and others (vv. 28 and 30), and also that her own accomplishments praise her, that is, they bring her honor and respect: "But a woman who fears the LORD is to be praised. Give her a share in the fruit of her hands, and let her works praise (*halal*) her in the city gates" (Prov. 31:30–31 NRSV).

The word *praise* occurs most frequently in the book of Psalms, that ancient Hebrew hymnbook that guides our prayers and worship. Many psalms start with the simple declaration "Praise the Lord!" Other psalms (see ***Lament***) may start with a question (like "Why?" or "How long?"), a cry for help (like "Rescue me"), or even a complaint ("O God, do not keep silent"), but they often end with praise—not because our circumstances have changed, but because God is worthy of it, regardless of our circumstances.

> Psalms 113–118 are traditionally referred to as the "Hallel Psalms," because they have to do with praise to God for deliverance from Egyptian bondage under Moses. . . . The word *halal* is the source of "Hallelujah," a Hebrew expression of "praise" to God which has been taken over into virtually every language of mankind.[1]

When we see the phrase "Praise the LORD!" it is a translation of the word *hallelujah,* meaning literally "Let us praise Yah" (short for Yahweh).

Just as there are many ways to praise God, there are many biblical words to describe it. Another word that occurs frequently is *yadah*. This Hebrew word, which means to give thanks, laud, or praise, is found 114 times in the Old Testament, seventy of which are in the Psalms. It is translated as "praise" most often, but also as "give thanks," "confess," "thank," and a few other similar ideas.

It's found in verses like "I will bless (*yadah*) the LORD at all times; his praise shall continually be in my mouth" (Psalm 34:1 ESV).

Other terms for *praise* include *barak,* which means to kneel or bless (see ***Blessing***); *shiyr,* which usually means to sing (Ps. 96:1);

*shabach*, to address in a loud tone, to praise; and *towdah*, which means to extend the hand, and is often translated "thanksgiving."

The word *tehillah* is found fifty-seven times in the Old Testament and can mean glory, praise, song of praise, or praiseworthy deeds. We find it in verses like Nehemiah 9:5 (which I remember singing as a worship chorus—that is, a *tehillah*): "Stand up and bless (*barak*) the LORD your God from everlasting to everlasting. Blessed (*barak*) be your glorious name, which is exalted above all blessing (*berakah*) and praise (*tehillah*)" (ESV). (See ***Blessing***.)

The word *zamar* means to celebrate in songs and music, praise, sing, or sing psalms. It is sometimes translated "sing praises":

> Make a joyful noise to God, all the earth;
> sing (*zamar*) the glory of his name;
> give to him glorious praise (*tehillah*).
> All the earth worships you;
> they sing praises (*zamar*) to you,
> sing praises (*zamar*) to your name.
> Bless our God, O peoples,
> let the sound of his praise (*tehillah*) be heard. (Ps. 66:1–2, 4, 8 NRSV)

It is significant that Psalms, the longest book of the Bible, is the one dedicated to helping us praise God. He is indeed worthy of our praise.

## PRAY/PRAYER

Prayer is both conversation and communion with God. It involves both speaking and listening; it is the means by which our relationship with God is established and flourishes—or not. It is both simple and miraculous: something a child can do, yet something even the most brilliant theologian cannot adequately explain.

*Eerdmans Bible Dictionary* defines prayer as

> a primary means of communication that binds together God and humankind in intimate and reciprocal relationship. Its foundational assumption is the belief that the Creator of the world is both available for human address and committed to a divine-human partnership.[1]

In his book *Prayer: Does it Make Any Difference?*, Philip Yancey writes, "Prayer invites me to lower defenses and present the self no other person fully knows to a God who already knows."[2]

In the Old Testament, the word *pray* is often used to mean ask or beseech, often toward another person, in the phrase "I pray thee" (KJV). In those cases, the word translated "pray" is *na*.

The word *palal* means pray or prayer; it also means to mediate or judge, or to intercede on behalf of someone else, a frequent occurrence in the Old Testament.

A word that derives from *palal* is *tephillah*, which also means prayer. While *palal* is specifically intercessory (most often), *tephillah* is more general. In some cases, this word refers to prayers that are set to music and sung during worship, as psalms.

Throughout the history of Israel as told in the Old Testament, we see a variety of types of prayers, from very informal to formal. The idea of prayer is often expressed without using either of these Hebrew words. For example, Genesis 4:26 says, "To Seth also a son was born, and he called his name Enosh. At that time people began to call upon the name of the LORD" (ESV). Seth was Adam's third son, born after Abel had been slain by his brother. So within two generations, the people of the earth began to call on (some versions say "invoke the name of" or "worship") God. The word is *qara*, which means to call out, summon, or proclaim. It is the same word used in the creation account, when it says things like "and God called (*qara*) the light Day, and the darkness he called (*qara*) Night" (Gen. 1:5 KJV).

Many of the Old Testament stories record what seem to be casual conversations between God and people. Again, neither *palal* or *tephillah* appear in these stories; they are simply recorded as dialogue. One dictionary notes:

> A large number of recorded prayers . . . begin with the simple statement 'and X said (*'mr*) to God,' an introduction that depicts prayer in theologically significant ways as analogous to the conversational dialogue routinely exchanged betweeen persons of equal stature.[3]

Prayer evolves throughout Old Testament history, but there are very few regulations governing it in the mosaic law. Another dictionary notes:

> The law did not prescribe any prayer for public worship except the confession of sin on the great Day of Atonement . . . and the thanksgiving on the occasion of the offering of the firstlings and tithes . . . yet it is certain that in Israel no act of worship was unaccompanied by prayer.[4]

By the time of Daniel, daily prayers at certain times had become customary. This continued through the time of the early church (Acts 3:1). While many religions prescribe prayers at set times, for many Christians, this has evolved to prayers before each meal, or at the beginning and/or end of the day. Paul wrote to the early church, "pray without ceasing" (1 Thess. 5:17). Perhaps we can obey this New Testament teaching by looking to the example of heroes of the Old Testament, who simply spoke with God as a part of their everyday lives.

## PRIEST

One of the defining characteristics of Yahweh, in sharp contrast to the gods of the other nations in the ancient Middle East, was his nearness. God dwelt among his people. He asked them to build a tabernacle—*mishkan*. The word means a dwelling place, and implies that the tabernacle was more than a tent—it was a symbol of the presence of God.

However, ordinary people could not approach God. In many ways, it is human nature to desire an intermediary, someone who can advocate on your behalf. In ancient Israel that role was reserved for priests. They offered sacrifices each day, officiated over various rituals, taught the people, and modeled holiness. The priests, especially the high priest, were living symbols of the coming Christ, our ultimate high priest (see the book of Hebrews, especially chapter 4).

The priests were to be holy—set apart. They wore distinctive clothing (see ***Ephod***). After being consecrated, they were able to offer sacrifices on behalf of the people. They officiated at the altar, offering sacrifices. The high priest, first mentioned in Leviticus 16:32, was the only one allowed to enter the Holy of Holies, and that only once a year, on the Day of Atonement. On that day, he would offer prayers on behalf of the entire nation and would place the sins of the people symbolically on a scapegoat. (See Leviticus 16 for details on the elaborate ritual involved with this holy day.)

One dictionary notes:

> Though all the people were to follow the *tora* and are commanded to be holy (Lev. 19:2), the priests were the paradigm holy people (Ezra 8:28). They were to be as the people they prayed for should be.[1]

The book of Leviticus spells out many of the duties of the priests. The priests were called to a higher level of purity, and yet, if you look at biblical history, you can see that eventually the power of the priests led to some corruption.

The priests were called on to determine what God was saying to the people, often by using the precious stone lots Urim and Thummim (see ***Lots*** and Num. 27:21). They also were to give instruction on the law. Every seven years, during the festival of booths, they were instructed to read the entire law to the people of Israel (Deut.

31:9–12). Why? So that the people "may hear and learn to fear the LORD your God and to observe diligently all the words of this law" (Deut. 31:12 NRSV). If people are to learn, it follows that someone is teaching them. That teaching was part of the role of the priest.

The Hebrew word translated priest is *kohen*, which appears 750 times in the text. It describes not only priests of Yahweh but also of other gods—specially designated men who handled sacrifices and rituals of each religion. The word *kahan*, which derives from *kohen*, appears twenty-three times and means to officiate as a priest.

God commanded Moses to establish Aaron and his sons, members of the tribe of Levi, to serve as priests (Ex. 28–29). But before Moses, the head of each family or clan served as its priest. "Abraham, Isaac, and Jacob built altars, offered sacrifices, purified and consecrated themselves and their households (Gen. 12:7; 13:18; 26:25; 33:20; 35:1–3)."[2]

Another dictionary notes, "The Hebrew word *kohen*, also attested in Phoenician, Punic, Ugaritic, Arabic and Aramaic, designates not only Jewish priests but also those who served in temples dedicated to other gods."[3]

Once Israel was established, priests had many duties in addition to offering sacrifices. For example,

> When a person suffered a disease or physical sign of impurity, the purification rites were performed by a priest. The methods of purification included things like waiting a specific amount of time, bathing, washing one's clothes, being sprinkled with water by the priest, and bringing a sacrifice the blood of which would be sprinkled on one's behalf by the priest.[4]

## PROPHET

As the history of God's people unfolds in the Old Testament, we see a disturbing pattern. The children of Israel would follow

God and obey him for a while, but then, often quite quickly, be distracted from their devotion. They would turn away from God, either going their own way (the Bible puts it "everyone did what was right in his own eyes"—see Judges 17:6 NKJV; Proverbs 12:15) or following the false gods of their neighbors.

When we go astray, we have the Holy Spirit within us to convict and guide us—although we too ignore this voice from God. But prior to Pentecost, God's people did not have the constant access to the Spirit that we enjoy. Rather, the Spirit came upon certain people who communicated God's message—the prophets.

The prophet was a person given a message from God who would call people to repentance. Prophets spoke to people on God's behalf, but the reverse is also true—they would speak to God on people's behalf. Sometimes the people would listen to God's spokesperson, but sometimes they would ignore the prophet. Other times, they would choose to listen to someone who claimed to speak for God but was actually a false prophet (see Jeremiah).

The Hebrew word translated "prophet" is *nabiy*. Prophets are also designated with the words *roeh* and *hozeh*, which both mean one who sees (often translated "seer").

The Bible mentions prophets not only of God but also of false gods (such as the prophets of Baal, whom Elijah challenges in 1 Kings 18). Whether of Baal or Yahweh, the word for prophet is *nabiy*. In 1 Samuel 28, Saul unwisely consults a medium or witch, who is able to conjure up Samuel for him. But consulting this person has serious consequences for Saul. (The Hebrew word is *owb*, meaning a necromancer, one who can conjure the dead.)

In English, we think of prophets as those who can foretell the future. While that was a part of what the prophets did—wrote prophecy, most often pointing to God's judgment or to the coming Messiah—they were more frequently serving as the conscience of the nation, calling people to repent to avoid God's coming wrath. They revealed God's will and helped people understand how to follow it. The prophets called people to greater faith and reminded them that their actions did not go unnoticed by God.

Aaron, who was a priest (see previous entry), was also a prophet, according to Exodus 7:1. When Moses resisted God's call to lead the Hebrews out of Egypt, God promised Aaron as a helper, who would speak for Moses. God explained to Moses, "He indeed shall speak for you to the people; he shall serve as a mouth for you, and you shall serve as God for him" (Ex. 4:16 NRSV).

> In addition to the declaration of God's will, the denunciation of His judgments, the defense of truth and righteousness, and bearing testimony to the superiority of the moral to the ritual, prophecy had an intimate relation to God's gracious purpose toward Israel.[1]

Scholars divide the Old Testament prophetic books into the Major Prophets and Minor Prophets. These designations do not reflect the importance of each, but rather, the length of the books they wrote. Indeed, the prophet Elijah, considered important enough that he and Moses were the only ones who showed up at the transfiguration, was known as an "oral prophet" because he didn't write down his prophetic words (they are mostly reported in the book of 1 Kings).

The prophets mentioned in the Old Testament are almost all men, but this role is not limited to males. There are a handful of women who are named as prophetesses of God. And as the prophet Joel declared, "I will pour out my Spirit on all people. Your sons and daughters will prophesy . . ." (Joel 2:28). This prophesy was fulfilled on the day of Pentecost and continues to be fulfilled today.

The prophetic books make up more than half of the Old Testament. While many prophets addressed a specific situation, their overall mission to call people back to right relationship with God is one that continues to be necessary and relevant to our lives. We, like the people of old, tend to go our own way or chase after false gods of ambition, money, and success. The Old Testament prophets also call out to us, asking us to turn back from these gods to follow Yahweh.

## RELENT

The word *relent* appears only in certain translations of the Bible. Older versions use the word *repent* to describe a turning around, a change of heart, whether it is people or God doing the repenting. But later translations tend to use the word *relent* when speaking of God's changing his mind or deciding to stay his hand of punishment (and save the word *repent* to describe the actions of people who have turned from sin). The Hebrew word is *nacham*.

When the Old Testament describes the repentance of human beings, we sometimes find the word *nacham*, but more frequently the word *shuwb*, which essentially means to turn around, go back, or come back. The idea is a 180-degree turn away from sin. Most frequently, the word *shuwb* is translated "repent."

*Nacham,* on the other hand, means to be sorry, console oneself, repent, regret. It also means to comfort, be comforted, be moved to pity, or have compassion.

It is translated both "repent" (forty-one times) and "comfort" (fifty-seven times) in the King James Version. Its original meaning is to sigh, implying pity or consolation. In the majority of its occurrences, it describes God's repentance.

For example, we often find that because of the sin of the people, God declares that he will destroy or punish them. When a prophet tries to intercede on their behalf, they are sometimes able to convince God to relent. For example, in Exodus 32, Moses goes up on the mountain to receive the Ten Commandments. While he is gone, things get out of hand very quickly, and soon the Israelites are dancing around a golden calf. God threatens to destroy them and even offers Moses a sweet deal—he says he'll wipe out the Israelites and make a whole new nation with Moses as its patriarch. But Moses, not even knowing what they had done yet, intercedes, asking God to relent. He appeals to God's reputation among the nations. He essentially bargains with God. And surprisingly, the text says, "And the LORD relented (*nacham*) from the disaster that he had spoken of bringing on his people" (Ex. 32:14 ESV).

Now, when Moses went back down to the camp and saw what was going on, he was angry, and there were still consequences and punishment for the sin he found there. However, God did not destroy the nation. There is something comforting about the fact that God's mind can be changed by the argumentative prayers of the faithful. We serve a God who is angered by sin but can be convinced to relent, even when it seems illogical to do so. The Israelites had blatantly disobeyed God and deserved to have him abandon them. And God was ready to do that. But he relented of his anger and gave them another chance.

The word *nacham* can also mean to be compassionate or empathetic. For example, Judges 2:18 says, "Whenever the LORD raised up judges for them, the LORD was with the judge, and he delivered them from the hand of their enemies all the days of the judge; for the LORD would be moved to pity (*nacham*) by their groaning because of those who persecuted and oppressed them" (NRSV). Other versions say the LORD "relented because of their groaning."

The combined ideas of compassion and a change of heart are found in verses like this: "And when the angel stretched out his hand toward Jerusalem to destroy it, the LORD relented (*nacham*) from the calamity and said to the angel who was working destruction among the people, 'It is enough; now stay your hand' " (2 Sam. 24:16 ESV; see also 1 Chron. 21:15).

The word *nacham* describes more than just limiting or avoiding punishment (i.e., how God is reactive), but also his compassionate initiatives (how God is proactive): " 'So do not fear; I will provide for you and your little ones.' Thus he comforted (*nacham*) them and spoke kindly to them" (Gen. 50:21 ESV).

That God is a God who will relent, who does not treat us as our sins deserve, is an amazing truth. The word *nacham* is a picture of God's grace.

## RESCUE

While God is a God of judgment, he is also a God of mercy. God saves, he delivers. When his people get into trouble, he rescues them. The word *rescue* in the Old Testament is a picture, again, of God's grace. It also is a prophetic theological concept, pointing toward the ultimate rescue from sin and its deadly consequences. It prophesies the coming of Jesus, the deliverer.

In fact, Jesus' name in Hebrew, *Yeshuw'ah*, means deliverance or salvation—it carries the idea of God's power to rescue.

The word most often translated "rescue" in modern translations—*natsal*—is often translated "deliver" or "save" in older versions. (See ***Deliver***.) It can refer to God's rescue of people, or one person's rescue of another, as it does in the story of Joseph's brothers when they plotted to kill him. His eldest brother, Reuben, saved his life by redirecting their plans:

> When Reuben heard this, he tried to rescue (*natsal*) him from their hands. "Let's not take his life," he said. "Don't shed any blood. Throw him into this cistern here in the wilderness, but don't lay a hand on him." Reuben said this to rescue (*natsal*) him from them and take him back (*shuwb*) to his father. (Gen. 37:21–22 NIV)

In this instance, the word *shuwb*, which we learned in the previous chapter means to turn around or take back, is literal rather than metaphorical.

More typically, *natsal* refers to divine rescue, often as part of a prayer asking God to intervene:

> Then they cried to the Lord, and said, "We have sinned, because we have forsaken the Lord, and have served the Baals and the Astartes; but now rescue (*natsal*) us out of the hand of our enemies, and we will serve you." (1 Sam. 12:10 NRSV)

> As your life was precious today in my sight, so may my life be precious in the sight of the Lord, and may he rescue (*natsal*) me from all tribulation. (1 Sam. 26:24 NRSV)

> Save us, O God of our salvation, and gather and rescue (*natsal*) us from among the nations, that we may give thanks to your holy name, and glory in your praise. (1 Chron. 16:35 NRSV)

*Natsal* can also mean to rescue by snatching away: "I snatched (*natsal*) you from the power of Egypt and from the hand of all your oppressors. I drove them from before you and gave you their land" (Judg. 6:9). Other translations say rescued or delivered instead of snatched.

Rescue is not so much removing our pain as supporting us and leading us to a new place, as we see when we look at parallel ideas in the Psalms like this one:

> They confronted me in the day of my disaster,<br>
>  but the Lord was my support.<br>
> He brought me out (*yatsa'*) into a spacious place;<br>
>  he rescued (*chalats*) me because he delighted in me.<br>
>  (Ps. 18:18–19)

In verses like this, we find two other Hebrew verbs that convey the idea of rescue. The first, *yatsa'*, means to deliver, lead out, come out. It appears in the Bible more than one thousand times, often translated as "brought forth," as in the opening pages of the creation story: "And God said, 'Let the earth bring forth (*yatsa*) living creatures according to their kinds . . .'" (Genesis 1:24 ESV). It is also used to describe how God brought Abram out of Ur, and how he brought forth a great nation from Abram (Gen. 15).

*Yatsa* conveys a sense of rescue in verses like this: "He brought them out (*yatsa*) of darkness and the deepest gloom and broke away their chains" (Ps. 107:14).

The word translated "rescued" in Psalm 18:19, *chalats*, means to draw out, to remove, equip, rescue. It can also mean to loosen, to strengthen, or arm (for battle). It is used in Job 36:15 in a similar way to the psalm: "But by means of their suffering, he rescues (*chalats*) those who suffer. For he gets their attention through adversity" (NLT).

We also find it in verses like this: "For You have rescued (*chalats*) my soul from death, My eyes from tears, My feet from stumbling" (Ps. 116:8 NASB).

Psalm 18:19 also makes a significant point by telling us why God rescues us: because he delights in us. We are his people, the sheep of his pasture, and he rescues us because he cares for us so deeply.

## ROBE

According to the flannel-graph Bible stories of my youth, everyone in Bible times appeared to be dressed in a bathrobe or long night-shirt, girded with a sash, or sometimes accessorized with a head covering. I couldn't help thinking Abraham and Moses dressed like Gandalf from *Lord of the Rings*. In fact, those Sunday school lessons were fairly accurate.

During Old Testament times, both men and women typically wore a *kethoneth*, a simple garment similar to what we would call a shirt, although *kethoneth* is typically translated "coat" or "robe." This was held to the body by a girdle and covered by a longer outer coat or robe, a *meiyl*. Easton's Bible dictionary notes, "An upper tunic (*meil*), longer than the 'coat' . . . is the mantle in which Samuel was enveloped; . . . the 'robe' under which Saul slept."[1] Easton notes that the outer garment is more like an exterior tunic, which hung to the ground, but is often called a robe or mantle. Often such robes were one piece of material with a hole for the head, like a long poncho, typically worn with a girdle or belt to hold it in place.

The word *kethoneth* is also used to describe Joseph's "coat of many colors," as well as the robes of the priests in Exodus 28:40; 29:8; and elsewhere. However, most often the robes of the priests worn for their religious duties are described by the word *meiyl* or *meil* (Ex. 28–29; 39).

Priests were to wear a robe, along with a turban, an ephod, and a breastplate (see ***Ephod***), according to Exodus 28, which contains carefully detailed descriptions of the robe, which was blue and decorated with pomegranates of purple and crimson, and a golden bell (Ex. 28:31–35).

When young Samuel was in training to be a priest, his mother would see him only once a year and bring a gift of a robe for him: "His mother used to make for him a little robe (*meiyl*) and take it to him each year, when she went up with her husband to offer the yearly sacrifice" (1 Sam. 2:19 NRSV).

The word *meiyl* is also used metaphorically, as it is in Job 29:14, "I put on righteousness, and it clothed me; my justice was like a robe (*meiyl*) and a turban" (ESV). Similar clothing metaphors appear in Isaiah 61:10: "For he has clothed me with the garments of salvation, he has covered me with the robe of righteousness" (NRSV).

Just as priests had special robes and clothing, prophets wore a special cloak, an outer robe also called a mantle. It is this outer robe that the prophet Elijah used to call his successor, Elisha. In 1 Kings 19, we read the story of how Elijah found Elisha working on his family farm, and simply walked up to him without a word and "passed by him and threw his mantle over him" (v. 19 NRSV).

It's obvious from the context that Elisha knew what this gesture symbolized, because he asked permission to say good-bye to his family, which Elijah quickly granted. He then went with Elijah.

The word in this passage is *addereth*, meaning a cloak made of fine material, but also meaning glory or splendor. A mantle in this context is not just a garment but a legacy. The word also appears in Genesis 25:25 and Jonah 3:6: "When the news reached the king of Nineveh, he rose from his throne, took off his royal robes (*addereth*), covered himself with sackcloth and sat down in the dust."

Another word translated "robe" is *eder*, which is used only once to describe a luxurious garment, and then, metaphorically: "But you rise up against my people as an enemy; you strip the robe from the peaceful" (Mic. 2:8 NRSV).

The Hebrew text has two words for robe, so the King James Version translates this phrase "ye pull off the robe (*eder*) with the garment (*salmah*) . . ." *Salmah* means outer garment or mantle as well, yet sometimes evokes images of royal splendor, as it does in Psalm 104:2, which describes God as being "dressed in a robe of light" (NLT).

Kingly robes or the "holy garments" of Aaron (Ex. 28:4) are sometimes described using the word *beged*, which can mean a garment, clothes, even a blanket, saddlecloth, or in one instance, rags. We find this word in the description of the kings of the divided kingdom in 1 Kings 22:10, with a tone of sarcasm or distain.

Another group of words is used to describe the robe worn by Mordecai in Esther 8:15: "Then Mordecai went out from the presence of the king in royal (*malkuwth*) robes (*lebuwsh*) of blue and white, with a great golden crown and a robe (*takriyk*) of fine linen and purple, and the city of Susa shouted and rejoiced" (ESV).

*Lebuwsh* means vestments or apparel and is found thirty-two times in the text. The adjective *malkuwth* means royal and appears ninety-one times. However, this is the only instance of the word *takriyk* in the Bible.

## ROCK

The Bible uses the word *rock* both literally and metaphorically. It refers repeatedly to God as our rock, a word picture that evokes strength, steadfastness, protection, and reliability.

The word *rock* appears first in Exodus 17:6, where Moses smites the rock in Horeb. God provides a miraculous response to the grumbling of the Israelites, who fear they will die of thirst in the desert. God instructs Moses to hit the rock with his staff, and water flows from the rocky ground. The text notes that the staff is the same one with which Moses "struck the Nile" (v. 5). When Moses struck the Nile, its water turned to blood—causing fish and animals to die and the Egyptians to suffer thirst (Ex. 7). Now the exact opposite occurs: Moses smites the dry, lifeless ground and water gushes forth, enough to provide water for the thousands of Israelites and their livestock. This was no little trickle; it had to have been a flow reminiscent of the Nile itself.

This story is recalled throughout the Old Testament as evidence of God's care and provision for Israel, a picture of how God makes possible what seems impossible. How can water spring from dry ground? And yet, that is what God does—a miracle remembered throughout the history of Israel. (See Ps. 78:20 and Isa. 48:21, for example.)

The word for rock in Exodus 17 is *tsur*, which can mean a rocky wall or cliff and often means a mountain or rocky hill. It appears seventy-eight times in the text and can also mean rock, strength, or even God or beauty.

Numbers 20:11 describes the same exact moment but uses a different word for rock: *cela*, which means a craggy rock, a fortress, or sometimes a refuge. This word appears about sixty times, typically as a noun, but also occasionally as an adjective meaning stony.

The word is found in verses like this one: "He drew me up

from the pit of destruction, out of the miry bog, and set my feet upon a rock (*cela*), making my steps secure" (Ps. 40:2 ESV).

Here, *rock* is used as a metaphor for stability and strength. But *tsur* is used metaphorically as an epithet for God himself, in verses like this: "He is the Rock (*tsur*), his works are perfect, and all his ways are just. A faithful God who does no wrong, upright and just is he" (Deut. 32:4).

Deuteronomy 32:31 compares other gods to Yahweh using the same word, *tsur*, for rock, but meaning two different things: "For their rock is not like our Rock, as even our enemies concede."

David praised God for delivering him from Saul by saying, "The Lord lives! Praise be to my Rock (*tsur*)! Exalted be God, the Rock, my Savior!" (2 Sam. 22:47).

The Bible sometimes mentions specific rocks or rock formations by name—not surprising because in a rocky land with few permanent buildings, rock formations or cliffs were landmarks. For example, "Within the passes, by which Jonathan sought to go over to the Philistine garrison, there was a rocky crag (*cela*) on the one side and a rocky crag (*cela*) on the other side. The name of the one was Bozez, and the name of the other Seneh" (1 Sam. 14:4 ESV).

In the Psalms we find, "The Lord lives! Praise be to my Rock! Exalted be God my Savior!" (Ps. 18:46). In this case, as in Deuteronomy 32:4 above, *tsur* is used as a name for God. It is somewhat ironic that although a rock is an inanimate object, it is coupled with the idea of life—because of the protection and strength it symbolizes.

"For in the day of trouble he will keep me safe in his dwelling; he will hide me in the shelter of his tabernacle and set me high upon a rock (*tsur*)" (Ps. 27:5). God can be a rock, or set us upon a rock.

God can also be a rock that is destructive to those who do not put their faith in him. This prophetic passage is talking about God, but also about his son Jesus, the Messiah, who would become both the rock and a stumbling block: "He will keep you safe. But to Israel and Judah he will be a stone (*eben*) that causes people to stumble, a rock (*tsur*) that makes them fall. And for the people of Jerusalem he will be a trap and a snare" (Isa. 8:14 NLT).

## ROD

A rod is basically a stick used for a variety of purposes. There are two Hebrew words, with unique meanings, translated "rod."

The first mention of a rod in Scripture is the one carried by Moses, called, in Exodus 4:20, "the rod of God." The word in Hebrew is *matteh*, which can mean a branch, a rod, or a walking staff, but is most often translated "tribe" (i.e., a branch of a family). Moses's rod was a scepter of sorts, a sign of his authority, and also a tool that God used to demonstrate his power. Each of the ten plagues was instigated by Moses's "stretching out his rod" or smiting something with it (Ex. 8). As we saw in the previous entry, he also used the rod to make water flow from a rock. Aaron also had a rod (Ex. 7:9), which symbolized his spiritual authority as a priest.

For some, discussions of biblical context for "rod" bring to mind the line "spare the rod and spoil the child." That exact phrase is not found in Scripture but was first coined in a line of seventeenth-century poetry (the context is political satire) by Sam Butler.

However, we do find similar sentiments in the oft-misquoted Proverbs 13:24: "Those who spare the rod hate their children, but those who love them are diligent to discipline them" (NRSV).

The parallel phrases tell us that a rod is a symbol of discipline, which is not the same thing as punishment. While many verses use the image of a rod as a metaphor for God's judgment or wrath, it is also used as a metaphor for guidance or protection. The Hebrew word in this verse is *shebet*, which again means branch, but like *matteh*, is most frequently translated "tribe." It can mean a rod or scepter—a symbol of authority. It is also a tool that a shepherd uses to care for his sheep, as mentioned in the famous line in Psalm 23:4, "Your rod and your staff, they comfort me." Like a shepherd guides and protects his sheep, parents are to guide (discipline) and protect their children.

Shepherds were common in the ancient world, but we rarely encounter them in our culture. Phillip Keller is an actual shepherd and author of *A Shepherd Looks at Psalm 23*. He notes that a rod was a club carved from a sapling. The knob where the trunk joined the roots of the tree was carved to fit a shepherd's hand. He would use it to defend the sheep from danger, often by throwing it. He might use it to strike at a predator, or if a sheep was wandering, he might throw it next to the sheep to startle it in order to send it back toward the herd.

The rod was also used to inspect the sheep, to make sure they were healthy. Keller writes:

> In caring for his sheep, the good shepherd, the careful manager, will from time to time make a careful examination of each individual sheep. As each animal comes out of the corral and through the gate, it is stopped by the shepherd's outstretched rod. He opens the fleece with the rod; he runs his skillful hands over the body; he feels for any sign of trouble; he examines the sheep with care to see if all is well. This is a most searching process entailing every intimate detail. It is, too, a comfort to the sheep for only in this way can its hidden problems be laid bare before the shepherd.[1]

This process of slowly letting sheep out of a pen, examining each one, was (and still is) called "passing under the rod." This is what God says he will do for each of us: "I will take note of you as you pass under my rod, and I will bring you into the bond of the covenant" (Ezek. 20:37). God does not watch over us from afar, but knows each of us intimately and cares for us tenderly.

## SABBATH

In the ancient world, various cultures kept track of time in different ways. Many looked to the cycles of nature to measure time: the predictable cycles of the sun, the moon, and the seasons. These natural phenomenon happened daily, monthly, or annually. Weeks, however, are not based on a visible pattern in nature, but rather are an arbitrary measure of time.

As a result, some ancient cultures did not even take note of weeks, only days and months (or moons). Others had five-day weeks, or even ten. The ancient Roman seven-day calendar named days for various "planets" (including the sun and the moon) that corresponded to their gods—Saturday was first called Saturn's Day, and Monday was originally Moon Day, for example.

The Hebrew calendar was instituted by God in the rhythm of creation. And it is in the pages of Genesis that we first see the idea of Sabbath: "By the seventh day God had finished the work he had been doing; so on the seventh day he rested (*shabath*) from all his work" (Gen. 2:2).

The English word *Sabbath* is a transliteration of the Hebrew word *shabath,* a verb that means to cease or to rest. The idea is a deliberate and mindful stopping. The noun *Shabbath* or *Shabbat,* meaning the Sabbath, has the verb as its root, and in fact that verb defines it: What we do on Sabbath is simply cease our labors and rest from them.

Thus we see the rhythm of life instituted by God: Work for six days, rest for one. Repeat. God modeled Sabbath-keeping long before he gave the Ten Commandments, first in creation, and then in the gift of manna in the wilderness.

When the Israelites were slaves in Egypt, they could not keep Sabbath. As Pharaoh's slaves, they did not have the freedom to have a day off. So God instituted a Sabbath for them (Ex. 16:23). Again, he modeled six days' work, one day rest in the way he provided food.

(See ***Manna***.) Later, he gave them the commandments, including the fourth one: Remember the Sabbath and keep it holy. The two lists of Ten Commandments each give a unique reason for this command: The Exodus list recalls creation; the Deuteronomy list reminds them of their freed status. God reminds them that Sabbath is about freedom—the freedom they did not have as slaves in Egypt (Deut. 5:15).

To keep Sabbath is to declare one's trust in God's miraculous provision—that he will turn six days of labor into seven days' worth of food and shelter. It is to believe that you will have enough.

Believing you have enough allows you to be generous, which is one reason the Sabbath laws were closely tied to God's concern for the poor. Both lists of the commandments make special note that the Sabbath was all-inclusive: men and women, slaves, and even animals were all to rest. In addition to weekly Sabbaths, God's people were to give the land a Sabbath, allowing it to lie fallow for one year every seven years (Lev. 25). During that year, the Israelites were not to sow or prune or harvest or reap. In the same year, slaves were to be set free (slaves in that culture were often those who had sold themselves into servant hood to pay off debts). The Sabbath year, and the related Jubilee year, were all about restoration of the poor. (See ***Jubilee***.)

The Sabbath for the land was a chance to see and trust the mighty provision of God. But God anticipates push-back on this rule and answers their objection before they even voice it with one of the most astonishing promises of Scripture:

> You may ask, "What will we eat in the seventh year if we do not plant or harvest our crops?" I will send you such a blessing in the sixth year that the land will yield enough for three years. While you plant during the eighth year, you will eat from the old crop and will continue to eat from it until the harvest of the ninth year comes in. (Lev. 25:20–22)

The Sabbath has eschatological and theological significance, pointing to both the rest we find in Jesus and the ultimate rest we will have in heaven. Sabbath-keeping was a visible sign of Israel's covenant with God and a way of declaring with the rhythm of their very lives that they trusted God's provision.

## SACRIFICE

The Old Testament sacrificial system was complex and specific. Particular kinds of sins required particular kinds of sacrifices: some of animals, others of grain, wine, or oil. Many required the intermediation of a priest, who would make atonement on a lay person's behalf or on the behalf of the entire nation.

Sacrifice precedes the priesthood and the giving of the law. The first mention of sacrifice in the Old Testament is in Genesis 8, when Noah offered sacrifices after he and the animals came safely off the ark. Prior to that, using a different word, the text implies that Abel sacrificed an animal from his flock as an offering to God. (See ***Offering***.) In Genesis 31:54, Jacob offers sacrifices as part of a covenant, an uneasy truce between him and his father-in-law, Laban. Even after the institution of the priesthood, the head of a family could offer sacrifices (Deut. 12:15).

The Hebrew words translated "sacrifice" are *zabach* (a verb meaning to slaughter or sacrifice) and *zebach* (a noun meaning the sacrifice itself or the flesh of the animal sacrificed). While other religions made sacrifices in order to appease the anger of their gods, Hebrews sacrificed to atone for their own sin.

Words translated "offering" can also mean sacrifice. A sacrifice that was completely burned was called a burnt offering (*olah*); an offering without blood (say of grain) was called a *minchah*; and a drink offering was called *necek*. A separate altar was constructed for burning incense. Exodus 30 describes this altar and its restrictions:

"Do not offer on this altar any other incense or any burnt offering (*olah*) or grain offering (*minchah*), and do not pour a drink offering (*necek*) on it" (v. 9).

One of the most important sacrifices in the Old Testament is described in Exodus 24, when Moses writes down all that God has told him, then reads it to the people. They respond (with good intentions, to be sure), "Everything that the Lord has said, we will do." And then Moses performs an elaborate ritual of building an altar with twelve pillars, sacrificing bulls, and sprinkling their blood on the altar and on the people themselves. He then proclaims, "This is the blood of the covenant that the Lord has made with you" (Ex. 24:8). This, more than any other sacrifice, clearly connects Israel with Yahweh and seals their covenantal relationship. It also foreshadows Christ's words at the Last Supper: "This cup is the new covenant in my blood, which is poured out for you" (Luke 22:20).

The law required that every sacrifice, whether of a bird, bull, or lamb, be a completely unblemished animal. Sickly or dying animals were not acceptable. Leviticus 3 spells out the procedure:

> You shall lay your hand on the head of the offering and slaughter it at the entrance of the tent of meeting; and Aaron's sons the priests shall dash the blood against all sides of the altar. You shall offer from the sacrifice of well-being, as an offering by fire to the Lord, the fat that covers the entrails and all the fat that is around the entrails. (Lev. 3:2–3 NRSV)

When the person making the sacrifice laid his hand on the head of the animal, he was symbolically transferring his sin, and the sin of his family, unto the animal.

The priests played a vital role in overseeing and handling the sacrifices. While the individual making the sacrifice would slay the animal, the priest was the one who poured out its blood onto the altar.

In Leviticus 17, we read of the regulations regarding blood, which Israelites were forbidden to consume, "for the life of the flesh is in the blood" (v. 11 NSRV). They could make their own sacrifices (vv. 5–7) but had to bring the animal to the tabernacle to have its blood poured on the altar by the priest. The blood is also a prophetic symbol of the coming Messiah, who would accomplish his mission by willingly allowing his own blood to be spilled. Sacrifice points out an important truth: There is no remission of sins without the shedding of blood (Heb. 9). Sacrifice is about substitution, meeting the demands of justice. It also continuously sealed the covenant between God and his people. By worshiping God with sacrifices, his people thanked God for

> their deliverance by him from Egypt and their adoption by him as his peculiar people. Through these gifts they were to enjoy the benefits and blessings of the covenant, forgiveness of sins, sanctification and true happiness.[1]

## SALT

Salt was an essential ingredient in the sacrifices and rituals of ancient Israel. As God spells out the various kinds of offerings and sacrifices the Israelites are to bring, he adds that salt is to be added to all of them, whether grain or meat. This was a symbol of the everlasting covenant: "Season all your grain offerings with salt. Do not leave the salt of the covenant of your God out of your grain offerings; add salt to all your offerings" (Lev. 2:13). Even today in the Middle East, sharing salt with a person (i.e., a meal) is a symbol of peace and connection.

Salt was used as a preservative, a purifying agent, and at times for chemical warfare (Judg. 9:45). In some cultures it was used as currency. Newborn babies were rubbed with salt as an antiseptic (Ezek. 16:4). The Hebrew word for salt is *melach*.

In the Old Testament, many of the ritual sacrifices and religious activity were connected with salt. The phrase "a covenant of salt" means "a covenant which was never to be broken."[1]

"Whatever is set aside from the holy offerings the Israelites present to the LORD I give to you and your sons and daughters as your regular share. It is an everlasting covenant of salt before the LORD for both you and your offspring" (Num. 18:19).

*Smith's Bible Dictionary* notes: "As one of the most essential articles of diet, salt symbolized hospitality; as an antiseptic, durability, fidelity and purity. Hence the expression 'covenant of salt,' . . . as betokening an indissoluble alliance between friends."[2]

Another encyclopedia notes:

> This custom of pledging friendship or confirming a compact by eating food containing salt is still retained among Arabic-speaking people. The Arabic word for "salt" and for a "compact" or "treaty" is the same. Doughty in his travels in Arabia appealed more than once to the superstitious belief of the Arabs in the "salt covenant," to save his life. Once an Arab has received in his tent even his worst enemy and has eaten salt (food) with him, he is bound to protect his guest as long as he remains.[3]

Similarly, even the incense burned on the altar of incense was to be combined with salt, which was a purifying agent and was again a symbol of the lasting covenant between God and his people: "And make an incense blended as by the perfumer, seasoned with salt, pure and holy" (Ex. 30:35 ESV).

Right after Elijah is taken up in the whirlwind and Elisha inherits Elijah's cloak, Elisha goes back the nearby city, where people honor him as a prophet. He does a miracle for them, using salt to purify the spring that supplies water to their city (2 Kings 2:19–22).

In quite a different usage, salt is a punishment, or perhaps a consequence. As Lot and his wife flee from Sodom as it burns, she cannot help but stop to watch her home as it is destroyed. The text says, "But Lot's wife, behind him, looked back, and she became a pillar of salt" (Gen. 19:26 ESV). Hers was not likely a quick glance over the shoulder. Some scholars believe that she stood gazing at her home as it burned, and was overcome by the ash and soot, which could have burned her body so that it appeared to look like salt. Others point out that this could be a mistranslation, as the similar word *malach* can mean to season with salt, but also means to vanish away, disappear. If Lot's wife lingered behind, she would have been consumed by the fire and would have "vanished away."

The Salt Sea is mentioned in Numbers 34 as a boundary of the Promised Land. This sea was also known as the Sea of Arabah (Deut. 3:15; Josh. 3:16) and is known today as the Dead Sea, an inland sea with an unusually high content of salt and minerals. The sea and natural salt mines in the land provided the valuable resource of an almost limitless supply of salt to the Israelites—yet another way that God blessed them.

## SATAN

For the amount of press he gets in religious circles today, Satan's mentions in the Bible are surprisingly rare. Satan is mentioned only eighteen times in the Old Testament, fourteen of those in the book of Job. In that book, he is a major character. He wagers with God that Job, a faithful man of God, loves God's blessings more than God himself. He claims that Job would fall away from faith if he faced hardship and trials.

God disagrees and allows Satan to bring suffering to Job. Two important theological points in what is believed to be the oldest book in the Bible: one, Satan is an agent of suffering whose aim is to destroy our faith; and two, he is limited in his power by God's decree (Job 2:6). However, God does not stifle him completely, but allows him to roam the earth (Job 1:7). The New Testament corroborates this fact in 1 Peter 5:8, comparing Satan to a lion seeking someone to devour.

The name of Satan, an angelic being, comes from the Hebrew word *satan,* which means adversary or opponent, and is sometimes used to describe a human adversary. This word is used a handful of times in the Psalms to describe an enemy or opponent: "Those also who render evil for good, They are my adversaries (*satan*), because I follow what is good" (Ps. 38:20 NKJV), and, "My accusers (*satan*) will be clothed with disgrace and wrapped in shame as in a cloak" (Ps. 109:29).

Zechariah 3 begins with the prophet's vision of Joshua, standing before God and Satan, the accuser:

> Then he showed me Joshua the high priest standing before the angel of the LORD, and Satan standing at his right side to accuse him. The LORD said to Satan, "The LORD rebuke you, Satan! The LORD, who has chosen Jerusalem, rebuke you! Is not this man a burning stick snatched from the fire?" (vv. 1–2).

In this vision, which painted a picture of the process by which Israel would be restored, Satan appears to play the role of prosecutor in a courtroom where God is judge, again showing that his power is subject to God's.

The seemingly related word *devil* does not appear in the Old Testament. Its plural, *devils,* as a synonym for false gods to whom people sacrificed, appears just four times.

In some instances, the word *satan* actually refers to God, in the specific role of an adversary, usually of evil. For example, when Balaam wanted to go to Moab to curse Israel, God told him not to. When he went anyway, God sent an angel with a sword to block his way: "But God's anger was kindled because he went, and the angel of the LORD took his stand in the way as his adversary (*satan*). Now he was riding on the donkey, and his two servants were with him" (Numbers 22:22 ESV).

Balaam's donkey could see the angel, but Balaam could not, and then God allowed the donkey to speak. To me this conversation was not so extraordinary in that the donkey spoke, but that Balaam was so mad that he started arguing with the donkey, not seeming to notice that anything was out of the ordinary!

Another mention of Satan is in the parallel passages of 2 Samuel 24:1 and 1 Chronicles 21:1, where "Satan rose up against Israel and incited David to take a census of Israel." David's advisors thought this was a bad idea, and God was displeased. Why? Because David was counting his warriors? Many times in the history of Israel, they had won battles where they were overwhelmingly outnumbered. David's advisor reminded him of this truth, but David told him to count them anyway. Was David's sin pride or lack of trust? Some scholars think he was not only counting his warriors but exacting a tax from each person. Was he making plans for some sort of conquest when God had not told him to do so? Was he becoming power hungry, money hungry, or just bored? Or, as the text implies, did he succumb to Satan's temptation?

At least one dictionary says that the correct translation of "satan" in 1 Chronicles 21:1 is "an adversary," not the particular person of Satan.

We can see that Satan is a tempter, accuser, and adversary, but his power is limited and his influence is not nearly as devastating to Israel as their own stubbornness. Rather than blaming Satan for temptation or sin in our own lives, we ought to notice how infrequently this accuser is mentioned and take responsibility for our own choices to follow God or not.

## SHEOL

Numbers 16 is one of the strangest stories in the Bible. I definitely never heard it taught in Sunday school, nor heard a sermon preached on the text. In it, a Levite named Korah, along with a band of his kinsmen, challenges Moses's power and ends up getting "pitched alive into Sheol" (vv. 28, 31) when the ground opens and swallows him and his extended family, then closes up again.[1]

Then, fire shoots from God and burns up another 250 men. As if that weren't enough, the next day the people complain about the loss of these lives, and God gets even angrier. He tells Moses he is going to destroy the whole nation, and the only thing that prevents total destruction is that Moses sends Aaron into their midst with a censer of incense, telling him to hurry and make atonement for the people. He does so and stops a deadly plague in its tracks, but only after 14,700 people have died on the spot.

It's the kind of story that leaves you scratching your head.

It does bring up an interesting question, though: Do people go to hell after they die, or do they sometimes go straight to hell while still alive?

The Hebrew word *Sheol* means the place of the dead, the grave, or hell, depending on which translation (or sometimes, which verse) you read. Many just use the Hebrew word in the text.

The Old Testament never mentions *Sheol* as a place of punishment, but rather as the abode of the dead and a place of nothingness. However, being sent there alive was definitely the fate of the wicked. God rescued others from it: "O Lord, you have brought up my soul from *Sheol*; you restored me to life from among those who go down to the pit" (Ps. 30:3 ESV).

But everyone went there, at least at first. The Bible says that God could rescue people from staying there: "But God will ransom my soul from the power of *Sheol*, for he will receive me" (Ps. 49:15 ESV).

The word *Sheol* is interesting because its use shows us how Hebrew theology evolved as the Bible was written. As the prophecies for the Messiah came to Israel, they began to shift their ideas about the afterlife. In Isaiah 25, the prophet predicts: "On this mountain he will destroy the shroud that enfolds all peoples, the sheet that covers all nations; he will swallow up death forever" (vv. 7–8 NRSV). This prophecy was the first of its kind in the Old Testament and planted a new seed of hope for resurrection and eternal life.

One dictionary notes:

> Toward the end of the Old Testament, God revealed that there will be a resurrection of the dead (Isa 26:19). Sheol will devour no longer; instead God will swallow up Death (Isa 25:8). The faithful will be rewarded with everlasting life while the rest will experience eternal contempt (Dan 12:2). This theology developed further in the intertestamental period.[2]

Sometimes *Sheol* is used metaphorically for feelings of desperation and despair, or to paint a picture of separation from God:

> For the waves of death encompassed me,
>   the torrents of destruction assailed me;
> the cords of Sheol entangled me;
>   the snares of death confronted me.
> In my distress I called upon the LORD;
>   to my God I called.
> From his temple he heard my voice,
>   and my cry came to his ears. (2 Sam. 22:5–7 ESV)

When a person died, they were placed in a physical tomb or grave; the Hebrew word is *qeber*. For example: "He laid the body in his own grave (*qeber*), crying out in grief, 'Oh, my brother!'" (1 Kings 13:30 NLT).

In Sheol, the dead still exist, but in a weakened, unhappy state. Isaiah 14:9–10 describes it this way:

> The realm of the dead below is all astir
> to meet you at your coming;
> it rouses the spirits of the departed to greet you—
> all those who were leaders in the world;
> it makes them rise from their thrones—
> all those who were kings over the nations.
> They will all respond,
> they will say to you,
> "You also have become weak, as we are;
> you have become like us." (ESV)

There was little hope of escape from this limbo unless God chose to intervene. But because of Jesus, we have assurance of being in his presence when this life ends.

## SHEPHERD

The word *shepherd* describes a pastoral occupation, and for Christians is obviously loaded with meaning—we cannot help but think of Jesus the Good Shepherd. But to those who were living when the Old Testament was written, sheep keeping was a way of life—an occupation many families had practiced for generations. It is a profession as old as time: Adam's son Abel was the first shepherd mentioned in the Bible. King David was a shepherd as a boy. Many modern urban dwellers, on the other hand, have never even seen a sheep.

*Ra'ah* means to pasture or to shepherd. It's what a shepherd does by leading his sheep to pasture to allow them to feed.

Genesis 46:34 declares that shepherds were detestable to the Egyptians. The word *shepherd* translates two words: *tso'n* (flocks, cattle) and *ra'ah* (to tend or shepherd).

The noun form, *ro'eh*, appears sixty-two times in the Old Testament and is used both literally and metaphorically, for both human leaders and God himself (first in Gen. 29:24).

When the Israelites were wandering in the desert, they had with them many flocks, and so their daily occupation was to be shepherds: "And your children shall be shepherds (*ra'ah*) in the wilderness forty years and shall suffer for your faithlessness, until the last of your dead bodies lies in the wilderness" (Num. 14:33 ESV). Some versions says "wander" instead of "be shepherds." Because much of Israel is a desert, shepherds have to be nomads in order to find enough grass to feed their sheep.

Sheep were frequently required for sacrifices, and thus for food, so keeping herds was part, in a way, of following God and keeping the covenant with him. (See ***Sacrifice, Offering***.)

One dictionary says, "Shepherding was the chief occupation of the Israelites in the early days of the patriarchs" but then adds that "the Hebrew word for shepherding is often translated 'feeding.' "[1]

Both men and women served as shepherds, as we can see from Genesis 29. Rachel, who eventually becomes Jacob's wife, is a shepherdess.

In Genesis 48:15, Joseph refers to God as his shepherd, and of course, the well-known analogy in Psalm 23 refers to the Lord as our shepherd. According to that psalm, God "restores my soul" (v. 3 NKJV). The Hebrew word translated "restore" is *shuwb*, which means to return, to bring back, to recover. The image evoked is of a sheep that has wandered off and is gently sought out and brought back to the fold, an act of care and protection.

The tending and leadership necessary to be a shepherd made it an apt metaphor for the role of a leader or ruler of people. This reference is often made as power is transferred from one leader to another, as it is when Jesus tells Peter, "feed my sheep" (John 21:17). The Greek word for feed, *poimain•;* can also mean to tend a flock—as it can in Hebrew as well.

As Moses is preparing to die, we read:

> Moses said to the LORD, "May the LORD, the God who gives breath to all living things, appoint someone over this community to go out and come in before them, one who will lead them out and bring them in, so the LORD's people will not be like sheep without a shepherd." So the LORD said to Moses, "Take Joshua son of Nun, a man in whom is the spirit of leadership, and lay your hand on him." (Num. 27:15–18 NIV)

Similarly, when David is anointed King of Israel, they summoned the one who had been a shepherd of sheep to fulfill his calling as a shepherd of God's people:

> All the tribes of Israel came to David at Hebron and said, "We are your own flesh and blood. In the past, while Saul was king over us, you were the one who led Israel on their military campaigns. And the LORD said to you, 'You will shepherd my people Israel, and you will become their ruler.'" (2 Sam. 5:1–2)

The metaphor continued as a frequent image in messianic prophecy:

> He will feed his flock like a shepherd;
> he will gather the lambs in his arms,
> and carry them in his bosom,
> and gently lead the mother sheep. (Isa. 40:11 NRSV)

What a beautiful picture of God's care for those he loves.

## SHIELD

Battles and military exploits dominate much of the Old Testament narrative. A central event is Israel's takeover of Canaan, which they accomplish by force (with plenty of divine assistance). Years later, their subsequent exile occurs because of their military defeat (precipitated by their rebellion against God, which results in his withdrawn protection).

In such a war-focused culture, it makes sense that the word *shield* would be used not only literally but figuratively. There were two types of shields—a large one carried by a shield bearer and a small one used in hand-to-hand combat (known as a buckler because it buckles onto the arm). The larger shield, large enough to shield a man completely, is a *tsinnah*. The smaller shield, or buckler, is a *magen*.

Both were used in warfare, as evidenced by verses like this: "Prepare buckler (*magen*) and shield (*tsinnah*), and advance for battle!" (Jer. 46:3 ESV).

King David, who was both a warrior and a poet, used the word *magen* often in his poetry. He often describes God in military terms: "My God, my rock, in whom I take refuge, my shield (*magen*), and the horn of my salvation, my stronghold and my refuge, my savior; you save me from violence" (2 Sam. 22:3 ESV). A *magen* also refers to a symbol, as the Star of David, which is called the "magen David" even today.

In another, earlier story of David, we find a description of the larger shield—*tsinnah*. When David was just a boy, he faced the giant Philistine Goliath. First Samuel 17:7 describes Goliath: "His spear shaft was like a weaver's rod, and its iron point weighed six hundred shekels. His shield (*tsinnah*) bearer went ahead of him" (NIV).

The text reveals something I never saw depicted in my Bible picture books: Goliath, for all his fierceness, had another man with a huge shield in front of him, even to face a little shepherd boy! "Meanwhile, the Philistine, with his shield (*tsinnah*) bearer in front of him, kept coming closer to David" (1 Sam. 17:41).

The word *shield* is also used metaphorically in the Old Testament. Most often, the word *magen* is used as a metaphor for God's protection and assistance: "After this, the word of the

LORD came to Abram in a vision: 'Do not be afraid, Abram. I am your shield (*magen*), your very great reward' " (Gen. 15:1). It is interesting that God's protection is not referred to as a *tsinnah*, a giant shield that keeps anything from hitting us, but rather a *magen*, a small shield that is used in hand-to-hand combat. God's protection doesn't isolate us from struggles but equips us to prevail against them.

Similarly, "Blessed are you, O Israel; Who is like you, a people saved by the LORD, Who is the shield (*magen*) of your help and the sword of your majesty! So your enemies will cringe before you, and you will tread upon their high places" (Deut. 33:29 NASB).

> As for God, his way is perfect;
>   the word of the LORD is flawless.
> He is a shield (*magen*)
>   for all who take refuge in him. (2 Sam. 22:31)

A third word for shield, used a handful of times, is *shelet*, which refers to a literal shield, probably a larger and more ornate one, taken as plunder: "David took the gold shields (*shelet*) that belonged to the officers of Hadadezer and brought them to Jerusalem" (2 Sam. 8:7).

When we find the verb *to shield* in the text, it is sometimes a translation for the Hebrew word *cabab*, which means to lead about, to turn around, or when translated "shield," to enclose or envelop. For example: "In a desert land he found him, in a barren and howling waste. He shielded (*cabab*) him and cared for him; he guarded him as the apple of his eye" (Deut. 32:10).

This word has several meanings, such as to go around something or to protect by shielding.

While we may not be engaged in military battles, we know what it is to battle against evil and temptation. In those moments, we can trust that God will indeed be our shield, allowing us to prevail against sin.

## SOUL

The Hebrew word for soul is *nephesh*. Many times it stands not only for the inner self, but for the person in totality. For example, Leviticus 5 contains numerous regulations on cleanliness, many of which begin "If a person touches . . ." or "if a person swears . . ." The Hebrew word translated "person" is *nephesh*, and the King James Version translates these phrases "If a soul . . ." It is sometimes translated with a personal pronoun (I or me).

While *nephesh* is translated with a wide variety of English words, it is different from the word *soul* in the New Testament or today. Rather than the part of a person that lives on after death, *nephesh* is a person's (or even an animal's) vitality, their life in the sense of their aliveness. It is what secularists might call a person's life-force.

This life is God-given and can be taken away by God. Genesis 2:7 says that the very breath of God made Adam, a pile of dust, into a living being (*nephesh*); in Job 27:8 and elsewhere we read that God can take away a person's soul, or life.

In the first chapter of Genesis, *nephesh* is sometimes combined with the Hebrew word *chay*, meaning living or alive, to designate "living creatures," i.e., animals.

The psalmist often prays, "Bless the Lord, O my soul (*nephesh*)," to designate worship with the whole self—"all that is within me." The soul in part reflects the image of God and is also to be devoted to God. At times it seems like the psalmist is addressing his soul as a separate entity: "Why are you cast down, O my soul, and why are you in turmoil within me?" (Ps. 42:11 ESV). This poetic convention creates a perfect image of the internal struggle between good and evil that wages in the soul of every person.

Each day, Old Testament Jews would pray the *Shema*, a prayer from Deuteronomy 6:4–5: "Hear, O Israel: the Lord our God, the

Lord is one. You shall love the LORD your God with all your heart (*lebab*) and with all your soul (*nephesh*) and with all your might (*me'od*)" (ESV).

Similarly, Deuteronomy 26:16 says, "The Lord your God commands you this day to follow these decrees and laws; carefully observe them with all your heart and with all your soul (*nephesh*)." The idea is not just to mentally assent to the statutes of God, but to live them, or as the text says, to "observe" them. The King James Version says, "Thou shalt therefore keep and do them."

For the Old Testament Jew, to believe was to obey—to "keep and do." However, their theology did not ignore the fact that deception was possible and a temptation. In their understanding, there was an important distinction between the inner and outer person. "The inner person is *nephesh*, while the outer person, or reputation, is *shem*, most commonly translated 'name.' "[1] One represented how you saw yourself, the second how others saw you. The way to bring these into alignment was to do what God had commanded, to observe the law.

The Bible promises that God will redeem our soul (Ps. 49:15), deliver our soul from death (Ps. 56:13), satisfy our soul (Ps. 63:5), delight our soul (Prov. 29:17). Our soul is our point of connection with God, the place where he can minister to us. The soul is not our emotions, which may react involuntarily. Rather, it is the self, which we can choose to instruct and take control of, even to encourage or rally. We can engage in spiritual practices like fasting or confession to humble our souls: "When I humbled my soul with fasting" (Ps. 69:10 NRSV). When we do this, we will find connection with God, although we must be prepared to pay the price—it sometimes results in alienation from others, or the scorn of our enemies (Ps. 69:11).

Nevertheless, we can find contentment and peace by choosing to still our souls before God:

> But I have stilled and quieted my soul;
> like a weaned child with its mother,
> like a weaned child is my soul within me. (Ps. 131:2)

When we trust God and choose to quiet our soul, it becomes, in the lovely image of the psalmist, "like a weaned child"—no longer rooting and needy, but content, resting in the presence of God.

## TABERNACLE

*Tabernacle* is a rich, multifaceted word in Hebrew, from which several other important words derive. It was the central symbol of Israel's God, who dwelt not far off in the heavens or on a distant mountaintop, but among them.

Exodus 25 and 26 spell out in careful detail a construction project that the children of Israel undertook while on their way from Egypt to Canaan. They were to build a portable tent, made with curtains and poles, to house the ark of the covenant. The tabernacle, or Tent of Meeting, was God's home among them, and because they were nomads (or more accurately, pilgrims), this home was to be mobile.

It was also to be constructed by skilled workers—God cared about the quality of his home and wanted his people to honor him by bringing their best work and materials to him. It was ornamented with gold, brightly colored cloth and embroidery, and fine workmanship.

The Hebrew is *mishkan*, which essentially means a residence or a dwelling place. It comes from the word *shakan*, "to dwell." God's instructions to build it expressed a desire of his heart for community with his people—he wanted to dwell with them. It referred to the physical tabernacle and later the temple, but it also was understood to represent the indwelling presence of God. It is the root of the term *shekinah*, which Jews used for centuries to refer to the active and real presence of God. *Mishkan* is also related to one of the Hebrew words for neighbor, *shaken*. It reminds us that God wants to be our neighbor, live among us. It is, of course, a prophetic symbol of the incarnation. (See ***Dwell***.)

God tells Moses, "Then have them make a sanctuary (*mishkan*) for me, and I will dwell (*shakan*) among them" (Ex. 25:8) and "I will dwell (*shakan*) among the people of Israel and will be their God" (Ex. 29:45 ESV). We also find *shakan* translated as "settled" in the idea of settling down or even lying down, but always with the underlying idea of presence. "Whenever the cloud lifted from above the Tent, the Israelites set out; wherever the cloud settled (*shakan*), the Israelites encamped" (Num. 9:17).

In my previous book *Rest*, I wrote, "By building a tabernacle for God, his people were, paradoxically, sheltered by God. They had a physical reminder of a spiritual reality: God is with us, wants to dwell with us, wants to rest with us. God is not just in one place, but dwells among us, can move with us."[1]

The tabernacle is usually called the *mishkan*, but it is also called the Tent of Meeting. One dictionary notes,

> Two compound phrases (*'ohel moed* and *ohel haeduth*) are used in the Bible to designate this tent: "the tabernacle of the congregation" (Ex. 29:42, 44), literally the "tent of meeting" (NRSV, NIV, NAS, REB) and the "tabernacle of witness" (Nu. 17:7) or "tent of witness." In both cases it was the place where the God of Israel revealed Himself to and dwelled among His people.[2]

Both names are sometimes used in the same verse:

> And he set the altar of burnt offering at the entrance of the tabernacle (*mishkan*) of the tent (*ohel*) of meeting (*mow'ed*), and offered on it the burnt offering and the grain offering, as the LORD had commanded Moses. (Ex. 40:29 ESV)

*Ohel* means tents, and *mow'ed* means an appointed place, but it can also mean an appointed time, a season. *Haeduth* means witness.

An *ohel* can be any tent; it refers not only to the tabernacle but the homes nomadic people dwell in, or even sometimes the barns for their flocks and cattle. Prior to the construction of the tabernacle, God met with Moses in a tent outside of the camp.

The tabernacle was the site of all sacrifices and offerings, which were to be brought to its doorway. There was an outer court, an inner tent (the Holy Place), and the innermost chamber called the Holy of Holies, which no one was allowed to enter except the high priest, and then only once per year on the Day of Atonement.

Some have likened the setup of the tabernacle with its various chambers to the human heart, wherein God dwells.

## TEMPLE

The books of 1 Chronicles and 2 Samuel tell the story of David's ascension to the throne of Israel. Eventually, he takes power, brings back the ark of the covenant to Jerusalem, and defeats the dreaded Philistines.

However, once he is established on the throne and living in the palace, he realizes something is amiss:

> Now when David settled in his house, David said to the prophet Nathan, "I am living in a house of cedar, but the ark of the covenant of the LORD is under a tent." Nathan said to David, "Do all that you have in mind, for God is with you." But that same night the word of the LORD came to Nathan, saying: Go and tell my servant David: Thus says the LORD: You shall not build me a house to live in. For I have not lived in a house since the day I brought out Israel to this very day, but I have lived in a tent and a tabernacle. Wherever I have moved about among all Israel, did I ever speak a word with any of the judges of Israel,

> whom I commanded to shepherd my people, saying, Why have you not built me a house of cedar? (1 Chron. 17:1–6 NRSV; see also 2 Sam. 7)

Throughout the passage, the word *house* translates the Hebrew word *bayith*, which can mean a literal building that serves as a residence or a family or clan, i.e., the household of a person. It appears that God is content to live in a tent. He never asked for a house, of cedar or anything else.

Then God goes on to tell David, through Nathan, "The LORD will build you a house (*bayith*). When your days are fulfilled to go to be with your ancestors, I will raise up your offspring after you, one of your own sons, and I will establish his kingdom. He shall build a house (*bayith*) for me, and I will establish his throne forever" (1 Chron. 17:10–12 NRSV). This prophetic word refers to David's son Solomon, who eventually does build a magnificent temple. But the verse contains a riddle: Is David's son Solomon to build the house for God, or is God building a house for David's family? The answer is yes; it's both. He is giving his people permission to build a more permanent structure, which will be a symbol both of his presence and the selection of David's "house" as part of God's plan. And eventually we come to learn that David's lineage leads us to Jesus.

David humbly responds, "Who am I, O LORD God, and what is my house, that you have brought me thus far? And even this was a small thing in your sight, O God; you have also spoken of your servant's house for a great while to come" (1 Chron. 17:16–17 NRSV). Again, the word *house*, which in these verses means family or household, is also *bayith*.

The word *bayith* is also sometimes translated "temple." For example, in a description of *bayith Yehovah,* or the house of the LORD, in 2 Kings 11, we find the word *bayith* repeatedly. Some versions render it "house," others use "temple," as it is obviously referring to the temple.

Often, however, "temple" is a translation of the Hebrew word *heykal,* which can mean a palace, God's temple, a hall, or even a heavenly temple. (See Ps. 5:7; 18:6; 27:4, for example.)

First Kings 5–7 provides an elaborate description of the temple's construction. The word in these chapters is *bayith*, which some versions translate as "house," others as "temple."

The temple was ornate, with floors of gold and walls trimmed with cedar. Its design was based on the tabernacle's dimensions, only it was much larger and more ornate—the altar area and all the bowls, censers, and equipment were made of gold. It was solid, made of huge hewn stone blocks. It took seven years to construct (1 Kings 6:38).

Later kings did not protect the temple as they should (1 Kings 14), and enemies stole its treasure. The condition of the temple often reflected the spiritual condition of God's people: When they wandered from him, the temple was destroyed. *Holman's Bible Dictionary* comments:

> Jeremiah in his great Temple sermon warned all who came into the Lord's house in Jerusalem that if they trusted primarily in the Temple, instead of the Lord, He could destroy Solomon's Temple just as He had the previous one at Shiloh (Jer. 7:1–15; 26:1–6).[1]

The temple is again a prophetic symbol, not of the church, but of our hearts, which are to be the temple of the Holy Spirit (1 Cor. 6:19).

## TRANSGRESSION

To transgress is to rebel, to go against. The Bible refers to people's transgressions against other people, against God, or sometimes a nation's transgression against another nation. Transgression is a specific kind of sin.

The most common Hebrew word translated "transgression" is *pesha'*, which can be used in any of these contexts. It literally means a revolt and is used to describe a willful rebellion against godly living:

> Thus says the LORD: "For three transgressions (*pesha'*) of Judah, and for four, I will not revoke the punishment, because they have rejected the law of the LORD, and have not kept his statutes, but their lies have led them astray, those after which their fathers walked." (Amos 2:4 ESV)

In fact, verses like this throughout the book of Amos provide clues to the meaning of *pesha'*.

As God was sending the Israelites into Canaan, he told them,

> I am going to send an angel in front of you, to guard you on the way and to bring you to the place that I have prepared. Be attentive to him and listen to his voice; do not rebel against him, for he will not pardon your transgression; for my name is in him. (Ex. 23:20–21 NRSV)

While God's angel was a warrior and leader, and was charged with upholding and meting out the justice of God, he could not pardon sin. However, God could, if he so chose:

> The LORD, the LORD, a God merciful and gracious, slow to anger, and abounding in steadfast love and faithfulness, keeping steadfast love for thousands, forgiving iniquity and transgression (*pescha'*) and sin (*chatta'ath*), but who will by no means clear the guilty, visiting the iniquity of the fathers on the children and the children's children, to the third and the fourth generation. (Ex. 34:6–7 ESV)

Even as he forgives, God does not shield us from the fruit of our rebellious and foolish decisions. The consequences of a parent's sin will be felt for three or four generations. But—and this is where our hope lies—the love of God will prevail and will outlast our mistakes for a thousand generations.

In Exodus 16, we read the religious ritual to be followed for the Day of Atonement, which was the only time the priest was allowed into the Holy of Holies. In this passage, we find the word *transgression* and two similar terms:

> Thus he shall make atonement for the sanctuary, because of the uncleannesses (*tum'ah*) of the people of Israel, and because of their transgressions (*pesha'*), all their sins (*chatta'ath*); and so he shall do for the tent of meeting, which remains with them in the midst of their uncleannesses. (Lev. 16:16 NRSV)

Note the parallel phrasing that links these three words: uncleannesses (*tum'ah*), transgressions (*pesha'*), sins (*chatta'ath*). (See ***Unclean***.)

We see a similar parallel phrasing in the first occurrence of the word *trespass* in the Bible: "Then Jacob was angry and rebuked Laban, and Jacob answered and said to Laban: 'What is my trespass (*pesha'*)? What is my sin (*chatta'ath*), that you have so hotly pursued me?'" (Gen. 31:36 NKJV).

As it does in Greek, the Hebrew word for sin means to miss the mark (as an archer shooting at a target), or to go off the path. The word *chatta'ath* also means a sin offering or the guilt associated with sin.

Similarly, to transgress means to cross a line, to go off the road of obedience.

Because we are human, transgressions are inevitable. But the Bible shows us that when we repent, God forgives transgressions: "Blessed is the one whose transgression (*pesha'*) is forgiven, whose sin is covered" (Ps. 32:1 ESV).

Less frequently we see the word *ma'al*, which is often translated "trespass." It means to be unfaithful. We find it in verses like this: "So Saul died for his transgression which he committed against the LORD" (1 Chron. 10:13 KJV). Most other versions use *unfaithfulness* instead of *transgression* to translate *ma'al*.

All of these words illustrate an essential truth of Christian theology: Every human being falls short of God's standard of holiness and stands in need of forgiveness.

## TRIBE

The nation or people (*'am*) of Israel was divided into tribes. They were descendants of Jacob, who was also called Israel. Each tribe descended from one of Jacob's twelve sons. The tribes were further divided into clans (*mishpachah*), again based on their ancestry. In fact, *mishpachah* is often translated "family," meaning an extended family. Within each clan, there were families designated by their father or patriarch.

In our culture, single families often live far from their extended families and move frequently. This was not the case in the ancient world. In a way, this is what is so radical about what God asks Abram to do—follow him to a distant land. God uproots Abram and transfers him, so to speak, to a new place. (See ***Wander***.)

The Hebrew words for tribe are *matteh*, which originally meant a branch, and *shebet*, a branch or stick. Both words can also mean rod or staff. (See ***Rod***.) A rod and staff are tools (sometimes used as weapons) used by a shepherd, but both words are most frequently used to mean tribe. Both meanings convey the meaning of strength and power; a tribe, especially in that culture, was a group of people who protected and supported one another, just as a rod protected and supported the shepherd. Both Moses and Aaron carried rods that were both symbols and actual sources of their spiritual power and authority.

When Israel entered and conquered the Promised Land, each tribe (except the Levites) was given a section of it (Josh. 13–20).

The land was divided by lot. (See ***Lot***.) The Levites, the tribe who served as priests, did not receive a territory: "But to the tribe (*shebet*) of Levi Moses gave no inheritance; the LORD God of Israel is their inheritance, as he said to them" (Josh. 13:33 NRSV). However, the Levites were given cities, scattered throughout Canaan, and also were supported by the other tribes (Josh. 20).

The twelve tribes are often described using the word *shebet*: "So Joshua called together the twelve men he had appointed from the Israelites, one from each tribe (*shebet*)" (Josh. 4:4).

Often, the words seem interchangeable: "Moses gave an inheritance to the half-tribe (*shebet*) of Manasseh; it was allotted to the half-tribe (*matteh*) of the Manassites according to their families" (Josh. 13:29 NRSV).

The "half tribe" of Manasseh were so called because half of the tribe received an allotment of land on one side of the Jordan River, the other half on the other side. Manasseh and his brother, Ephraim, were not sons of Jacob, but grandsons—they were the two sons of Joseph. However, they were each considered one of the tribes.

The tribes did not always get along—in fact, skirmishes between tribes may have been what caused the division of Israel into the northern and southern kingdoms. The so-called "tribal period" lasted until Israel demanded and received a king.

The name "Lion of Judah" refers to the fact that Jesus came from the tribe of Judah, one of the twelve (see Rev. 5:5).

The tribes are listed several times. Genesis 49 records Jacob's blessing of each son, or tribe. Moses goes through each tribe and offers a blessing just before he dies, as recorded in Deuteronomy 33. The song of Deborah in Judges 5 also lists nearly all of the tribes, naming their role in the battle. Some, like Zebulun and Naphtali, fought alongside of her; others, like Reuben and Dan, hung back (vv. 16–17).

The Bible often explains someone's identity by telling what tribe and clan they come from. Leviticus 24:10–11 describes a situation with a man whose mother was an Israelite and whose father was an Egyptian. Because his father was Egyptian, his lineage as an Israelite came through his mother. The text clarifies: "His mother's name was Shelomith, the daughter of Dibri, of the tribe (*matteh*) of Dan" (v. 11 ESV). Another example is found in Exodus 31: "See, I have chosen Bezalel son of Uri, the son of Hur, of the tribe (*matteh*) of Judah" (v. 2).

The significance of this word becomes clear in the New Testament, where we read that followers of Jesus are a part of the people of God, and we are a "branch grafted in" to the tribes of Israel (Rom. 11).

## UNCLEAN

God told Noah when stocking the ark, "Take with you seven of every kind of clean animal, a male and its mate, and two of every kind of unclean animal, a male and its mate" (Gen. 7:2). The context makes no mention of how to discern whether animals are clean or unclean, but it seems to assume that Noah understands the distinction. Later in biblical history, we find a very specific list of what is clean and unclean, and how things can be purified if they become unclean, or defiled.

The Hebrew word *tame'* means to be unclean, defile, or pollute. The related adjective, spelled in English with the same transliteration, means foul, unclean, defiled. The word carries a connotation of guilt. If someone is unclean, even because they touch a dead animal, for example, they are considered guilty (Lev. 5:2).

The cleanliness rules stem from God's injunctive that his people be holy and set apart. God tells his people, "And you will be my kingdom of priests, my holy (*qadowsh*) nation (*goy*)" (Ex. 19:6 NLT). To be holy means to be separate, pure. So God's people needed guidelines for that purity.

A person could become unclean by what they touched or ate, or via an infection. Also, bodily emissions and childbirth rendered people unclean for varying amounts of time. In what seems like a misogynistic rule, women were considered unclean after childbirth, and the length of time required for purification after the birth of a girl was twice as long as that for the birth of a boy. A woman was also considered unclean for seven days while she had her monthly period—a rule that women actually may have welcomed, as it gave them a break from having to meet their husband's sexual demands.

Certain animals were prohibited from being eaten, or even touched. Even things those animals touched became ceremonially unclean. In Leviticus 11, God tells Moses and Aaron, "You may eat any animal that has a split hoof completely divided and that chews the cud" (v. 3).

God goes on to give numerous examples, just to clarify. No camels or rabbits because, although they chew the cud, neither has a split hoof. No pigs because, although they have a split (or cloven) hoof, they do not chew cud. The examples seem excessive, to drive home the point that both criteria (not just one!) must be met for an animal to be considered a clean food source.

Animals that creep along the ground were also forbidden, and again the restrictions are very specific: "Of the animals that move about on the ground, these are unclean for you: the weasel, the rat, any kind of great lizard, the gecko, the monitor lizard, the wall lizard, the skink and the chameleon" (Lev. 11:29–30). Birds of prey and animals with paws, along with bottom feeders in the ocean, were also prohibited—only fish with scales *and* fins were considered clean.

Why all these rules? The last verse in Leviticus 11 gives us a hint: "You must distinguish between the unclean and the clean, between living creatures that may be eaten and those that may not be eaten" (Lev. 11:47). God wants his people to develop discernment and to live with intention. You didn't just grab anything you saw and gobble it up thoughtlessly. The rules of clean and unclean forced God's people to think before they acted and to exercise self-control over their appetites. Those are valuable life lessons.

The most notable infection causing uncleanness was leprosy—in Hebrew, *tsara'ath*—which referred to various skin diseases and infections. Leprosy, which caused the body to decay before death, was seen as a symbol of death.

On a deeper level, the clean and unclean rules went beyond mere sanitation. God's stated intention for his people was holiness, and these rules were more significant spiritually than physically. Their faith was expressed in every aspect of life—eating, bathing, even what they could and could not touch.

The Levitical regulations also spell out very clearly how that which is unclean can become clean: typically through ablution (washing with water) or sacrifice, or both. In the same way, under the new covenant, we are washed in baptism and cleansed by Christ's sacrifice on our behalf.

## UNLEAVENED

Unleavened bread is bread baked without leaven (or yeast). It has both practical and symbolic significance in the Old Testament.

Unleavened bread, *matstsah* (or *massah*) in Hebrew, is most closely associated with the feast of Passover. Exodus 12, where the word *matstsah* appears six times, spells out for the Israelites what to expect in the first Passover, and how to commemorate it in years to come.

This festival was so significant that God told his people to reset their calendar, to make this festival the first month of their year (Ex. 12:2). The Passover was the final plague God sent to ensure Israel's escape from slavery in Egypt. The angel of death would come and kill the firstborn son of every family (even animal families). Only those who had the blood of a lamb on their doorpost would be spared. God's people were to slaughter a yearling lamb, smear its blood on the doorpost of their home, and then cook the entire lamb over a fire. The people were to eat roasted lamb, bitter herbs, and unleavened bread—highly symbolic foods—and they were to eat them as if they were getting ready to bolt out the door to escape Egypt (which they were).

"This is how you shall eat it: your loins girded, your sandals on your feet, and your staff in your hand; and you shall eat it hurriedly. It is the passover of the LORD" (Ex. 12:11 NRSV). Unleavened bread was the original fast food.

This chapter gives instructions for the ritual that will protect the Israelites from death, and tells them to commemorate their emancipation by reenacting this hurried meal each year thereafter. Passover was also later called the Festival of Unleavened Bread. (See ***Feast***.) Other festivals and sacrifices also required unleavened bread, which was seen as more pure than bread with yeast, because the yeast ferments and, in essence, decays what it is mixed with. (See ***Bread***.)

At Passover, the Hebrews were not only to eat unleavened bread, they were to completely remove any yeast or leaven from their homes. Traditionally, Jews do a total housecleaning before Passover to make sure there is no leaven lurking in the back of a cupboard. God instructed his people on that first Passover to remember their emancipation by eating unleavened bread for a week. The festival was bookended by solemn assemblies on days when no work was done.

> Seven days you shall eat unleavened bread (*matstsah*). On the first day you shall remove leaven (*se'or*) from your houses, for if anyone eats what is leavened, from the first day until the seventh day, that person shall be cut off from Israel. (Ex. 12:15 ESV)

The word *matstsah* is often combined with the word *'uggah,* which means cakes, especially unleavened cakes made with eggs but not yeast, as it is in Exodus 12:39:

> They baked unleavened (*matstsah*) cakes (*'uggah* ) of the dough (*batseq*) that they had brought out of Egypt; it was not leavened, because they were driven out of Egypt and could not wait, nor had they prepared any provisions for themselves. (NRSV)

Unleavened bread was also part of the sacrifice offered for certain special occasions, such as the taking of a Nazarite vow (Num. 6). Grain offerings offered throughout the year, when made as cakes, were to be unleavened:

> When you bring a grain offering baked in the oven as an offering, it shall be unleavened loaves of fine flour mixed with oil or unleavened wafers smeared with oil. (Lev. 2:4 ESV)

Sometimes, unleavened bread or cakes were made because it was simply more expedient than waiting for bread to rise. The first use of the word *matstsah* in the Bible has nothing to do with sacrifice or festival. Lot receives unexpected visitors and makes bread that can be baked quickly.

> But he pressed them strongly; so they turned aside to him and entered his house. And he made them a feast and baked unleavened bread, and they ate. (Gen. 19:3 ESV)

However, almost every other usage of the word *unleavened* has to do with its ceremonial significance. Unleavened bread symbolizes the purity God calls his people to have and reminds them of their deliverance from slavery.

## VEIL

A veil is a piece of fabric that covers something else, shielding it from view. The Old Testament contains several words that are translated "veil" (or in the King James Version, "vail").

Some texts indicate that Old Testament women did not wear veils out of modesty but because of shameful professions. For example, when Judah is seduced by his daughter-in-law Tamar, the text seems to indicate that a veil—*tsa'iyph* in Hebrew—was the mark of a prostitute:

> And when Tamar was told, "Your father-in-law is going up to Timnah to shear his sheep," she took off her widow's garments and covered herself with a veil (*tsa'iyph*), wrapping herself up, and sat at the entrance to Enaim, which is on the road to Timnah. For she saw that Shelah was grown up, and she had not been given to him in marriage. When Judah saw her, he thought she was a prostitute, for she had covered her face. (Gen. 38:13–15 ESV)

Genesis 24:65, where Rebekah meets Isaac for the first time, seems to indicate that women would wear a veil for modesty—but that modesty was not required for everyday situations. Several verses that comment on women like Sarah, Rebekah, and Rachel being noticed for their beauty indicates that women did not wear veils as part of their everyday clothing. While Rebekah puts on a veil to meet Isaac, that means she did not wear one as part of her regular wardrobe.

Another word for veil is *macveh*. This word is used to describe the veil that Moses put on his face after meeting with God. Exodus 34 says that when Moses would meet face-to-face with God, his face would shine with such an otherworldly glow that people were afraid of him:

> Whenever Moses went in before the LORD to speak with him, he would remove the veil (*macveh*), until he came out. And when he came out and told the people of Israel what he was commanded, the people of Israel would see the face of Moses, that the skin of Moses' face was shining. And Moses would put the veil (*macveh*) over his face again, until he went in to speak with him. (Ex. 34:34–35 ESV)

This passage shows us the unique relationship that Moses had with God, that he was able to speak to him face-to-face, like a friend (Ex. 33:11). This passage is also a prophetic story, which we can only fully understand by reading 2 Corinthians 3, particularly verses 15–16: "Indeed, to this very day whenever Moses is read, a veil lies over their minds; but when one turns to the Lord, the veil is removed" (NRSV).

Another word translated "veil" is the Hebrew word *poreketh*. This word refers to the veil or curtain that was before the ark of the covenant, sometimes called the veil (*poreketh*) of the testimony (*'eduwth*).

This elaborate curtain was to be made according to very specific instructions and was to serve as a barrier to the Holy of Holies:

> And you shall make a veil (*poreketh*) of blue and purple and scarlet yarns and fine twined linen. It shall be made with cherubim skillfully worked into it. And you shall hang it on four pillars of acacia overlaid with gold, with hooks of gold, on four bases of silver. And you shall hang the veil (*poreketh*) from the clasps, and bring the ark of the testimony in there within the veil (*poreketh*). And the veil (*poreketh*) shall separate for you the Holy Place from the Most Holy. You shall put the mercy seat on the ark of the testimony in the Most Holy Place. And you shall set the table outside the veil (*poreketh*), and the lampstand on the south side of the tabernacle opposite the table, and you shall put the table on the north side. (Ex. 26:31–35 ESV)

Other versions translate *poreketh* with the word *curtain*. The English Standard Version uses the word *curtain* earlier in the text to describe the outer walls of the tent, but *veil* to describe that last barrier between people and God.

It is this veil that was split when Christ died on the cross, opening the way to the Holy of Holies. As a result, we can approach the throne of grace with confidence (Heb. 4:16). The veil has been taken away.

## WALK

As it does in English, the word *walk* in the Bible can refer to both the literal physical action of moving one's legs to propel yourself in a given direction, or it can refer figuratively to one's behavior.

Two Hebrew words are translated "walk" or "walking" in the Old Testament. The first and most frequent is *yalak*, a word that appears 1,043 times in the text but is translated with a variety of words, including not only "walk" but "go," "come," follow," and many other related words.

The second word is *halak*, which appears five hundred times and also means to go, walk, behave. Translated "go" more often than "walk," this word is often used figuratively to describe how a person lives, the manner in which they walk through life.

The first incidence of the word *walk* in the Bible is in Genesis 3:8: "Then the man and his wife heard the sound of the LORD God as he was walking (*halak*) in the garden in the cool of the day, and they hid from the LORD God among the trees of the garden."

What, exactly, did the "LORD God as he was walking" sound like? Thunderous footsteps? A rustling wind? The New Revised Standard Version translates the phrase "the cool of the day" as "at the time of the evening breeze." Adam and Eve apparently walked with God, both literally and figuratively, until that fateful day when instead of joining him on the evening stroll, they hid themselves.

Either word can be used to refer to literal walking: "Go, walk (*halak*) through the length and breadth of the land, for I am giving it to you" (Gen. 13:17).

Certain godly people in the Old Testament were said to have "walked with God," meaning not only did they have a particularly intimate relationship with God, but that relationship manifested itself in righteous behavior.

The Bible mentions several individuals who provide for us an example of this kind of faith: Enoch, Noah, and Abraham (Gen.

17:1; 24:40), to name just a few. It is interesting that all three of these men lived before the Mosaic law was given (and one could argue that Moses also walked with God, i.e., had an intimate friendship with him).

"Noah was a righteous man, blameless in his time; Noah walked with God" (Gen. 6:9 NASB). This parallel phrasing defines what "walked with God" meant: to be righteous and blameless. To the ancient Hebrew, belief and obedience were inextricably linked. Faith was not mental assent to truth but living out that truth by obeying God's law. To describe such faith as a walk, with its connotations of action, direction, following, balance, and focus, makes perfect sense.

When Solomon dedicated the temple, his prayer for the people was this: "The LORD our God be with us, as he was with our fathers. May he not leave us or forsake us, that he may incline our hearts to him, to walk (*yalak*) in all his ways and to keep his commandments, his statutes, and his rules, which he commanded our fathers" (1 Kings 8:57–58 ESV). Notice the emphasis on walking as obedience.

Enoch, the great-grandfather of Noah, was also said to have walked with God. He is one of the few people in the Bible who apparently was taken directly up to heaven without suffering physical death: "Enoch lived 365 years, walking (*halak*) in close fellowship with God. Then one day he disappeared, because God took him" (Gen. 5:23–24 NLT).

God also tells his people not to walk with other gods (Jer. 7:6–9) and condemns those who walk in the way of previous wicked generations (2 Chron. 21:6). To walk in God's statutes (Ezek. 20:19) meant not just avoiding sin, but proactively following God: to offer sacrifices, to love their neighbors, to care for widows and the poor, to keep the Sabbath and the festivals, to study the Torah.

> Then the LORD said to Moses, "Behold, I am about to rain bread from heaven for you, and the people shall go out and gather a

> day's portion every day, that I may test them, whether they will walk (*yalak*) in my law or not." (Ex. 16:4 ESV)

What was the test God alluded to? He had commanded the people not to hoard—to gather only one day's worth of manna. He wanted to know whether they would walk in his law, that is, whether they would trust him to provide for them.

While we walk in the light of grace rather than the law, we are still called to walk with God: to follow him, to trust him, and to go his way.

## WALL

One of the most inspiring stories of leadership in the Old Testament is found in the book of Nehemiah. After the exile, a remnant of Jews returned to find the once powerful city of Jerusalem in ruins—its wall had been destroyed. This left it vulnerable to further attack, and also served as a symbol of Israel's decimation as a nation.

Nehemiah was not living in Judah, but in Susa, where he served as cupbearer to King Artaxerxes. When he heard about Jerusalem and its wall, his first response showed his heart: He fasted and prayed.

Nehemiah was distraught about the state of affairs in his home city, but he did more than just pray. He was a man of action. He went to the king and, praying even as he spoke to the king, asked for permission to go and rebuild the wall of Jerusalem. He also asked for practical assistance, both in building materials and military protection. Nehemiah took a risk of making this bold request to the king, but felt strongly that he needed to restore both the city and its people.

Despite numerous obstacles and challenges, Nehemiah rebuilt the wall, and in so doing, began to rebuild the confidence and strength of the people of Israel.

There are several Hebrew words that mean wall. The one used in Nehemiah is *chowmah*. It often connotes a wall of protection, especially the walls that typically encircled ancient cities to protect them from enemies. (This same word is used in the description of the walls of Jericho in Joshua 2–6.) We also find *chowmah* in Exodus 14:22: "The Israelites went into the sea on dry ground, the waters forming a wall for them on their right and on their left" (NRSV). Here the literal walls of water are also a symbol of God's miraculous protection of his people.

*Chowmah* is also used figuratively of God's protection: "Violence shall no more be heard in your land, devastation or destruction within your borders; you shall call your walls Salvation, and your gates Praise" (Isa. 60:18 ESV). This symbolism—of walls constructed of God's saving power and gates made out of praise—is a promise of both the Messiah who will save our souls and our ultimate home in the New Jerusalem.

Another word that means wall is *qiyrah*. We find *qiyrah* often used to describe an interior wall, as it does in Ezekiel 8:7–10 and 2 Chronicles 3:11–12, where it describes a wall of the temple in Jerusalem. It is used in various ways seventy-four times in the Old Testament.

In Ezekiel 43, God gives the prophet a vision and tells him that he is angry that the Israelites are trying to worship both him and their idols, essentially putting their idols right next to God's temple, "with only a wall (*qiyrah*) between me and them" (v. 8). This is obviously not a fortified city wall but a thinner wall, and not enough separation; therefore, the holiness of the temple is defiled.

Another word that means wall is *shuwr*, which is found only four times in the text. It is found in David's poetic image, "In your strength I can crush an army; with my God I can scale any wall" (Ps. 18:29 NLT; see also 2 Sam. 22:30).

The word *gader* can mean wall, hedge, or fence. It is found in verses like this: "You have not gone up to the breaks in the wall to repair it for the house of Israel so that it will stand firm in the battle on the day of the LORD" (Ezek. 13:5). It often means an outer wall or hedge.

Walls can be obstacles in our way or God's protection for us. So sometimes, like Nehemiah, we are called to shore up that which is designed to protect God's people. Other times, we must tear down the walls that the enemy puts up to impede our progress or to cause division. Our job, with God's help, is to discern which is which.

## WANDER

In 1758, Robert Robinson penned these words:

> Prone to wander, Lord, I feel it,
> Prone to leave the God I love.[1]

Those words still ring true more than 250 years later—we are prone to wander away from God, even after we have experienced his blessings and love. Amazingly, God continues to call us back from our wanderings.

The Old Testament is a story of people who wander—sometimes led by God, other times wandering from him. There are several Hebrew words that can mean wander.

God built the nation of Israel through Abraham. Their relationship begins when God asks him to leave his home to wander (Gen. 20:13). The word for wander is *ta'ah*, which is most often translated "to err" or "go astray." We find this same word in the story of Hagar, the slave of Abraham's wife, Sarah, who is sent away because of Sarah's jealousy. In Genesis 21 we read her story of how she wandered in the desert, despairing. But God met her there.

A large portion of the Old Testament is focused on Israel's exodus from Egypt. At first they did not wander, but followed God, who led them as a cloud by day and a fire by night. But eventually, their rebellion led to a consequence: wandering through the wilderness.

"And your children shall wander in the wilderness forty years, and bear your whoredoms, until your carcases be wasted in the wilderness" (Num. 14:33 KJV). The word for wander in this verse is *ra'ah*, which most frequently means to feed or shepherd. (See ***Shepherd***.) The image is of a flock that is wandering but does not have a place to rest. God could have punished them by killing them right away—instead he punishes them while still taking care of them.

Several chapters later, we read, "The LORD's anger burned against Israel and he made them wander in the desert forty years, until the whole generation of those who had done evil in his sight was gone" (Num. 32:13). The Hebrew word in this verse is *nuwa*, which originally meant to waver or shake. It can mean to wander, or to be a fugitive.

We also see this word in Genesis. When Cain killed his brother, Abel, God told him, "When you work the ground, it will no longer yield its crops for you. You will be a restless wanderer on the earth" (Gen. 4:12). The King James Version says "a fugitive (*nuwa'*) and a vagabond (*nuwd*)." Both words mean quiver, totter, shake, to wander aimlessly. Interestingly, the word *nuwd* can also mean to have compassion on. The LORD was not sending Cain on vacation, but naming the consequence of his action of murdering his brother—he had fractured community, and would not be able to restore it.

Even when wandering is a consequence for sin, we are not out of God's sight. Consider this promise:

> You have taken account of my wanderings;
> Put my tears in Your bottle
> Are they not in Your book? (Ps. 56:8 NASB)

The word translated "wanderings" in this verse is *nod*, a derivative of *nuwd*. The idea is one of exile. Yet even in those times when we feel lost, God is aware of us and watching over us.

Wandering can also be a metaphor for sin—to wander away from truth. It stands in contrast to walking purposefully with God. But we are always to remember our heritage of wandering. In Deuteronomy 26, Moses tells the people that when they celebrate their conquest of the Promised Land by bringing tithes and firstfruits, they should say, "My father was a wandering Aramean, and he went down into Egypt with a few people and lived there and became a great nation, powerful and numerous" (v. 5). The word translated "wandering" is *'abad,* which essentially means to be lost or wander. It was often used to describe lost or wandering sheep. (See ***Shepherd***).

In 2 Kings 21:8, God promises not to make his people wander any more if they will follow him and live by his law. Again, the word is *nuwd*, which means to shake, waver, or wander. It can also mean to have compassion on. Even the curse of God is tinged with the mercy of God.

A recurring theme in Psalm 119 is the warning not to wander: "With my whole heart I seek you; let me not wander from your commandments!" (v. 10 ESV). The word for wander here is *shagah*. It means to stray or mistake, to cause to go astray.

The prophet Zechariah reminds us that our wandering illustrates our need for a savior: "Therefore the people wander like sheep; they are afflicted for lack of a shepherd" (Zech. 10:2 ESV). The Hebrew is *naca'*, which means to pull up or out, an image of pulling up tent stakes to move or journey.

We all wander, but God calls us to make our home in him.

## WINE

The Hebrews had two words for wine: *yayin*, used most often in contexts where it obviously refers to fermented, alcoholic wine; and *tirosh*, also transliterated *tiyrowsh*, which referred most often to sweet wine, or new wine—which many scholars would translate as unfermented wine or grape juice.

The Bible definitely condemns drunkenness and warns of the dangers of drinking too much wine. But it also seems to say that wine in moderation is appropriate for times of celebration or even as a normal accompaniment to a meal. The nation of Israel is sometimes referred to metaphorically as a vineyard.

In ancient times, wine was sometimes mixed with water or other drinks, perhaps to lower the alcohol content in the wine, or perhaps to kill the germs in the water. Many scholars believe that wine made in the ancient world was much lower in alcohol content than wine today.

The first vineyard mentioned in the Bible is the one Noah plants. The story goes that he drank some wine and got drunk and passed out, naked, in his tent (Gen. 9). The story implies that his drunkenness and nakedness are both shameful. But his career as a vineyard owner is not.

Drunkenness is a part of Lot's family dysfunction, as his daughters purposely get him drunk on wine in order to have sex with him. The story points to the moral failings of this family, rather than making a moral judgment about wine itself (Gen. 19).

Genesis 14:18 tells of Abram's interaction with Melchizedek: "And Melchizedek, the king of Salem and a priest of God Most High, brought Abram some bread and wine" (NLT). Abram had just won a military conquest, with God's help, and the text implies that the priest was commemorating and celebrating that with a meal.

In Genesis 27, we read of Jacob stealing his brother Esau's birthright. He brings his father a meal, including some wine. The Bible makes no moral judgment on this being part of the meal. In fact, part of the blessing Isaac gives him says:

> May God give you heaven's dew
> and earth's richness—
> an abundance of grain and new wine (*tiyrowsh*). (v. 28)

In the rules about the Tabernacle and the regulations for the priests, we read: "You and your sons are not to drink wine (*yayin*) or other fermented drink (*shekar*) whenever you go into the Tent of Meeting, or you will die. This is a lasting ordinance for the generations to come" (Lev. 10:9). *Shekar* is fermented drink or liquor, often made from dates or honey rather than grapes.

These prohibitions were specific directions to Aaron and his sons, for specific times: when they were going into the Tent of Meeting. They were to be sober when they were attending to their priestly duties. It is not a prohibition for all people at all times.

Grain, wine, and oil were considered blessings of God (Deut. 7:13—in this verse the word is *tirosh*), and were all offered as sacrifices but also enjoyed by God's people.

Wine was used in the sacrifices as a drink offering (Ex. 29:40; Lev. 23:13—the word in these verses is *yayin*).

When people took a Nazarite vow, they abstained from wine or strong drink. The fact that they would abstain for special reasons seems to imply that drinking wine would be unremarkable (Num. 6). And the text says that when the period of time for their vow was over, they were allowed to have wine. The text gives permission to drink wine, but of course, not to get drunk.

In Deuteronomy 14, God tells his people what not to eat, then reminds them of the good things they may eat and enjoy. The list of prohibited foods does not include wine. At the end of the chapter, God tells his people to set aside a tenth of what their fields produce, including grain and new wine (*tirosh*), and then to feast on that tithe. He then adds that he will decree a place for this feast, and if it is far away, the people can convert their tithe to silver, then use it to buy whatever they want and have a party: "Use the silver to buy whatever you like: cattle, sheep, wine (*yayin*) or other fermented drink (*shekar*), or anything you wish. Then you and your household shall eat there in the presence of the LORD your God and rejoice" (Deut. 14:26).

Wine that makes the heart glad, and oil and bread are listed among the blessings of God (Ps. 104:15). Like all of God's gifts, wine is something that we may enjoy but should never abuse.

## WISDOM

As we have said before, Old Testament religion was not focused on philosophy and thoughts about God, but on how one lived. To follow God, to walk with God, was to obey his law. To believe was to live in a certain way.

So wisdom, to an Old Testament Hebrew, was moral rather than intellectual. Wisdom was something you lived out, not something you knew intellectually. To be wise was to live wisely, that is, to live according to the precepts of God.

The books of Job, Proverbs, and Ecclesiastes are called the "wisdom literature" of the Bible. They focus not just on truth, but on how to live—on the process of wrestling with the questions of faith and attaining wisdom, little by little, as one lived.

One passage in particular, Proverbs 8, personifies wisdom as a woman. The chapter begins:

> Does not wisdom (*chokmah*) call,
>    and does not understanding raise her voice?
> On the heights, beside the way,
>    at the crossroads she takes her stand. (vv. 1–2 NRSV)

The word *chokmah* means both wisdom and skill. It is often combined with the word *ruach*, or spirit, in the phrase "a spirit of wisdom," or with the words *ruach eloyim*, the Spirit of God, in wisdom.

Proverbs 8 goes on to describe how "Wisdom" was present in the creation of the world and how she worked by God's side as the world and people were formed.

Some scholars believe this passage is talking about Jesus prior to the incarnation. One commentary that disputes that idea says:

> The context makes it clear that the writer does not see Wisdom as one with Yahweh but rather as an attribute of God and metaphorically, as the agency of divine action in creation. Wisdom is a metaphoric or allegorized figure akin to the allegorized attributes of God in Psalm 85:10, which medieval thinkers rendered as the Four Daughters of God—love, faithfulness, righteousness and peace.[1]

The first eight chapters of Proverbs contrast Lady Wisdom with a woman of folly, and urge the reader to choose to walk in the way of wisdom. In the next chapter, a slightly different form of the word, *chakmowth*, is used: "Wisdom has built her house, she has hewn her seven pillars" (Prov. 9:1 NRSV, see also Prov. 1:20; 14:1).

Several related Hebrew words describe various aspects of wisdom. *Chakam*, as a verb, means to be wise, or act wisely: "Hear instruction and be wise (*chakam*), and do not neglect it" (Prov. 8:33 NRSV).

*Chakam* (transliterated the same but slightly different in Hebrew), as an adjective, means both wise and skillful.

We often find this adjective translated "skillful" or "skilled." It is used several times in Exodus as God gives instruction for the building of the tabernacle. Being willing to work was not enough—God expects and in fact commands that his house be constructed by "skilled" workers, whether carpenters, workers of metal, weavers, embroiders, or carvers.

Apparently, God cared about excellence and expected quality. Just having a great attitude or a willing heart was not enough; the people who built God's house had to actually know what they were doing. Do we still have those standards of craftsmanship and skill in the church today? Do we still seek to live wisely?

Second Chronicles 1 and 1 Kings 3 tell how God appeared

to Solomon to offer answers to any prayer—almost like a magic genie granting a wish. Solomon does not see it that way, of course. He treats God with reverence and respect. One could argue that Solomon already displays wisdom with his answer—he asks for more wisdom. It's a request God smiles upon and liberally grants.

*Chokmah*, the noun form, means wisdom or experience. This word is used to describe the wisdom of Solomon. The text tells us also that he had *tabuwn*, meaning discernment, understanding, or intelligence, and that he had largeness or breadth of understanding (*leb*—see ***Heart***):

> God gave Solomon very great wisdom (*chokmah*), discernment (*tabuwn*), and breadth of understanding (*leb*) as vast as the sand on the seashore, so that Solomon's wisdom (*chokmah*) surpassed the wisdom (*chokmah*) of all the people of the east, and all the wisdom (*chokmah*) of Egypt. (1 Kings 4:29–30 NRSV)

The repetition for emphasis is a way of making or even exaggerating a point: Solomon had not only intelligence, but emotional intelligence to be able to apply that wisdom. Certainly we should follow Solomon's example in asking God for wisdom, which the Bible promises he will give generously to us (James 1:5).

# APPENDIX OF HELPFUL WEBSITES

When studying the Scriptures, it can be helpful to use search engines like Google, but remember that almost anyone can put up a website and write whatever they want, whether or not it is true, so some sites will have more credibility than others. This may seem obvious, but don't automatically trust Wikipedia or other sites that have no process for verification of the facts. Not everything you read on the Internet is true, so check it against other sources.

I did most of the research for this book in the reference section of the Wheaton College library, where I found hundreds of academic books published by credible publishers. A local Christian college or seminary is a great place to do serious research. Also, a copy of *Strong's Exhaustive Concordance* (which is available for all the major translations of the Bible) is an invaluable tool. You can get a print version or find an online version. Strong's lists every instance that each word in the Bible is used. So, for example, if you look up *hope* in Strong's, you'll find a list of the 132 verses that contain the word *hope* in the Bible. Each, with a short phrase of context, is listed, along with a number next to it. The numbers correspond to the Hebrew or Greek word that is used in that particular verse. In verses that translate the word *tiqvah* as "hope," you'll see the number 8615. You then go to the Hebrew dictionary section to see the definition and usage of *tiqvah*.

The most important tool when trying to understand the Scriptures is prayer. As you study, ask that the Holy Spirit would speak to you, that he would reveal truth and renew your mind. Additionally, there are online tools that are very helpful and accurate. Here are a few that I used while writing this book.

www.blueletterbible.org is a great site for studying without having to look up each individual word in a concordance. You can search by reference or by word. The KJV is the default version, and with that, if you look up a verse, you can see the Strong's concordance number after each word. Click on the number, and it takes you to a Greek or Hebrew dictionary with the word, its meaning, and all other verses the word is used in. Click on the icons to the left of each verse and you can see that verse in several other versions, read commentary, and more.

www.biblegateway.com has the Bible online in over twenty English translations and many other languages. You can compare the same verse or verses in different versions, do a keyword search (for one or more words), or look up a verse by typing in the reference (e.g., John 3:16 or Psalm 23). This is one of several online Bible sites. It's great for doing word study. It also provides access to several commentaries.

www.eliyah.com/lexicon.html has Strong's concordance online, along with a Hebrew and Greek lexicon. On this site, you can search by word, reference, or Strong's number. You can also search a thesaurus, encyclopedia, and other reference books.

www.biblestudytools.com is a very helpful site with dictionaries, encyclopedias, Bible translations, commentaries, and more, along with daily devotionals. Like biblegateway.com, it has over twenty English translations available to search, but www.biblestudytools.com has more extensive commentaries and dictionaries.

www.netbible.org contains commentaries, Strong's concordance, maps, sermon illustrations, and a lot of other resources, as well as the text of the Bible in various versions.

# NOTES

## Alien

1. See also Num. 11:4 and Josh. 8:35.

## Altar

1. *Eerdmans Dictionary of the Bible*, David Noel Freedman, ed. in chief (Grand Rapids, MI: Eerdmans, 2000), 45–46.

## Angel

1. Stephen D. Renn, ed., *Expository Dictionary of Bible Words* (Peabody, MA: Hendrickson Publishers, 2005), 32.

2. W. E. Vine, *Vine's Concise Dictionary of the Bible* (Nashville: Thomas Nelson, 2005), 11.

3. Lawrence O. Richards, *New International Encyclopedia of Bible Words* (Grand Rapids, MI: Zondervan, 1991), 44.

## Ark

1. Ibid., 72.

2. Vine, 17.

## Barren

1. Renn, 91.

2. Philip Yancey, *The Bible Jesus Read* (Grand Rapids, MI: Zondervan, 1999), 31.

3. Renn, 92.

## Bind

1. Ibid.

2. Richards, 125.

## Blessing

1. *Eerdmans Dictionary of the Bible*, 192.

2. Renn, 119.

## Blood

1. Walter A. Elwell, ed., *Baker's Evangelical Dictionary of Biblical Theology* (Grand Rapids, MI: Baker Books, 1996). As quoted on www.biblestudytools.com.

2. *Eerdmans Dictionary of the Bible*, 193.

## Bread

1. Renn, 140.

2. Eerdmans, 199.

## Cherubim

1. Ibid., 233.

## Covenant

1. Yancey, 29.

## Death

1. Paul Ferguson, "Death, Mortality," in *Baker's Evangelical Dictionary of Biblical Theology*. www.biblestudytools.com.

2. Ferguson.

## Deliver/Deliverer

1. Vine's, 88.

## Earth

1. Vine's, 108.

2. *Tyndale Bible Dictionary*, Walter A. Elwell and Philip W. Comfort, eds. (Wheaton, IL: Tyndale House Publishers, 2001), 402.

## Elder/Elders

1. Ibid., 414.

2. Richards, 243.

## Enemy/Enemies

1. A helpful Bible study blog, http://donna-connections.blogspot.com/2009/02/biblical-idioms.html, notes that "In Bible lands, almost everything was carried on the head," and further explains that most people kept fire for cooking and heating "in a metal container, or brazier, which they used for simple cooking as well as for warmth. It was always kept burning. If it ever went out, a family member took the container to a neighbor's house to borrow fire. Then she would lift the brazier to her head and start for home. If the neighbor was a generous person, she would heap the container full of coals. To feed an enemy and give him drink was like heaping the empty brazier with live coals which meant food, warmth, and almost life itself to the person or home needing it. 'To heap coals of fire upon

their heads' was a saying which symbolized the very finest generosity." The blog is written by Donna Nielsen, but she doesn't list her scholarly credentials on the site.

### Ephod

1. *The New Strong's Exhaustive Concordance of the Bible* (Nashville, TN: Thomas Nelson Publishers, 2001), Hebrew and Aramaic Dictionary section, 25.

2. *Tyndale Bible Dictionary*, 437.

### Evil

1. *Strong's Hebrew Dictionary*, 264.

2. Richards, 251.

3. William C. Williams, "Evil," in *Baker's Evangelical Dictionary of Biblical Theology*, www.biblestudytools.com.

### Exile

1. *The New International Dictionary of Old Testament Theology and Exegesis*, Willem A. VanGemeren, ed. (Grand Rapids, MI: Zondervan, 1997), 595.

### Face

1. Richards, 258.

### Father

1. C. S. Lewis, *Letters to Malcolm: Chiefly on Prayer* (New York: Harcourt Brace Jovanovich, 1964), 21.

### Feast

1. For more on this theory, see the YouTube video by Dr. Gavin Finley, *The Seven Feasts of Israel*. Also see www.gotquestions.org/jewish-feasts.html.

2. *Tyndale Bible Dictionary,* 480.

### Fight

1. We also find it somehow easy to forget that our own nation is engaged in a war in which we have killed our enemies, and many of our own people have died. If we ask, "How could God command killing?" we should also ask, "How can we tolerate killing?" If we believe war is necessary now, then we have to, for consistency's sake, concede that it may have been "necessary" then, or that it served some greater purpose that only God understood.

### Fool

1. *Strong's Hebrew Dictionary*, 133.

### Forever (Ever)

1. *Strong's Hebrew Dictionary*, 205.

### Forty

1. www.biblestudy.org/bibleref/meaning-of-numbers-in-bible/40.html. This site does not list authors, and I don't agree with all of its conclusions, but it provides a helpful overview of this topic and many others. Use it as you would any website—with discernment. Check its facts against other sources.

## Glory

1. *Tyndale Bible Dictionary*, 539.

2. Rob Bell, *Velvet Elvis* (Grand Rapids: Zondervan, 2005), 77–78.

## Harvest

1. From James Orr, MA, DD, gen ed. "Definition for 'HARVEST.' " "International Standard Bible Encyclopedia" as cited on *www.Bible-history.com*; 1915. www.Bible-history.com/isbe/H/HARVEST/

2. Ibid.

## Heart

1. Vine, 174.

## Help/Helper

1. Carolyn Custis James, *Lost Women of the Bible* (Grand Rapids, MI: Zondervan, 2005), 35–36.

## Holy

1. From Rob Bell's *Breathe*, part of his Nooma series of videos, published by Zondervan Publishing.

2. M. William Ury, "Holy, Holiness," in *Baker's Evangelical Dictionary of Biblical Theology*.

3. Ibid.

4. R. C. Sproul, *The Holiness of God* (Wheaton, IL: Tyndale, 1985), 40.

5. Ibid., 54.

## Hope

1. www.triumphpro.com/mikvah-measure-of-time.htm

## Israel

1. *Strong's Hebrew Dictionary*, 124.

2. Gerard Van Groningen, "Israel," in *Baker's Evangelical Dictionary of Biblical Theology*, www.biblestudytools.com.

## Jubilee

1. From "It Shall Be a Jubilee Unto You" on *www.yesmagazine.org/issues/living-economies/*532. Michael Hudson is distinguished research professor of economics at the University of Missouri, Kansas City, and author of *Super Imperialism: The Economic Strategy of American Empire*.

2. Ched Myers, *The Biblical Vison of Sabbath Economics* (Washington, D.C.: Church of the Saviour, 2001), 13.

## Judge

1. Vine, 200.

2. *Strong's Hebrew Dictionary*, 62.

## Just/Justice

1. Ronald J. Sider, *Just Generosity* (Grand Rapids, MI: Baker Books, 1999, 2007), 66.

## King

1. *www.enduringword.com/commentaries/0908.htm*

## Lament

1. M. Scott Peck. *The Road Less Traveled* (New York: Touchstone/Simon and Schuster, 1978), 15.

2. *Dictionary of the Old Testament Wisdom, Poetry, and Writings*, Tremper Longman and Peter Enns, eds. (Downers Grove, IL: InterVarsity Press, 2008), 384–385.

3. Ibid., 385.

4. *The IVP Women's Bible Commentary,* Catherine Clark Kroeger and Mary J. Evans, eds. (Downers Grove, IL: InterVarsity Press, 2002), 392.

## Lamp

1. John Walton, etc., *IVP Bible Background Commentary: Old Testament* (Downer's Grove, IL: InterVarsity Press, 2000), 522.

## Lion

1. For more detail, see www.biblestudytools.com/dictionaries/bakers-evangelical-dictionary/lion.html.

## Lord

1. See Rob Bell's Nooma video series DVD, "Breathe."

2. *Baker's Evangelical Dictionary of Biblical Theology*, www.biblestudytools.com/dictionaries/bakers-evangelical-dictionary/god-names-of.html.

3. *Tyndale Bible Dictionary*, Walter Elwell, ed. (Wheaton, IL: Tyndale, 2001), 540.

## Manna

1. Avram Yehoshua, "Passover and Jesus," *www.seedofabraham.net/feasts1.html*

## People

1. *Strong's Hebrew Dictionary*, 213.

## Praise

1. *Strong's Hebrew Dictionary*, 69.

## Pray/Prayer

1. *Eerdmans Bible Dictionary*, 1077.

2. Philip Yancey, *Prayer: Does it Make Any Difference?* (Grand Rapids: Zondervan, 2006), 30.

3. *Eerdmans Bible Dictionary*, 1077.

4. *The New Unger's Bible Dictionary*, R. K. Harrison, ed. (Chicago: Moody Press, 1988), 1025.

## Priest

1. *Eerdmans Bible Dictionary*, 1082.

2. Unger, 1029.

3. *The HarperCollins Bible Dictionary*, Paul J. Achtemeier, ed. (New York: HarperSanFrancisco, 1900), 880.

4. *HarperCollins Bible Dictionary*, 882.

## Prophet

1. Unger, 1042.

## Robe

1. M. G. Easton, *Illustrated Bible Dictionary*. Thomas Nelson, 1897. Public domain. As quoted on www.biblestudytools.com.

## Rod

1. Phillip Keller, *A Shepherd Looks at Psalm 23* (Grand Rapids, MI: Zondervan, 1990), 90.

## Sacrifice

1. *Unger's Bible Dictionary,* 1099.

## Salt

1. *The New Bible Commentary,* D. Guthrie and J. A. Motyer, eds. (Grand Rapids: Eerdmans, 1991), 187.

2. Dr. William Smith, "Salt," *Smith's Bible Dictionary,* 1901, www.biblestudytools.com/dictionaries/smiths-bible-dictionary/salt.html.

3. *International Standard Bible Encyclopedia,* James Orr, ed. (Grand Rapids, MI: Eerdmans, 1939), www.internationalstandardbible.com/S/salt.html.

## Sheol

1. The quote is from The Message translation, which I found the easiest to understand when reading this peculiar tale.

2. *Baker's Evangelical Dictionary*, www.biblestudytools.com/dictionaries/bakers-evangelical-dictionary/sheol.html.

## Shepherd

1. *Holman Bible Dictionary,* Trent Butler, general ed. (Nashville, TN: Holman Bible Publishers, 1991), 1263.

## Soul

1. *Vine's Bible Dictionary*, 353.

## Tabernacle

1. Keri Wyatt Kent, *Rest: Living in Sabbath Simplicity* (Grand Rapids: Zondervan, 2009), 184.

2. *Holman Bible Dictionary*, 1316.

## Temple

1. *Holman Bible Dictionary*, 1325.

## Wander

1. "Come Thou Fount of Every Blessing." By Robert Robinson, 1758. Find the full lyrics on www.cyberhymnal.org.

## Wisdom

1. *The IVP Women's Bible Commentary*, Catherine Clark Kroeger and Mary J. Evans, eds. (Downers Grove, IL: InterVarsity Press, 2002), 327.

# ACKNOWLEDGMENTS

There's no way this book would have happened without divine intervention, so I first want to acknowledge and thank my Lord and Savior Jesus Christ.

I want to thank several people, of course, whom God used to bring this project to life:

First, to anyone reading this page—thank you for reading this book. My prayer is that through this resource, God will ignite in you a passion for his Word, that it would be a source of life and joy for you.

Thanks to my husband, Scot, and our terrific kids, Melanie and Aaron. Our teamwork allows me to put time and effort into writing, so thank you for playing an important part in this book. I appreciate and love you guys!

Thank you to everyone at Bethany House Publishers who has worked so hard to make this project a reality—from editorial, marketing, publicity, and sales. Each of you plays a critical role and I appreciate what you do. Special thanks to my editor, Andy McGuire, for having the vision for this project and for your encouragement during the writing process. And to my line editor,

Ellen Chalifoux, for your encouragement and excellent attention to detail.

Thank you also to my agent, Chip MacGregor, for finding projects that are a perfect fit for me, even when I don't realize it. Thanks for believing in me. It's an honor to be working with you.

A huge thank-you to the women of Redbud Writers Guild, my traveling companions on the writing journey. Thank you for reading my work, encouraging me, laughing and praying with me. You are an amazing group of women.

This book required a lot of prayerful research. I'm sure my former Bible professors at Wheaton College would be shocked at how much time I spent in the stacks at the Wheaton College Buswell Memorial Library pouring through commentaries, Bible dictionaries, and encyclopedias. (Way more time than I spent when I was a student there.) Thank you to all the library staff who answered questions, patiently directed me toward helpful resources, and so on. I'm grateful to have a treasure like this library (and its staff) so close to home.

**Keri Wyatt Kent** is the author of eight previous books and is a regular contributor to *Kyria.com* (formerly *Today's Christian Woman*), *Outreach* magazine, and *Momsense* magazine. She is a founding member of Redbud Writers Guild. Keri speaks at churches and retreats around the country and is a frequent guest on several shows on the Moody Broadcasting Network, including *Midday Connection*. Keri lives with her husband and two children in suburban Chicago. Connect with her at www.keriwyattkent.com.